A HUNDRED HORIZONS

A Hundred Horizons

THE INDIAN OCEAN IN THE
AGE OF GLOBAL EMPIRE

SUGATA BOSE

HARVARD UNIVERSITY PRESS
Cambridge, Massachusetts
London, England
2006

Library of Congress Cataloging-in-Publication Data

Bose, Sugata.
A hundred horizons : the Indian Ocean in the age of global empire / Sugata Bose.
p. cm.
Includes bibliographical references.
ISBN 0-674-02157-6
1. Indian Ocean Region—History.   I. Title.
DS340.B65 2006
909'.09824083—dc22   2005052767

Contents

Preface

"Beside you," Nietzsche once wrote, "is the ocean: to be sure, it does not always roar, and at times it lies spread out like silk and gold and reveries of graciousness. But hours will come when you realize that it is infinite and that there is nothing more awesome than infinity." I experienced many such hours of realizing that I was facing awesome infinity during the long years of researching and writing this book. My gratitude to the people who gave me courage during those hours is, therefore, deeply felt.

My early years as a historian were spent with peasants who worked the land. By the mid-1990s I was restless to leave the safety of the Indian shores and began to test the waters by dipping my feet under gentle waves. But I really set sail on my oceanic adventure during a year of leave I had as a fellow of the Guggenheim Foundation in 1997–1998. This book is a product of the riches I accumulated at various libraries and archives that served as my ports of call for the next few years. A log of my debts will be found in the notes to this book. I was also able to try out the wares I collected at seminars and conferences in various locations, including the Asiatic Society of Bangladesh in Dhaka, Presidency College in Calcutta, St. Stephen's College in Delhi, the Anglo-American History Conference in London, the Social Science Research Council workshops on the Mediterranean and the Indian Ocean in Aix-en-Provence and Oxford, the Centre of History and Economics at the University of Cambridge, Harvard University, Tufts University, Yale University, the University of Pennsylvania, the University of Chicago, Duke University, and Emory University.

When it comes to support for an intellectual enterprise, individuals are more important than institutions. The historians who came before me and whose work I admire are cited throughout this book. Among people at various institutions who gave me a sense of intellectual community are Rajat Ray of Presidency College, Christopher Bayly and Emma Rothschild of the University of Cambridge, Leila Fawaz of Tufts University, Jim Scott of Yale University, David Ludden of the University of Pennsylvania, and Karen Wigen of Duke, now at Stanford University. Chris Bayly, Emgoeng Ho, Mridu Rai, and Emma Rothschild read chapters of the manuscript and gave insightful comments and warm encouragement. I could always count on Leila Fawaz's friendship and confidence. My conversations with K. N. Chaudhuri and Michael Pearson on Indian Ocean history have been illuminating. I treasure Ranajit Guha's example and advice about the finer points of the historian's craft. I have been able to try out my ideas and arguments with my students in various courses; in particular, I have learned much and continue to learn a great deal from my graduate students, past and present. I have greatly benefited from reading the work of younger scholars like Ritu Birla, Prachi Deshpande, Semanti Ghosh, Farina Mir, Mridu Rai, and Chitralekha Zutshi. Faisal Iqbal Chaudhry, Kris Manjapra, Mandavi Mehta, Neeti Nair, Maarij Qazi, and Daniel Sargent have helped with my research at different times in the Boston area, and Seema Alavi's student Mohammad Sajjad of the Jamia Millia provided a useful stint of research assistance in Delhi. More recently, it has been a pleasure to welcome Sana Aiyar, Antara Datta, and Sandhya Polu into the ever-widening circle of my graduate students and to have the stellar assistance of Aliya Iqbal and Manjari Chatterjee Miller in my teaching duties.

My colleagues in the History Department at Harvard supplied a stimulating intellectual environment and several of them have been partners in forging a new way forward in comparative and connective scholarship. I wish to record a special word of thanks to Bill Kirby, who played a key role in building the History Department and in supporting the South Asia Initiative that I direct at Harvard. I have had the good fortune of working closely with a number of wonderful friends. I would like to specially mention Homi Bhabha, the innovator par excellence in the field of cultural studies, who joined me in chairing the "South Asia without Borders" conversations. The towering presence of Amartya Sen has been a true blessing. I have been learning from his vast repertoire of knowledge for the past twenty-five years and it was a sheer delight to teach a course with him at Harvard.

Two anonymous readers for Harvard University Press wrote reports on the penultimate version of the manuscript that were of great help in the final revision of the book. Joyce

Seltzer has been a splendid editor, encouraging me to write as fluently as possible for a wide audience. I am grateful to Rukun Advani of Permanent Black for his zeal in wanting to make this book available to readers in South Asia.

Whatever I have achieved in life I owe to my parents, Sisir Kumar Bose and Krishna Bose. I lost my father on September 30, 2000. Since then, my mother has bravely taken on the mantle of both parents. It is to her that I have dedicated this book in love and admiration. My younger brother, Sumantra Bose, has helped in many ways, including setting the pace and standards of scholarly excellence through his own books. During my years of research in Britain and India, my three nephews were a great source of joy. The eldest one, Aidan Samya (Tipu), has been, to borrow his phrase, my "favorite person in the whole world" and I hope he will soon be able to read and enjoy this book. Ayesha Jalal has been my inspiration. Needless to say, she read this book with a sharp and critical eye, even while busily researching and writing her own. She has been my constant companion during our shared intellectual *jihd-o-jihad* for more than a quarter of a century. I can only steal a line from Hafiz to say to her:

> Your heart and my heart
> Are very, very old
> Friends.

Let us together in the manner of the Sufis of old fill many more cups of wine.

A HUNDRED HORIZONS

I

Space and Time on the Indian Ocean Rim

On December 26, 2004, giant tsunami waves triggered by a magnitude 9.0 earthquake off the northwest coast of Sumatra devastated communities around the Indian Ocean rim. The quake at the interface between the India and Burma tectonic plates lifted up the sea floor in its vicinity by several meters. A massive displacement of water above the sea floor generated the tsunami that swept westward across the Indian Ocean as far as the east coast of Africa, wreaking havoc in Indonesia, Sri Lanka, India, Thailand, Somalia, Maldives, Malaysia, Myanmar, Tanzania, Bangladesh, and Kenya. It left a staggering death toll of over 200,000 and destroyed the livelihoods of many more victims. The tsunami took about half an hour to reach the Indonesian island of Sumatra and crashed into Thailand in less than two hours. It traveled the approximately two thousand kilometers to Sri Lanka and the southeast coast of India in less than three hours and was pounding the coast of East Africa, some five thousand kilometers away, within seven hours.[1] The unity of the Indian Ocean world had been demonstrated in the most tragic fashion by a great wall of water moving at the speed of a jet aircraft.

A tsunami, the Japanese word for "harbor wave," is unusual but not unknown in the Indian Ocean. The first modern tsunami hit the Indian Ocean more than a century ago on August 27, 1883. The trigger on that occasion was not an earthquake, but a volcano—the eruption of the Krakatau in the Sunda Strait. It unleashed tsunami waves up to thirty meters high that drowned 34,000 people on the coasts of Sumatra and Java. The tsunami radiated out toward Sri Lanka and the southeast coast of India, striking Aden on the southern tip of the Arabian peninsula in about twelve hours. A natural catastrophe in the Indian Ocean, the 1883 tsunami was also a global event in more ways than one. It caused small but significant sea-level oscillations in other oceans that were recorded as far as Hawaii, the west coast of the United States, and even the English Channel. It made front-page news—carried by a newly laid telegraph—in the world's newspapers. In 2004, too, energy from the Indian Ocean tsunami was reported to have "leaked into adjoining oceans, producing sea-level fluctuations at many places around the world."[2] In the age of the Internet, news and anxiety about the 2004 calamity certainly reverberated worldwide, even though experts at the Pacific tsunami warning center did not know whom in the Indian Ocean to warn of the impending disaster. The tsunami devastated Indian Ocean coastal communities, but Western tourists in seaside resorts were also caught up in its swirl.

Yet the devastation and aftermath of the 2004 tsunami also

brought to light the deep and unique bonds that tie together the peoples of this interregional arena of human interaction. Despite the global outpouring of sympathy, the sense of the peoples of the Indian Ocean rim sharing a common historical destiny was palpable. The ocean was—and, in many ways, continues to be—characterized by specialized flows of capital and labor, skills and services, ideas and culture.

The contemporary analogy of the tsunami makes vivid a novel contribution that this book seeks to make to our historical understanding of the modern process of globalization, namely, the continuing relevance of the Indian Ocean as an interregional space in a time of intense global interconnections. Just as waves in one ocean produce fluctuations in sea levels in others, the human history of the Indian Ocean is strung together at a higher level of intensity in the interregional arena while contributing to and being affected by structures, processes, and events of global significance. A radically new perspective on the history of globalization can, therefore, be offered by focusing on the historical space that intermediates between the levels of nation and globe. Such a focus may enable us to tease out both the power and the limits of globalization as a historical phenomenon.

After the 2004 tsunami tragedy, an assertion made in 2003 that "it is people, not water, that created unity and a recognizable Indian Ocean that historians can study" may sound like a case of human beings tempting Providence.[3] While nature's fury provides a stern reminder of the limits of human capability, the claim about people forging unity in an interregional arena such as the Indian Ocean still has merit. It also makes more challenging the task of sketching spatial boundaries. "For what boundaries can be marked," the great historian of the Mediterranean Fernand Braudel asked, "when we are dealing not with plants and animals, relief and climate, but men, whom no barriers or frontiers can stop?" He answered: "Mediterranean civilization spreads far beyond its shores in great waves that are balanced by continual returns . . . We should imagine a hundred frontiers, not one, some political, some economic, and some cultural." Having used an oceanic metaphor, Braudel was convinced that the "wheel of human fortune" had "determined the destiny of the sea," rather than the other way around.[4] In exploring Indian Ocean history in all its richness, we have to imagine a hundred horizons, not one, of many hues and colors. This book, too, will emphasize the role of human agency, imagination, and action, while being a little more humble in respecting the power of the sea. The people of the Indonesian islands, in particular, seem to be in need of some mercy from the goddess of the southern ocean whom they have revered through the ages and who appears to have abandoned them at this moment.

Spatial Boundaries of an Interregional Arena

According to Bernard Bailyn, "There comes a moment when historians . . . blink their eyes and suddenly see within a mass of scattered information a new configuration that has a general meaning never grasped before, an emergent pattern that has some kind of enhanced explanatory power. That happened somewhere along the line in the past three decades, to bring the idea of Atlantic history into focus." A very similar claim can be made about the idea of Indian Ocean history as it has evolved in the minds of many historians across many seas, but there is one major difference: "Nobody I know," Bailyn asserts, "is or has been poetically enraptured by the Atlantic world."[5] Whatever the relationship might be between Atlantic history and poetry, there is no question that the history of the Indian Ocean world is enmeshed with its poetry and in some ways propelled by it, as will be clear from my engagement with a problem even as prosaic as that of spatial and temporal boundaries.[6]

"Space," writes K. N. Chaudhuri, "is a more fundamental, rational and *a priori* dimension for social action than time-order and succession." For example, it is possible to mark on a map "the sites of all the important historical battlefields, great urban centres, caravan routes, and the commercial emporia in the Indian Ocean," regardless of when they were active. Such an exercise enables one to sift out the elements of structural importance in Indian Ocean history. Further, the continuity of a spatial surface and an idea of its limits are dependent not only on physical structure but also on the cognitive domain of mental processes. It was not the geographical morphology but the *interpretation* of "the distant grey silhouette of the Girnar mountain" of Gujarat that marked for sailors in the western Indian Ocean the welcoming, yet perilous, gateway to the inner domain of Hind. Space "takes precedence" in historical understanding over its complementary field of chronology.[7]

The history and historiography of the Indian Ocean can be introduced, as a seascape artist might do, in broad strokes of the brush: once dipped in the sources of many archives, the picture as a whole will emerge more textured and complex. The issue of spatial boundaries helps us theorize and place in historical context the Indian Ocean as an interregional arena of political, economic, and cultural interaction. Then temporal thresholds will be addressed to define a meaningful scheme of periodization for Indian Ocean history. Some thematic and methodological issues concerning structure and narrative may help lend coherence to a field of study that demands an ability to engage in fairly large-scale comparisons. Such an effort is necessary to clear the deck as a prelude to a series of sea voyages across the Indian Ocean.

The Indian Ocean is best characterized as an "interregional arena" rather than as a "system," a term that has more rigid connotations.[8] An interregional arena lies somewhere between the generalities of a "world system" and the specificities of particular regions. Regional entities known today as the Middle East, South Asia, and Southeast Asia, which underpin the rubric of area studies in the Western academy, are relatively recent constructions that arbitrarily project certain legacies of colonial power onto the domain of knowledge in the postcolonial era. The world of the Indian Ocean, or for that matter, that of the Mediterranean, has a much greater depth of economic and cultural meaning. Tied together by webs of economic and cultural relationships, such arenas nevertheless had flexible internal and external boundaries. These arenas, where port cities formed the nodal points of exchange and interaction, have been so far mostly theorized, described, and analyzed only for the premodern and early modern periods.

They have not generally formed the canvas on which scholars have written histories of the modern era. If the Mediterranean was seen to have been swamped by a world capitalist system with a global reach, the organic unity of the Indian Ocean rim was widely assumed to have been ruptured with the establishment of European political and economic domination by the latter half of the eighteenth century.

The Portuguese presence in the Indian Ocean in the sixteenth century and the Dutch role there in the seventeenth century have been the subject of some interesting revisionist work, but insightful scholarship on the Indian Ocean as an interregional arena and level of analysis in the period after 1750, and especially after 1830, is still in its early stages.[9] Colonial frontiers came to obstruct the study of comparisons and links across regions and left as a lasting legacy a general narrowing of scholarly focus within the framework of area studies. Macro-models such as the world-systems perspective, while transcending these limitations, have tended to view an omnipotent West as the main locus of historical initiative and are too diffuse to take adequate account of the rich and complex interregional arenas of economic, political, and cultural relationships.[10] Micro-approaches, such as subaltern studies, have done much to recover the significance of marginal actors, but have been overall a little too engrossed in discourses of the local community and the nation to engage in broader comparisons.[11] One way to disturb the stereotyped views of India or Islam that have been colonialism's legacy is to unravel the internal fragments; the other is to render permeable and then creatively trespass across rather rigidly drawn external

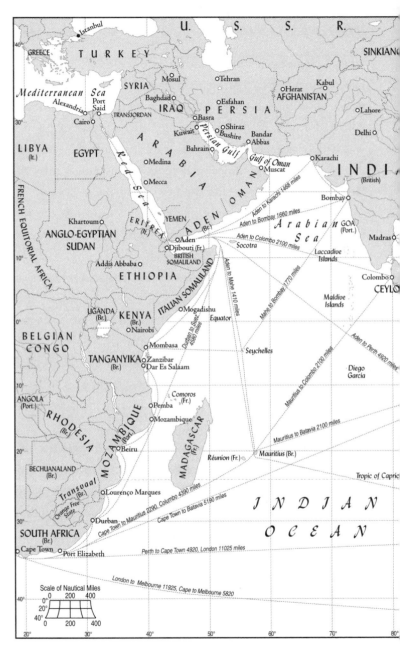

1.1. The Indian Ocean, 1935. Philip Schwartzberg, Meridian Mapping.
Map based on Alexander Gross, Map 9180/1935, Pusey Library, Harvard
University.

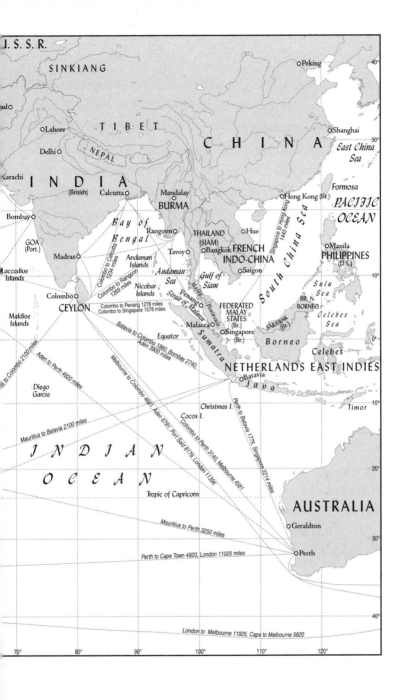

boundaries. It is to the latter effort that a reconceptualization of the Indian Ocean as an interregional arena can lend some much needed momentum.

It is hard to deal with spatial boundaries to the exclusion of temporal thresholds, but it may be worthwhile to pause and concentrate for a moment on the ways in which the problems of spatial limits and elements of unity of the Indian Ocean region can be approached. Although the ocean referred to in old Arab navigational treatises as *al bahr al Hindi* has long been perceived to have some kind of unity, there can be no single answer to the question of its geographical extent. The spatial boundaries of the Indian Ocean have varied according to the nature of cultural, economic, and political interactions under consideration and have certainly altered over time.[12] For the 1500 to 1800 period it is plausible to suggest outer boundaries drawn by the East African coast north to the Red Sea and extending east all the way along the Asian coast through the Arabian Sea and the Bay of Bengal to the Strait of Malacca. It can be argued that in the early nineteenth century southern Africa and even western Australia were drawn more emphatically into the orbit of the human history of the Indian Ocean.

More important for any project aimed at unraveling the symbiotic activities of people on land and at sea is a discussion of the principles of unity and disunity that have been seen to have undergirded the Indian Ocean as an interregional arena of economy and culture. At the broadest level the rhythms of long-distance oceanic trade have been recognized as having provided a basis for the unity of the Indian Ocean until the eighteenth century.[13] The overemphasis on trade has tended to obscure much else that went along with it, especially the flow of ideas and culture. The exploration of the Indian Ocean as a cultural milieu is quite as important as its role as a trading zone.

The problem of unity and commonalities has been addressed in a variety of ways by different historians of the Indian Ocean. Among them, K. N. Chaudhuri has made the most deliberate attempt to have his history from the rise of Islam to 1750 be informed by a "rigorous theory of the concept of unity and disunity, continuity and discontinuity, ruptures and thresholds."[14] The unity of economic and social life in the Indian Ocean realm takes on "analytical cohesion," according to Chaudhuri, "not from the observable unity of a spatial construct but from the dynamics of structural relations."[15] Yet it remains an open question whether the recourse to mathematical precision fares much better than a historian's intuitive presumptions in resolving the problem of the spatial limits of an interregional arena of human interaction. In Chaudhuri's scheme the Indian Ocean blends imperceptibly into Asia, comprising four distinct but comparable "civilisations"—Islamic, Sanskritic Indian, Chinese, and Southeast Asian.[16] If Braudel's gaze from the south of France failed to acknowledge the historical actors on the southern and eastern shores of the Mediterranean, the limitations of Chaudhuri's perspective become apparent in the marginalization of Africa. "The exclusion of East Africa from our civilizational identities," he writes, "needs a special word of explanation. In spite of its close connection with the Islamic world, the indigenous African communities appear to have been structured by a historical logic separate and independent from the rest of the Indian Ocean."[17] This special word on Africa seems to fall short of an explanation.

Other historians less ambitious about contributing to a grand theory have offered alternative typologies of unity amid diversity in the Indian Ocean region. One alternative advances an argument about three layers of unity: racial, influenced by patterns of migration; cultural, emanating out of India; and religious, shaped primarily by the spread of Islam.[18] M. N. Pearson sees "considerable unity in matters of monsoons, ports, ships and sailors." Another unifying factor can be noticed in "the widespread distribution of certain products from particular areas." For example, from the sixteenth to the eighteenth centuries the great majority of the inhabitants across the Indian ocean wore Indian cottons that came from one of three major production centers in Gujarat, Coromandel, or Bengal.[19] Among several other elements of commonality, if not unity, one of the more important was supplied by religious activities, especially the Muslim hajj, which was crucial to the working of a large and complex cultural and trade network in the premodern and early modern periods.

Did the Indian Ocean rim continue to be a coherently definable interregional arena after the imposition of European economic and political domination by the first half of the nineteenth century? If so, it will be useful to inquire what principles of unity might have sustained this level of economy and culture in an age when it had become part of and in many ways subservient to a global set of interconnections. Most historians of the Indian Ocean have preferred to assume that it stopped being a system or arena around the mid- to late eighteenth century. But histories of agrarian regions in colonial India have shown that migrant capital and labor played a crucial role in forging between 1850 and 1930 a system of interregional specialization and interdependence across the Bay of Bengal involving the old settled agrarian zones, newly developed rice frontiers, and the plantations and mines sector.[20] Rajat Kanta Ray has suggested in a very substantial and thoughtful essay that "the imposition of the hegemony of Western capital and the disruption of the older Indian Ocean economy constitutes a process much more complex than is to be comprehended in terms of a unidimensional history of the expansion of 'the capitalist world economy.'" In fact, he argues that the Indian and Chinese chain of trade and finance stretching from Zanzibar to Singapore formed "a distinct international system that never lost its identity in the larger dominant world system of the West."[21] The bazaar nexus occupying the intermediate tier of a three-tiered system—with European capital at the top and the world of peasants, peddlers, and pawnbrokers below—provided the critical link across the Indian Ocean during the nineteenth century. The concept of the bazaar here is quite removed from the narrow and ahistorical notion of it as atomistic person-to-person transactions. Instead, the bazaar refers to wholesale commerce above the level of local markets and even more importantly to "the indigenous money market which finances, through promissory notes, bills of exchange (suftajas, hundis, etc.) and other negotiable instruments, the wholesale and forward trade over the longer distances." The "colonial expansion of the international capitalist economy of Europe and the rise of the new pan-Asian economic formation dubbed the bazaar" have been interpreted as related historical processes of the modern era.[22]

There were strands other than the ties of intermediary capital that sustained the Indian Ocean rim as an interregional arena of economy and culture. From about 1800 to 1930 preexisting interregional networks were utilized, molded, reordered, and rendered subservient by Western capital and the more powerful colonial states, but never torn apart until these networks came under severe strain during the 1930s. Almost throughout the age of European colonialism, the Indian Ocean rim was characterized by specialized flows of capital and labor, administrative skills and professional services, and ideas and culture. Not to be mistaken for continuity between the precolonial and colonial eras, such a reinterpretation requires a new paradigm for the European colonial and paracolonial enterprise of domination as well as a subtler understanding of the unities and distinctive features of the cultures and idioms of anticolonial resistance. The fortunes and fears of migrant Indian merchants, moneylenders, soldiers, and laborers make it imperative to blend imaginatively the dimensions of economy, politics, and culture in rethinking the Indian Ocean as an interregional arena in the nineteenth and twentieth centuries. But if theory is not to be disconnected from history and space from time, I need at this stage to turn to that part of the canvas where temporal thresholds can be sketched in and juxtaposed with the sweeping lines of spatial limits.

Temporal Thresholds

The Indian Ocean has been traversed by a number of distinguished historians with a penchant for describing long- and medium-term movements in trade and culture. Whether they have taken on a whole millennium or just a couple of centuries, most have chosen to concentrate on the premodern and early modern periods. What emerges from these studies of the Indian Ocean until the eighteenth century is a picture of a well-integrated interregional arena of economic and cultural interaction and exchange. Particularly important connections of material life, politico-military organization, economic institutions, and social-religious ideology were forged across the ocean during the millennium that stretched from the eighth to the eighteenth century. The modification of these links in the late eighteenth and early nineteenth centuries critically influenced the nature of the colonial transition in South and Southeast Asia and European ascendancy in the Middle East.[23] The direct links of political economy of the recent decades since the oil boom of 1973 have also been written about by economists and political scientists. The study of linkages and the comparative context is now beginning to receive the attention it deserves in historical research spanning the period from circa 1830 to 1970. It is this apparent hiatus between the early colonial and contemporary periods that my discussion of the matter of temporal thresholds will primarily address.

The ancient, if not eternal, quality of the Indian Ocean has appealed not just to historians, but to poets and philosophers as well. Although coastal trading links between India and Mesopotamia go back nearly five millennia, it was the cracking of the code of the *mausim* or monsoon, probably in the seventh century B.C., that "dramatically extended the range of human movement across the Ocean, making possible increased direct contact between the Middle East, South Asia and Southeast Asia."[24] The thriving agrarian and urban economies of the Achaemenid and Mauryan empires provided the basis for the exchanges between the Middle East and South Asia, which predated the crafting of close links between South and Southeast Asia. By the beginning of the common era, there was a perceptible shift in the balance, from the earlier emphasis on luxuries, to staple goods in the commodity composition of the Indian Ocean trade. At key centers throughout this realm sprang up important expatriate communities of South Asian merchants, who appear to have been more direct agents of cultural diffusion in Southeast Asia than in the Middle East.

The old Indian Ocean arena managed to cast a spell on the imaginative mind of a leading twentieth-century Bengali poet. In his famous ode to the eternal woman "Banalata Sen," Jibanananda Das evoked its atmosphere:

> A thousand years have I been roaming the world's
>   pathways,
> From Ceylon to Malaya in darkness of night across
>   oceans

Much have I traveled; in the grey universe of
    Bimbisara, Ashoka,
Yes, I was there; deeper in the darkness in Vidarbha
    metropolis,
A weary soul, I, life's waves all around foaming at the
    crest,
A moment or two of peace she gave me, Natore's
    Banalata Sen.

Her hair, darker than the darkest Vidisha night,
Her face, Sravasti's carved ivory; on the distant
    sea
As a lost sailor of a rudderless ship
Sees on a sudden the line of an island's green
Have I seen her in the darkness; she has asked, "Where
    have you been, so long?"
Raising her eyes like a bird's nest, Natore's Banalata
    Sen.

At day's end, like the sound of dewdrops
Evening descends; the seagull wipes the sun's scent
    from its wings;
When all the colors of the world have faded, the
    Manuscript prepares
For stories then in colors of fireflies, glowing,
All the birds come home—all the rivers—life's
    transactions end;
There remains only darkness, and to sit face to face
    with Banalata Sen.[25]

In another, less well-known, epigrammatic poem he let his imagination fly in a westerly direction:

> A thousand years just play like fireflies in the darkness
> Pyramids all around, the stench of the dead,
> Moonlight on the sand, palm-shadows scattered
> Broken pillars, as if: Assyria stands dead, pale.
> The smell of mummies in our bodies, life's transactions
>   have all ended.
> "Do you remember?" she asked, and I gasped,
>   "Banalata Sen."[26]

South Asian mariners and merchants played the key integrative role in the economy and culture of the Indian Ocean arena during the first millennium of the common era. After the third century their ties were closer with Southeast Asia than the Middle East, as Arabs and Persians began to play a more active role in the western Indian Ocean during the decline of the Roman Empire. The Chinese mercantile presence in Southeast Asia began a serious rivalry with that of the South Asians, but also formed another strong link in the Indian Ocean chain, from the tenth century. Meanwhile, in the eleventh century, Arabs and Persians as well as a few South Asians began to draw the Somali and Swahili coast of East Africa more firmly into the Indian Ocean network. The rapid spread of Islam across the Indian Ocean between the thirteenth and fifteenth centuries wove a new pattern of economic and cultural unity throughout this vast interregional arena. By the fifteenth century Arab and Indian merchants, mostly Muslim but some Hindu and Jain as well, were in the vanguard of maritime economic activity from the Mozambique coast in the west to the Moluccas islands in the east. At the same time, Sufi preachers fanning out from the port cities into the agricultural hinterlands were creating a common world of religious-cultural ambience and sensibility. It is this so-called high medieval period—from the fourteenth to the sixteenth centuries—that Ashin Dasgupta has identified as the peak of indigenous maritime activity in the Indian Ocean region.[27]

Did the early European forays into the Indian Ocean in the sixteenth and seventeenth centuries fundamentally alter or undermine the principles of economic and social integration in the region? The Portuguese certainly introduced a new kind of armed trading and a novel assertion of sovereignty over the waters of the Indian Ocean. Yet these two centuries have been characterized as "an age of partnership" between Europeans and Asians or as "an age of contained conflict" in India and the Indian Ocean. Scholarship on this period of Southeast Asia's history has disabused us of any simplistic notions of economic and societal decline.[28] Overall, Ashin Dasgupta has claimed, after the first "violent overture" the Portuguese in the sixteenth century "settled within the structure and were, in a way, swallowed by it." The English and the Dutch in the seventeenth century also worked to a certain extent within the indigenous structure, "and except the few pockets in Indonesia claimed by the Dutch, they were everywhere one more strand in the weave of the ocean's trade."[29] Recent scholarship, however, has suggested that the early European incursions were rather more disruptive of Asian economic and political arrangements than has been recognized by early modern historians of the Indian Ocean.[30]

Indian Ocean historians, so adept at defying the constraints of arbitrary spatial boundaries imposed by conventional area studies, have been by and large remarkably diffident about crossing the great temporal divide of the eighteenth century. But that has not prevented many of them from making confident assertions about the decisive end of a millennium in Indian Ocean history. A few examples will suffice. One distinguishes "five successive stages" in what is called a "millennium of Islamic expansion." This scheme locates the fifth stage in the eighteenth century when "finally, India's core position is subordinated to metropolitan British control and the integrative network of Indian Ocean relations is destroyed."[31] Another has written of 1750 as marking the end of "a life-cycle of human civilisation."[32] A third views the "most important change" that occurred in the eighteenth century as "the growing importance of the European factor in the Indian Ocean and the eventual sundering of the organic unity of trade and shipping towards the close of the period."[33] Finally, a general history of the Indian Ocean is quite sanguine that "by the eighteenth century . . . [the Indian Ocean] world was crumbling as it was overwhelmed, physically and economically, by European merchants and soldiers."[34] Something dramatic certainly happened in the eighteenth century. Yet paradoxically, the abandonment by most historians of the Indian Ocean as an interregional arena of analysis—on the assumption that its organic unity had been sundered—made it especially difficult to ferret out the key elements of change during the transition to colonialism. This in turn has hampered the development of a historical method that would unsettle the discredited, yet entrenched, notions of a West versus rest and other accompanying dichotomies. The challenge in this regard is to keep in play an Indian Ocean interregional arena of economic and cultural interaction as an analytical unit while avoiding the pitfalls of assuming any uncomplicated and unsustainable thesis about continuity.

The question of colonial insertion into the political economy of India and, by extension, of the Indian Ocean needs to be addressed in more complex ways. One way is to note the qualitative differences between precolonial and colonial capitalism. The portfolio capitalist, a ubiquitous figure on the Indian scene since 1500, was "an entrepreneur who farmed revenue, engaged in local agricultural trade, commanded military resources (war animals, arms and human labour), as well as on more than the odd occasion had a flutter in the Great Game of Indian Ocean commerce." The beginnings of the process of erosion of one significant item on the portfolio—independent seaborne commerce—lay in tough competition from European private trade at the turn of the eighteenth century. (One of the ultimate beneficiaries of the shift was a university on the east coast of the United States, Elihu Yale having been prominent among the rising private traders of that moment on the Coromandel Coast.) These "nabobs" were different from the typical Asian portfolio capitalist in two ways: they were linked to the English East India Company and eventually to the colonial state, and they dramatically altered the scale of British remittance out of India. By around 1820 the company's state in India had taken a series of measures to cut the cord between commerce and political power, which had contributed to the undoing of the indigenous states and had the potential to threaten the colonialists once they began acquiring state power (from 1757 onward). The building of networks and portfolios by Indian expatriates in Southeast Asia and the Middle East later in the nineteenth century borrowed "much more from the 'Chinese model' of overseas intermediation than from South Asian portfolio capitalism."[35]

While there were certain analogies between the Chinese and Indian patterns of interregional links across the Indian Ocean in this period, the Indian variant also bore some of the unmistakable marks of colonial difference. The spatial boundaries and temporal thresholds shaping the Indian Ocean's modern and postmodern history might be lent some further perspective and depth by painting in a set of important, related themes that will clarify the elements of comparison, continuity, and change.

Comparisons and Connections

A comparative examination of three broad themes will help frame our understanding of the colonial and postcolonial periods in Indian Ocean history. A point of entry into explorations of these themes can be found by embarking with early twentieth-century travelers on a number of sea voyages. This literary and methodological device is crucial in order to avoid the high degree of abstraction that characterizes so much of global, oceanic, interregional, and comparative histories in which real human beings and their agency vanish from view. While accepting the broad framework of a movement in time from the imposition of colonial and paracolonial domination to the articulation of anticolonial resistance on an interregional plane, I tell my stories in the form of a series of nonlinear narratives. The weaving of broad patterns of interregional networks is matched in each chapter by the unraveling of individual tales of proconsuls and pirates, capitalists and laborers, soldiers and sailors, patriots and expatriates, pilgrims and poets. An analysis of the large flows of goods and money is balanced with an interpretation of the perceptions and experiences of people who were key actors in the Indian Ocean interregional arena in modern times.

We launch into the role of colonialism in restructuring states and redefining ideologies of sovereignty by setting sail in Chapter 2 with Lord George Nathaniel Curzon, viceroy of India, from Karachi harbor toward the Persian Gulf, guns booming and masthead flags fluttering in the breeze. By tuning our ears to his public rhetoric and eavesdropping on his private conversations with His Majesty's government, we try to get a sense of how the British went about the task of making the sovereignty of some small princes one of the foundations of the supremacy of the almighty British sovereign of India in the waters of the Indian Ocean. The British raj has been typically regarded as having its basis in the territorial landmass of the Indian subcontinent and its external relations have been studied following the longitudinal axis that linked metropolitan Britain and colonial India. Curzon's voyage illuminates the latitudinal connections of India across the Indian

Ocean and opens a route for a reinterpretation of the British Empire, locating it in its oceanic spatial domain. Curzon's claim that "a hundred years ago . . . almost every man [in the Indian Ocean world] was a marauder or a pirate" provides an opportunity to cast a glance backward in time to revisit the debate about the myth and reality of piracy.[36]

The violence embedded in state-making processes in early modern Europe and the export of violence abroad by European "warrior nomads who differed little from the Mongols or the Mughals" are by now well-worn themes in world history.[37] By the late eighteenth and early nineteenth centuries, however, the character of state violence engaged in by the British colonial state was qualitatively different from the warfare of the age of Mughal ascendancy and hegemony. It has been quite accurately observed that the "centralized state which was created in the colonial period was an entirely new political innovation in the Indian Ocean region."[38] Its key novel feature in India was one of the largest European-style standing armies in the world, which came into being during the Revolutionary and Napoleonic wars. In the early nineteenth century, the soldiers of this colonial army crossed the *kalapani* (dark waters) to fight in Ceylon, Java, and the Red Sea area. Later in the nineteenth century and during the first half of the twentieth century, Britain's Indian army was deployed even more widely in imperial operations in Africa, the Middle East, Southeast Asia, and China. The story of these soldiers, their movements across the seas, and their memories of these movements are taken up in Chapter 4. From the early nineteenth century onward, the state penetrated society much more deeply than it had before and reshaped several institutions in law, landed rights, religion, and some customs. It was at this time that wandering peoples on land were either forcibly settled or branded "criminal tribes" and their counterparts at sea termed "pirates." Piracy may have been an old profession, but it was now infused with a new meaning.

The change in the meaning of sovereignty was fraught with even greater consequences. Precolonial states and polities generally possessed a shared and layered concept of sovereignty, which had helped create certain autonomous spaces for the inhabitants of port cities. Surat and Aden, for instance, had been part of the great land-based Mughal and Ottoman Empires, "yet they had autonomy enough not to be unduly harassed by their inland masters."[39] The notion of indivisible and unitary sovereignty imported under colonial conditions from Europe represented a major break from ideas of good governance and legitimacy that had been widespread in the Ottoman, Safavid, and Mughal domains and their regional successor states. Moreover, the British juxtaposed with their own monolithic sovereignty a particularly fake version of sovereignty invested in reinvented "traditional" rulers in post-1857 India (such as that in Kashmir), and extended it to coastal polities in the Arabian Sea, the Persian Gulf, and the Bay of Bengal around the turn of the century.[40] Later sections of Chapter 2 investigate the clash of Burmese pride with British paramountcy and the reconfiguration of the relationship between Malay sultans and British power extended from India. This process went on at the same time as "traditional states" were being formed in the Gulf under the watchful eye of British residents. The sovereignty accorded to some of the Gulf sheikhdoms was, as Curzon let slip in 1903, no more than the other side of the coin on which the supremacy of British power was clearly engraved. The Indian Ocean realm experienced a sea change in the concept of sovereignty in the age of high imperialism, which has lingered as colonialism's most poisoned legacy.

The second theme is the relationship of Asian intermediary capital and migrant labor with the broader structures of colonial and paracolonial capitalism. Historians of India have been pointing out the brief congruence of interests of indigenous merchants and bankers with the East India Company, which facilitated the transition to colonialism.[41] Yet it is also becoming clear that once the company had state power within its grasp, it generally clobbered indigenous merchant capitalists within most Indian regions. In other words, there was a significant decline in the position of most intermediate groups on whose collaboration colonial rule had initially rested. Indeed, the British had made "considerable strides by 1830 towards wiping the middle ground clean" of portfolio capitalists.[42] The timing of the erosion of these figures varied with the progress of colonial conquest. The Jagat Seths, for example, whose deep purse had aided the conquest of Bengal in 1757, were forced in the early 1760s—during the brief revival of power of the nawab of Bengal under Mir Kasim—to pay what was owed to the British and then move bag and baggage from their mansion in Murshidabad to live in virtual detention in Monghyr. In another case, several Hindu and Parsi financiers of cotton production and trade who helped finance the British takeover of Gujarat in 1803 had reasons to regret their alliance by the 1810s. The Hotchand family, which bankrolled the British possession of Sind in 1842, paid for their sins by rapidly losing out in shipping and seaborne trade (although they survived as landlords and bureaucrats).

Significantly, it was precisely in certain sectors of seaborne commerce, which is supposed to have dropped out of the portfolio of Indian men of capital in the eighteenth century, that some found opportunities for profit in the nineteenth century. The rise of the Omani empire stretching from Muscat to Zanzibar in the early nineteenth century gave certain Gujarati communities the opening they needed to create a lucrative niche in the interregional arena of Indian Ocean revenue-gathering and trade. Later in the century, Indian traders and financiers followed the British imperial flag to engage in what was perhaps dependent seaborne commerce but which nevertheless enabled them to carve out sectors or pockets of local dominance in Southeast Asia, East Africa, and the Middle East. Indian intermediary capital was of critical importance to business in the rice frontiers of Burma, Thailand, and Vietnam; laborers in need of capital on the rubber plantations of Malaya; the sugar industries of Natal and Mauritius; initially the slave trade and later the cloves economy in Zanzibar; the ivory trade and the coconut and cashews economy in Mozambique; the pearl economy of the Gulf and the Red Sea; the coffee economy of Yemen; and the bazaars of southern Iran. In addition to their role as financiers, Indians were selling agents for British, Indian, and finally Japanese manufactured products, including textiles.

While their long historical experience in handling money

enabled Indian, Baghdadi Jewish, and Chinese specialist communities to adjust to the age of European colonial capitalism and dominate the bazaar economy of the Indian Ocean, a couple of caveats are in order.[43] The Bhatias and Memons from Kutch who rose to prominence in East Africa and the Middle East, and the Chettiars from Tamil Nadu who came to the fore in Southeast Asia, were new dominant groups—not the same old banking communities from an earlier age. Also, one needs to be careful not to write out of history the dogged resistance of sailing communities in the Arab and Malay worlds, even while acknowledging the dominance that European shipping came to exercise in the waters of the Indian Ocean. The Arab dhow and Malay prahu boats, with all they represent, had a much longer afterlife than is commonly supposed. An overemphasis on the relevance or irrelevance of earlier skills in the age of the communications revolution of the later nineteenth century runs the risk of falling into a technological determinism; historical outcomes were actually being influenced by a more complex interplay of domination, collaboration, and resistance among economic and political actors. With the solitary exception of the Sassoons, none of the Asian intermediary capitalists was able to break into the arena of high finance in the colonial era. The entire intermediary structure was also vulnerable to the possibility of coming unhinged as a result of crises at the higher echelons of the capitalist architecture and the foundation of agrarian production below, as was to become dramatically apparent during the 1930s depression.

The so-called Indian and Chinese models of interregional links were different in the ways in which the flows of capital were related to the flows of labor. In the case of the Chinese in Southeast Asia, the movement of labor seems to have been tied in a dependent relationship to the movement of intermediary capital, and while Chinese capital and labor in Malaya were integrally connected, the Kling laborers and Chettiar capitalists were distinct immigrant groups.[44] In the Indian instance the flows of labor and capital were often quite separate, and the colonial state played an important part in regulating the movement of indentured labor across the Indian Ocean, as well as farther afield to the Caribbean and Fiji islands. The Indian flows of the colonial era also contained a significant component of professional and service workers. The relationship of these migrants with local peasants and laborers often became fraught with deep tensions and constitutes one of the more important subplots in the story of anticolonial and postcolonial nationalisms in Southeast Asia and Africa. In the colonial era, the cosmopolitan array of peoples in the port cities and their hinterlands no longer translated readily into a cosmopolitan attitude. During the early decades of this century not only was the pace of anticolonial nationalisms quickened at these sites, but also related sectarian and "communal" conflicts were accentuated. Such conflicts cannot be explained without addressing the seemingly continuous but indeed transformed interregional flows of capital and labor in the colonial era.

These flows of capital and labor are considered most fully in Chapter 3. The voluminous and valuable colonial records on Indian intermediary capital and migrant labor available in archives in London and New Delhi are the very best for a reconstruction of the economic history of the Indian Ocean in-terregional arena. But in order to probe the memories and meanings of migration, we turn to memoirs, travel accounts, and letters as well. Statistical evidence is offset by textual sources, the quantitative aspects of trade and finance balanced by a range of qualitative source materials that tend to be more evocative.[45]

J. H. Parry had once commented on the modern period of oceanic history: "All the seas of the world are one."[46] Indeed, the sea of the Indian and Chinese merchants, bankers, and financiers effectively extended from East Africa to Southeast Asia. Yet the fact that none of the Asian intermediary capitalists except the Sassoons could enter London's financial world suggests that there were some glass ceilings in the capitalist architecture. Psychological obstacles were certainly as important as material barriers. The nineteenth-century movement of indentured labor monitored by the British colonial state to the Caribbean across the Atlantic and to Fiji in the middle of the Pacific may have been part of a connected economic system along with migration to plantations in different parts of the Indian Ocean arena. But a recovery of the voices of indentured laborers indicates that these movements were experienced and felt by them in rather different ways, with some implications for understanding the outer limits of al-Hind in the modern, colonial period.[47]

It is not easy to breathe life into things. But each of the key commodities in Indian Ocean trade have engendered vibrant stories, some of which I try to record in Chapter 3. The focus here is on the relationship of people to commodities and the interregional networks of capital and labor that made their production and marketing possible. To construct my narrative of interregional links across the Arabian Sea, I examine under a microscope a primary product—pearls—that had to be extracted from the seabed and then introduce the tasting of a spice—cloves—that was grown on the tiny islands of Zanzibar and Pemba. For the flows across the Bay of Bengal a plantation product—rubber—cultivated on the Malay peninsula and rice grown on the great Irrawaddy delta are my commodities of choice. Work on the plantations was almost invariably done by migrant laborers while capital was supplied on the rice frontiers by Indian and Chinese intermediaries. The power of European capital seemed to lie in its ability to choose its clearly delimited spheres of operation.

The third and broadest theme is the role of extraterritorial identity and universalist aspiration among the people of the Indian Ocean arena in the age of global empire. The dreams and goals of the colonized were never fully constrained by the territorial frontiers of colonial states.[48] Nationalism and universalism, far from being in an adversarial relationship, were bound in a strong symbiotic embrace. Anticolonialism as an ideology was both tethered by the idea of homeland while strengthened by extraterritorial affiliations. Islam in particular and religiously informed universalism in general provided an overarching unity in their varied regional and cultural settings. Premodern and early modern historians of the Indian Ocean have shown that Islam signified both integration and cosmopolitanism in that wide realm. I seek to reappraise the experiences of Muslim encounters with European colonialism in the Indian Ocean arena, long objectified by a weighty Orientalist tradition that has come under serious challenge but has not yet been laid to rest. A comparative approach regarding the strengths and weaknesses, bonds and fissures, of Islam as an ideology of anticolonial resistance in the nineteenth and twentieth centuries is an eminently worthwhile exercise. For example, what went through the minds of Indian Muslim soldiers as they fought under the British imperial flag during World War I and served in an army of occupation in parts of the Middle East? In the same period, how did leading Indian Muslim thinkers invoke Islam to justify their conscientious objection to World War I? Why did so many Indians become deeply concerned with the fate of the sultan-caliph toward the war's end? The Khilafat movement of 1919 was, after all, the first mass nationalist movement to span all of India.[49] Islam had been one key element in the unity of the Indian Ocean in an earlier age; what was its role in the age of high imperialism and its aftermath?

Chapter 4 journeys with the soldiers who fought for and eventually against the British Empire in the wide Indian Ocean realm. The sources here include censored letters of Indian subalterns, the depiction of soldiers' experiences in the imagination of realist literature, depositions in courts-martial as well as memoirs of different sorts. The study of these soldiers explores the interplay among loyalties to empire, religion, and nation and, in the process, contributes to an understanding of the simultaneous pulls of universalism and nationalism. We enter the world of patriots and expatriates in Chapter 5 by waiting with Mohandas Karamchand Gandhi outside Durban harbor on his second voyage to South Africa. Gandhi, it must be stressed, came to Natal as a lawyer to represent Indian business interests. During his twenty-one-year stay in South Africa, he did not take more than a fleeting interest in the condition of Indian indentured laborers, men and women, who worked on the sugar plantations in Natal. We also accompany Gopāl Krishna Gokhale, the moderate leader of the Indian National Congress, on his voyage to South Africa in 1912. This chapter analyzes the relationship between various castes, classes, and communities in the emerging politics to protect "Indian" interests in South Africa. It also asks what lessons, if any, Gandhi might have taken from South Africa for his political career in India, especially regarding the challenge of accommodating religious difference. This question, after all, was prominent in Gandhi's mass movements of 1919–1922, which sought to fuse together Indian nationalism with Islamic universalism. We then take a ninety-day submarine journey—including a transfer from one submarine to another in a rubber boat off the coast of Madagascar in the Indian Ocean with national leader Subhas Chandra Bose and his trusted lieutenant Abid Hasan—to reach the Indian expatriates in Southeast Asia who took part in a patriotic movement from 1943 to 1945. Here too we examine the role of Indians of various castes, classes, and communities in the independence movement and seek some insights into what motivated Indians, some of whom had never seen India, to fight for the freedom of their distant or imaginary homeland.

During the twentieth century, the peoples of the Indian Ocean rim witnessed both oppression and liberation, terrible

destruction and remarkable creativity. For all the conflicts
between rival empires, nation-states, sects, and communities,
there were also voices extolling the ocean as a symbol of universal humanity—its unfathomable depths matched by its
hundred horizons, if not a horizonless infinity. In this spirit,
Chapters 6 and 7 turn to the theme of pilgrimage. Chapter 6
tries to recreate the experience, atmosphere, and meanings of
the Muslim hajj in the modern period by using firsthand accounts as well as annual reports and enquiry committee reports on the hajj produced by the colonial government of India. Chapter 7 turns to the form of pilgrimage embarked on
by poets and philosophers, who sought to discover elements
of India's history and identities outside the strict territorial
borders of the subcontinent. In particular, the chapter travels
with Rabindranath Tagore on his later oceanic journeys, including one in search of "greater India" across the Bay of
Bengal and another that traced the lineaments of the universal
brotherhood of Sufi poets bridging the Arabian Sea.

On his visit to Shīrāz in 1932, Rabindranath Tagore claimed
close kinship with the medieval Sufi poets Saadi and Hafiz; the
only difference, he said, was that he spoke in the language of
the modern age. A leading historian of premodern trade and
civilization in the Indian Ocean wrote in 1985:

There are few studies which examine the historical past
of the Indian Ocean countries before 1800 as a single
subject. The tendency of history schools to divide themselves into regional branches has led to intense speciali-
sation, adding greatly to our knowledge of finer details;

but the task of integrating this knowledge into a general mosaic of interpretation is still incomplete. The purpose of this work is to begin a personal pilgrimage along that long road.[50]

Walking on the same path of pilgrimage, displaced only by time, I seek in this work to make a similar advance in our understanding of this vast interregional arena by reintegrating the modern history of culture, politics, and economy of the Indian Ocean rim.

2

The Gulf between Precolonial and Colonial Empires

It is fast becoming conventional wisdom that the power of the United States today closely resembles that of the United Kingdom roughly a century ago.

—NIALL FERGUSON

About one hundred years ago, on November 3, 1903, Lord George Nathaniel Curzon, viceroy of India, led a flag-waving naval flotilla out of Karachi harbor into the western Indian Ocean. The relative positions of the ships were so admirably maintained that "the lights of the squadron as seen by the night . . . presented an apparently stationary pageant." The coast of Oman was sighted just after sunrise on November 18, 1903—"an apparently unbroken line of precipitous cliffs, rising diaphanous and opalescent out of the pale blue waters of the Indian Ocean."[1] Addressing the sheikhs of Trucial Oman in a durbar (court) room "fitted up and decked with gold-worked carpets and handsome embroideries" on board the

Argonaut on November 21, 1903, Curzon explained why Great Britain sought dominance in the region:

> The history of your States and of your families, and the present condition of the Gulf, are the answer . . . We found strife and we have created order . . . The great Empire of India, which it is our duty to defend, lies almost at your gates . . . We are not now going to throw away this century of costly and triumphant enterprise; we shall not wipe out the most unselfish page in history. The peace of these waters must still be maintained; your independence will continue to be upheld; and the influence of the British Government must remain supreme.[2]

In Curzon's imperious public rhetoric the sovereign independence of the Gulf sheikhdoms and the supreme influence of the British sovereign had been neatly placed on two sides of the same coin. On November 18 and 19 the viceroy had met the sultan of Muscat whose demeanor, he had been pleased to report privately to His Majesty's Government, was "that of a loyal feudatory of the British Crown rather than of an independent sovereign." It was observed at Bahrain on November 26 that the sheikh had "kept his sandals on throughout the interview" with the viceroy, but the indiscretion was forgiven because "his omission to remove them was evidently due to nervousness."[3]

On November 28, 1903, the viceroy of India landed in Kuwait. He was delighted with the "great reception" he received from the sheikh and his forces, "cavalry, camel-cavalry and

2.1. Lord and Lady Curzon with staff on the Persian Gulf tour. British Library.

foot." Surrounded by "a shouting, galloping crowd, firing guns with ball cartridge into the air or onto the ground," the viceroy and sheikh made their "state entry into the town." The sole vehicle of Kuwait that they rode was later in the day "kicked to pieces by the two Arab horses who drew it."[4] But the visit on November 28 and 29 to Kuwait, which had been made a British protectorate in 1899, was reported by Curzon to have been "regarded by the ruler as finally . . . setting the seal upon the protection and overlordship of the British Power." Even so, the "success and completeness of the

2.2. Curzon's landing at Kuwait. British Library.

Viceroy's tour," J. G. Lorimer tells us, "were to some extent marred" by a diplomatic incident at Bushire (Büshehr), where the Iranian authorities refused to be reduced to the status of the sultan of Muscat.[5] Unable to get his way on the definition of sovereignty and the corresponding protocol, Curzon abandoned plans of disembarking at the Iranian port.

Curzon's voyage to the Gulf marks the high point of a sea change in sovereignty during the late nineteenth and early twentieth centuries that distinguished the nature of the British colonial empire from its precolonial variants. Recent exhortations by neo-conservative polemicists and strategic analysts calling on the United States to take up Britain's imperial mantle and India to adopt a Curzonian strategic doctrine in relation to its neighbors reflect a selective amnesia concerning the history of empires.[6] This amnesia has two aspects: first, the exclusion of most historical models of empire in a celebration of an imagined genealogy leading from Rome through Britain to the United States; and second, the erasure of the subjecthood of the colonized and with it the degradation of colonial rule. The bluster of today's political rhetoric, which imagines the British Empire beckoning the United States to its true calling, is best contested by scholars through a subtle deployment of historical allegory. One has to be careful about switching too easily between the past and present tenses of empire. Yet there is much to be gained from a serious rather than a superficial recourse to the drawing board of history. To be allusive and to leave room for some ambiguity is not to be elusive or hesitant to make comparisons between the British and U.S. empires.[7] Instead, a multifaceted and expansive intellectual approach may supply some indirect insights into the contemporary predicament of the U.S. empire in light of the British Empire a hundred years ago.

Proconsuls, Pirates, and Princes

Lord Curzon was the last viceroy of India in the Victorian era, which came to an end roughly a century ago. His political legacy in the Indian Ocean arena was as weighty as the marble monument he erected in memory of the queen-empress in Calcutta. In 1877 at an "Imperial Assemblage," Queen Victoria had been proclaimed with much pomp and ceremony to be "Kaiser-i-Hind," the "only appropriate translation of the title of the Empress of India."[8] The assemblage was held in the old Mughal capital, Delhi, rather than Calcutta, then the second city of the British Empire. Curzon held another Delhi durbar in 1903 before embarking on his journey to the Gulf. Imitation and adaptation of Mughal customs remained a characteristic feature of British imperial authority during both the East India Company raj and Crown raj before and after the great revolt of 1857. Yet even by the early nineteenth century the meanings of Mughal ritual had changed, with "a ritual of incorporation" under Indian rulers metamorphosed into "a ritual marking subordination" under the British.[9] The suppression of the great revolt of 1857 desacralized the Mughal emperor, under whose sovereignty the rebels had sought to reconstitute the legitimate eighteenth-century state system after destroying the illegitimate rule of the East India Company.[10] The Mughal imperial center, like its Ottoman and Safavid counterparts, had always aspired to be the repository of the highest level of sovereignty, leaving room for negotiating the terms of imperial unity with a plethora of regional and local governments. In periods of decentralization, as in the eighteenth century, real power seeped downward within this architecture of layered sovereignty. But Mughal legitimacy among the Indian people long outlasted Mughal power.[11]

The renewed centralizing impulse in the Ottoman domains in the mid-nineteenth century did not wholly abandon older notions of sovereignty that enabled Istanbul to be the center of a somewhat loosely organized "galactic polity."[12] Centralization and westernization may have been the slogans of the Tanzimat reforms of 1839–1876, but "this was paradoxically meant to transform the Ottoman Empire into a sort of sprawling unitary state, rather than into a colonial empire in the European style."[13] Yet the reformulation in India of political authority in the decades following 1857 had both structural and ideological dimensions. The centralized, modern structure of the colonial state was buttressed with new ideological concepts of sovereignty. The spectacles of British imperial power in the late nineteenth and early twentieth centuries, therefore, showed an obsession with Mughal form while rejecting its substantive basis.

The great rebellion of 1857 had been the last gasp of resistance by disaffected Indian kings and nobles against the rule of the East India Company. The new Crown raj took calculated steps from 1858 to disarm any cultural resistance to colonization, making sure that the preservation of ceremonial trappings and a measure of internal autonomy transformed the princely states into solid bulwarks of empire. At the same time, the raj strengthened the power of the Indian princes and Gulf sheikhs over their subjects. While the princes may have been weakened in relation to the paramount power, the British guarantee of personalized sovereignty, for example of the Dogra ruler of Jammu and Kashmir, obviated the need for the ruler to seek legitimacy through the time-honored practices of cultural patronage and material munificence toward one's subjects.[14]

The buttressing of princely autocracy was one of the key changes brought about by colonialism in the latter half of the nineteenth century, and it involved a very dramatic shift in ideas about sovereignty and legitimacy throughout the Indian

Ocean arena. The rhetorical claim was that these sovereign princes occupied "thrones which were filled by their ancestors when England was a Roman Province."[15] In practice they were often of more recent vintage, the Dogra chieftain of Jammu, for example, having acquired the vale of Kashmir as recently as 1846. Between 1858 and 1877, however, he was transformed into an ancient, "traditional" ruler—a good, old "Rajput," no less—governing under the authority of the queen-empress.[16] The colonial state had imported from post-Enlightenment Europe the notion of unitary sovereignty, which replaced the concept of layered and shared sovereignty that had characterized Indian and Indian Ocean polities of the precolonial era. The British raj, for example, would not encourage any substantive move toward the acquisition of citizenship rights. In colonial India and the paracolonial rim of the Indian Ocean, there were to be only subjects of the empire and of "traditional" princes. There were to be no citizens.

In the colonial discourse the princes and chiefs of the Indian Ocean arena certainly stood for "order" and with the aid of a Curzonian flourish, if not flight of fancy, for "freedom" as well. During Curzon's speech to the Gulf sheikhs on November 21, 1903, described by his faithful chronicler as "an epitome of British history in the Arab waters of the Gulf during the preceding century," the mighty proconsul claimed that "a hundred years ago there were constant trouble and fighting in the Gulf; almost every man was a marauder or a pirate."[17] The stigma of piracy has provoked heated historical and political debate without always shedding much new light on its meaning and substance. J. G. Lorimer, in his narrative on the suppression of piracy, played his part in the early twentieth century in affixing the label "the pirate coast" to the shores of the Arabian Gulf from the Qatar peninsula to Oman. Another colonial administrator added insult to injury by turning it into the title of a book based on the diaries of a British military officer who took part in the antipiracy campaigns of the early nineteenth century. "The Pirate Coast," in his view, "was an ideal place for sea robbers. It [was] studded with little islands, indented with narrow, twisting creeks, protected by treacherous sand banks, and jagged coral reefs . . . often only a few feet below the water level."[18] A scion of a ruling family of the region made a spirited scholarly attempt to debunk what he saw as "the myth" of Arab piracy in the Gulf by delving into a range of primary sources from the early nineteenth century. While exposing the stereotypical images of Arab piracy drawn by historians unable to read self-serving colonial accounts against the grain, the claim that the Gulf was "always a peaceful waterway" and that there were no pirates but for one solitary exception went a little too far in the opposite direction.[19]

There can be little question that with the European intrusion into the Indian Ocean arena, piracy acquired a new connotation as "a category of subversive Asian activity." The Portuguese had pioneered this transformation, which merely was taken to its logical conclusion when the English East India Company became involved. Prior to the European challenge, Indian rulers had not typically claimed sovereignty over the seas. Their attitude was best encapsulated in a Gujarati ruler's statement: "Wars at sea are merchants' affairs and of no concern to the prestige of kings." But once Europeans had asserted exclusive control over the seas and sought to regulate shipping through a system of *cartazes* (passes issued by the Portuguese), merchants responded with a variety of methods of everyday resistance without making any "counter-claim to sovereign control." It was only gradually, over the course of the seventeenth and eighteenth centuries, that Indian coastal potentates began to see themselves as coastal sovereigns, triggering "a fundamental clash between notions of sovereign authority" and inviting the charge of piracy.[20] Meanwhile, European seamen also came to be viewed as pirates within Indian society, as demonstrated by hidden transcripts in the form of Malayali chronicles and Bengali ballads.[21] The struggle for supremacy between these foreign and indigenous "pirates" remained unresolved until the English East India Company scored a decisive victory, both military and discursive, in the early decades of the nineteenth century.

At the turn of the nineteenth century the tussle between "pirates" of different stripes took on a new intensity across the Indian Ocean from East Africa to Southeast Asia—and for good reason. Various maritime peoples and states had been stoutly resisting the monopolistic trading practices of the European powers during the eighteenth century. Perhaps the most successful resistance was put up by the Sulu sultanate in Southeast Asia, which was able to maintain its own trading patterns for a long time by fending off the incursions of the Spanish, the Dutch, and the British. In the European view, Sulu was the quintessence of "an Islamic world whose activities centered about piracy and slavery." Yet commerce, marauding, and servitude were bound in an intricate symbiosis: the testimony of fugitive captives from the Sulu sultanate, for example, suggested a certain status of "acquired persons" and the possibility of their upward mobility—none of which appeared in denunciatory narratives on uniform categories of piracy and slavery.[22] So far as the Europeans could see, piracy was rife in the Malay, Indian, and Arab maritime worlds alike throughout the eighteenth century. Only success against organized indigenous resistance on the Indian subcontinent would enable the English East India Company to combat piracy in the Gulf in the second decade of the nineteenth century.

Having successfully surmounted "various internal troubles in India" between 1814 and 1817, the company raj could turn to making "an end to piracy in the Persian Gulf."[23] The Mysore sultanate had already fallen to British troops in 1799 and the last embers of Maratha resistance were snuffed out by 1818. In November 1819 an expedition set sail from Bombay under General William Grant Keir to sort out "the Arab chiefs of the pirate coast." An earlier expedition in 1809 had inflicted no more than a temporary setback to the recalcitrant Qawasim tribal confederation based in Ras al Khaima. The 1819 force was the largest ever sent to the Gulf and consisted of three thousand men, of whom about half were European artillery and half "native Indian infantry." Three ships of the British navy—the HMS *Liverpool*, HMS *Curlew*, and HMS *Eden*—were supplemented by nine cruisers of the East India Company. Ironically, the best-known pirate of the region, Rahmah bin Jabr of the Jalama tribe, was, willy-nilly, on the British side in this antipiracy campaign. As Francis Loch, captain of the *Eden,* recorded in his diary: "He was as great a pirate as those of the Joasmi [Qawasim] tribe with this exception, he protected British trade, and was at peace with Basra and Bushire, but at war with every other part of the Gulf."[24] The warming of British relations with the Sultanate of Oman, which controlled the stretch of sea from Muscat to Zanzibar, had contributed to the casting of their common enemy, the Qawasim, as pirates. A battle broke out between the British-Indian expeditionary force and the Qawasim on December 3, 1809. The Qawasim were forced back "with great slaughter, taking care to carry with them the greater part of their dead and wounded, many of whom were females who had joined in the sortie." Loch's journal records "a loss of about 200 in killed and wounded, including several officers" among the British and Indian troops, "the pirates neither giving nor expecting quarter and, owing to their savage brutality, they received none from our troops."[25] The citadel of Ras al Khaima was captured on December 9, 1819, paving the way for the first "truce" by the signing of a "General Treaty of Peace" with Arab chiefs of the coast, including the sheikhs of Bahrain. In the British lexicon the "Pirate Coast" was now metamorphosed into the "Trucial Coast" (after "truce"), even though the Arabs of the region were understandably not enamored of either description.

As usual, it was easier to declare peace than to enforce it. General Grant Keir's interpreter, Captain Perronet Thompson, had successfully inserted an antislavery clause into the treaty. A Methodist from Yorkshire whose parents were friends of William Wilberforce, founder of the Anti-Slavery

Society, Thompson was made the "Political Agent" to deal with matters concerning the Arab tribes and left in command of the garrison at Ras al Khaima once the main expeditionary force was withdrawn in July 1820. A better ideologue than a soldier, he promptly led a small force of British and Indian troops into a humiliating defeat at the hands of the Bani Bu'Ali tribe. This necessitated the dispatch of another large expedition from Bombay of more than 1,200 British and nearly 1,700 Indian soldiers, which in alliance with the Sultanate of Oman brought the Bani Bu'Ali to heel.[26] There followed in the next few decades seven more treaties with Arab chiefs. The "Maritime Truce" was reached in 1839 and periodically renewed until the grander "Treaty of Perpetual Peace" was concluded in 1853. Curzon was able to sermonize to the Arab chiefs in 1903, "Out of the relations that were thus created, and which by your own consent constituted the British Government the guardian of inter-tribal peace, there grew up political ties between the Government of India and yourselves, whereby the British Government became your overlords and protectors and you have relations with no other Power."[27]

Of the essence here is the interregional strategic and political link that had been forged across the Arabian Sea between India and the Gulf. From the second decade of the nineteenth century the two major British political residencies at Bushire and Basra reported to India, in particular to the provincial government of Bombay, from which it drew its salaries in Indian rupees. As an increasingly centralized, modern state came to be constructed in India under colonial auspices in the middle decades of the nineteenth century, the government of India took over powers previously held at the provincial level. From 1843, the political residency and agencies in Ottoman Iraq reported to Calcutta, the capital of British India, rather than to Bombay, even though a comparable switch of political authority was not effected in the Persian Gulf for another three decades.

The great mutiny and revolt of 1857 caused a temporary rupture in the interregional strategic link between India and the Gulf. Worries about the loyalty of Indian soldiers and sailors led to the abolition of the Indian Navy in 1863. The Royal Navy, slated to step into the breach, was not especially well equipped to do so and, consequently, "British political interests suffered severely in the Persian Gulf, in the Red Sea, and elsewhere." In 1864–1865 the British resident at Bushire complained that he did not have the naval power to either restrain the slave trade or keep the peace among rival Arab chiefs. Convinced of the indispensability of India's interregional role, British policy-makers decided to permanently lease six ships of the British admiralty to the government of India for £70,000 a year. At Indian taxpayers' expense, these vessels were to be on "constant and exclusive service in the Persian Gulf, where they were to perform police duties and prevent the Arab chiefs from rendering navigation and commerce insecure by piratical expeditions and from engaging in the slave trade." In 1872 the central government of India sought full responsibility for "the relations of the British Government with the foreign powers and states to the West of India, *viz.*, Muscat, Zanzibar, those on the coast of Arabia, and those on the littoral of the Persian Gulf," which the provincial government of Bombay ceded in 1873.[28]

Colonial India's interregional links stretched eastward as well, across the Bay of Bengal toward Burma and Malaya. The Straits Settlements on the Malay peninsula remained under the administrative jurisdiction of Calcutta until 1867. These included Penang, acquired by the East India Company in 1786; Singapore, founded by Stamford Raffles in 1819; and Malacca, obtained as a result of the Anglo-Dutch Treaty of 1824, which demarcated the Strait of Malacca as the dividing line between the British and Dutch empires in Southeast Asia. As free ports, these served as convenient stopping points for company vessels as long as the China tea trade remained of vital importance in the early nineteenth century. Once the revision of the Charter Act in 1833 had taken away the company's monopoly over trade with China, the Indian government's interest in the Malay peninsula began to wane. A transformation in sovereignty in this sector of the Indian Ocean rim followed. In a trajectory somewhat different from what has been outlined for the Persian and Arabian Gulf, it was the snapping of the interregional administrative bond and the 1867 transfer of the affairs of the Straits Settlements from the Indian government to the Colonial Office in London that enabled capitalist interests, British and Chinese alike, to press for a more interventionist policy at a time when tin mining was altering the economic landscape of Malaya. The reported plunder in June 1871 of a British merchant ship by Chinese and Malay "pirates" in Selangor triggered the policy discourse on how best to assure "order and freedom."[29]

It only required the presence of an aggressive proconsul to make Malaya part of the larger story of a new imperialism—a story that endured for the last three decades of the nineteenth century. Anarchy in Perak, too close for comfort to the British settlement of Penang, led Andrew Clark, governor of the Straits Settlements, to intervene in the name of order. On January 14, 1874, his emissary concluded with a pliable chief of Perak the Pangkor Engagement, by which the sultan agreed to receive a British resident whose advice he was bound to accept on all matters except those concerning Malay religion and customs. The terms of the Pangkor treaty were soon extended to the states of Selangor and Sungei Ujong.

The resident system in the Malay peninsula had an inauspicious beginning. The British and their Malay wards did not see eye to eye on what in fact constituted the domain of Malay religion and custom. The overzealous first resident, James W. Birch, stepped on Malay sensitivities and was assassinated in November 1875. British and Indian troops had to be rushed from India and Hong Kong to fight a little Perak war.[30] The anti-British elements were quickly overwhelmed and the errant sultan, who was seen to have provided them succor, banished to the Seychelles. Pahang was brought within the purview of the resident system in 1888, followed by Negri Sembilan, a conglomeration of nine Minangkabau states, in 1889. If India and the western Indian Ocean experienced a transition to two versions of sovereignty—the unitary kind in provinces directly ruled by a British-dominated center and the personalized sort vested in subservient, yet autocratic, princes and chiefs—colonial Malaya presented the unique spectacle of a fusion of centralization and indirect rule within the same territories. In 1895 the Malay states of Perak, Selangor, Pahang, and Negri Sembilan were amalgamated into what was misnamed the Federated Malay States with a British resident-general at their head. Frank Swettenham, who had advocated the unlikely marriage of centralization and federation, brought theory and practice together, becoming the first holder of this exalted office.[31]

Burma was connected to Britain's Indian concerns by land as well as by sea. The conquest of Burma presents a case of continuously creeping imperialism throughout the nineteenth century rather than a dramatic territorial grab in its final decades. The East India Company's prized possession, Bengal, had to be defended in the early nineteenth century against the ambitions of the Burmese sovereign, who claimed tributary relations with a range of states in northeast India. The first Anglo-Burmese war of 1824–1826 was a bitterly fought contest waged on the British side mostly by a large contingent of Indian military personnel. By the time of the second Anglo-Burmese war of 1851–1852 leading to the conquest of Lower Burma, economic considerations, such as the attractiveness of teak for the British navy and the importance of Rangoon as a port, had entered imperial calculations. In the decades that intervened between the second and the third Anglo-Burmese war of 1885, Burmese kings stoutly refused to be dragged down to the position of princes and chiefs of India, the Gulf, and the Malay peninsula. The clash of sovereignties was exacerbated by an inability of the British to acquire information about the Burmese throughout the nineteenth-century colonial advance into Burma. As C. A. Bayly writes, "No ethnic Burmese were found to write digests and reports on their homelands to help the conquerors, and even if there had been, the British could not yet read them."[32] The final reply of the Burmese monarchy on November 4, 1885, to an ultimatum delivered by the British a few days earlier, was dignified and firm in not parting with the accoutrements of real sovereignty. The Burmese did agree to the stationing of a British resident in Mandalay, but denied that his intervention would be necessary in a legal dispute with the Bombay Burmah Trading Corporation, in which the Burmese judiciary's ruling remained supreme. The sovereign of Burma was also not prepared to conduct his state's foreign policy in the manner to which Indian princes acknowledging British paramountcy had been compelled.[33]

It took the British and Indian military forces a mere two weeks to reach Mandalay and depose the king of Burma. Refused a last ride out of his capital on an elephant, the monarch and his family were bundled onto ox-carts to be exiled to India. The novelist Amitav Ghosh perhaps best captures the mood of that moment:

An anguished murmur ran through the crowd: the captives were moving, alighting from their ox carts, entering a ship. Rajkumar jumped quickly into the branches of a nearby tree. The river was far away and all he could see was a steamer and a line of tiny figures filing up a gang-plank. It was impossible to tell the figures apart. Then the ship's lights went out and it disappeared into the darkness. Many thousands kept vigil through the night. The steamer's name was *Thooriya,* the sun. At daybreak, when the skies lightened over the hills, it was gone.[34]

The way was now clear for Randolph Churchill to make a New Year's Day gift of Burma to Queen Victoria. On January 1, 1886, it was proclaimed:

> By Command of the Queen-Emperor, it is hereby noti-fied that the territories governed by King Theebaw will no longer be under his rule, but have become a part of Her Majesty's dominions, and during Her Majesty's pleasure be administered by such officers as the . . . Gov-ernor-General of India may from time to time appoint.[35]

Burma had not yet been annexed as a province of British India. Lord Dufferin, viceroy and governor-general of India, gave some thought to the possibility of alternatives, including turning the country into a protectorate. In a minute of February 17, 1886, he dismissed these alternatives. Upper Burma could not work as a buffer state like Afghanistan, sovereign in internal administration and submitting to British supervision in foreign relations, because it was too weak to defend itself and might drag Britain into war with China. Dufferin also saw difficulties with converting it into "a fully protected State, with a native dynasty and native officials, but under a British

Resident, who should exercise a certain control over the internal administration, as well as over its relations with foreign Powers." In Dufferin's view, Burmese rulers were not "highly civilized, intelligent, and capable persons" like Indian princes; therefore, a "puppet King of the Burmese type would prove a very expensive, troublesome, and contumacious fiction." Besides, there was "no Prince of the Royal House to whom the trust could be safely confided," one likely candidate being deemed too greatly under French influence.[36] Underlying Dufferin's prejudices about the inscrutable Burmese was a larger British failure on the northeastern fringe of their Indian empire to effectively penetrate Burmese information networks and knowledge systems. So without further ado, Burma was annexed to British India on February 26, 1886. Burma was to remain one of its provinces until the mid-1930s. But it required a five-year protracted "war of pacification" against tenacious guerilla resistance and a dismantling of local Burmese institutions before a semblance of colonial order could be introduced.

Sovereignty and Frontiers

The new concepts of sovereignty in the wake of colonial and paracolonial domination in the Indian Ocean arena were matched by some novel departures in the definitions of frontiers. It is not that precolonial states did not possess notions of territorial boundaries. But frontiers between states were more often than not nebulous zones not amenable to sharp demarcation.[37] Where borders were identified more precisely, markers such as boundary stones became points of reference only in specific instances of need or dispute.[38] A generalized cartographic anxiety over territorial possessions was new to the area and was spread via colonialism and paracolonialism from modern Europe to distant parts of the globe. Not only were attempts made to draw frontiers of the colonial state in the form of lines, such as the Durand Line of 1893 on the northwest frontier of British India, but on occasion this new sort of frontier dramatically severed age-old historical links. "For years a Rebel Colony has threatened our Frontier," wrote W. W. Hunter on the opening page of his 1871 book *The Indian Musalmans;* "from time to time sending forth fanatic swarms, who have attacked our camps, burned our villages, murdered our subjects, and involved our troops in three costly Wars. Month by month, this hostile Settlement across the border has been systematically recruited from the heart of Bengal."[39] What the British called the "North West Frontier" of India was historically no frontier at all but the "heart," to borrow Hunter's term for Bengal, of an expansive Indo-Persian and Indo-Islamic economic, cultural, and political domain that had straddled Afghanistan and Punjab for two millennia. For five hundred years, from the fourteenth to the nineteenth centuries, Bengal—the center of British India—may be seen to have constituted the inchoate, eastern frontier of that expansive domain.

Just as the British deployed two concepts of sovereignty from the mid-nineteenth century, so also there were at least two notions of frontiers. The close regulation of colonial frontiers of states etched unambiguously on maps often required the expansion of imperial frontiers in response to political and economic contingencies. This process of expansion led the British Empire in India into a collision course with the Ottoman Empire across the Persian and Arabian Gulf in the late nineteenth and early twentieth centuries.

Whatever the effect of European balance-of-power rivalries on the scramble for colonial territories in the nineteenth century, rival European empires shared a penchant for precise map-making and the drawing of lines to mark colonial frontiers once these colonies had fallen into their grasp. Even the sole Southeast Asian country that escaped formal colonization—Siam—imbibed the territorial obsession of a modernizing state that had seized the British and French-dominated colonial states to its west and east.[40] The British and Dutch colonial empires broadly respected the deals they struck in 1824 and 1871 to divide up their possessions, even though their colonial subjects took a different view of the matter—as was made clear in the late nineteenth century by the fierce resistance during the Acheh war against the Dutch and the Ashante war against the British. The British and French colonial empires held each other in deep suspicion, but eventually came to a common understanding on the nature of frontiers of modern colonial states. The same could not be said of the British colonial empire and the Ottoman precolonial empire, which despite episodic centralization by the Ottoman emperor since the mid-nineteenth century, believed in radically different notions of sovereignty and frontiers. The gulf between these two entities was as much conceptual as geographic.

No one articulated the connection between colonial and imperial frontiers better than the Kaiser-i-Hind's most dedicated viceroy, Lord Curzon. Before he became viceroy of India in 1899, Curzon published in 1896 a monumental study, *Persia and the Persian Question,* which advanced principles that he later tried to translate into policy. It was crystal clear to George Nathaniel Curzon that "without India the British Empire could not exist." "The possession of India," he wrote, "is the inalienable badge of sovereignty in the eastern hemisphere." Whatever the losses since the late eighteenth century in the Western Hemisphere, the British could take heart from the fact that they were "the rulers of the second-largest dark-skinned population in the world." He reckoned that it "ought not to be difficult to interest Englishmen in the Persian people" because they were of the "same lineage." "Three thousand years ago," in Curzon's historical vision, "*their* forefathers left the uplands of their mysterious Aryan home from which *our* ancestral stock had already gone forth." But now, Turkestan, Afghanistan, Transcaspia, and Persia were "the pieces on a chessboard upon which [was] being played out a game for the dominion of the world." The "connection of Persia with the larger problems of Asiatic politics" was therefore the "first object" he had in view in writing his book. Toward the end of his magnum opus—written while "skirting in a vessel the southern and maritime borders of Persia"—he called attention "to a country and a sea little known at home, to warring Arab tribes and piratical professions, to seaports, now dead and deserted, whose fame once sounded through

Europe." In Curzon's view, however faded the fame of these tribes and pirates, "the British name" was "still on these distant waters a synonym for order and freedom."[41]

A Gulf War between Empires

A little more than a decade after Curzon's tour of the Persian Gulf in 1903, tens of thousands of Indian troops in Britain's colonial army were hurled into the Mesopotamian campaign of World War I. From the start of the war in November 1914 until the end of Charles Hardinge's viceroyalty in April 1916, 210,000 Indian and 80,000 British troops were dispatched from India to fight in Mesopotamia, Egypt, East Africa, and France.[42] The Indian troops took the brunt of General Charles Townshend's folly during the Mesopotamian campaign of 1915–1916, which culminated in the debacle at Kut, and later spearheaded the entry into Baghdad in March 1917.[43] Soon after Britain's declaration of war on Turkey on November 5, 1914, an Indian expeditionary force was sent to the Gulf and within seventeen days succeeded in capturing Fao and Basra. The initial goal of this force was simply to protect the trade routes to India and the newly acquired oilfields in Persia, especially the terminus of a pipeline at Abadan. General Townshend arrived in Basra on April 22, 1915, and his spectacular success at Shaiba with the help of the 22nd Punjabis encouraged an opportunistic push up the Tigris to Amara. Townshend's "regatta," as it came to be called, was unimpeded: the Turks and those among the Arabs who supported them overestimated British and Indian strength. The first ever use of an aircraft in Mesopotamia operating from Basra brought the British news of the Turkish retreat.

The seizure of Amara emboldened Townshend's superior John Nixon to think of occupying Kut, farther up the river, as well as Nasiriyah, and to even contemplate an advance on Baghdad. The plans were put on hold because summer illnesses had laid low Townshend and his men. British policymakers in India enjoying the cool climes of the resort town of Simla, however, had warmed to Nixon's aggressive plans and were able to persuade a reluctant London to clear a limited advance to Kut. This new offensive commenced on September 12, 1915, and by the end of the month Kut was taken. The British then decided to tempt Providence once more by deciding to quickly move up to Baghdad. "I still hope to be the Pasha of Baghdad," Hardinge wrote on October 9, 1915, "before I leave India!"[44] When the cabinet in London approved the advance on October 21, 1915, only two veterans, the old rivals Curzon and Lord Kitchener (who had disagreed in 1906 on British strategy regarding India), argued against such a rash venture. Two days later, on October 23, 1915, Hardinge took the momentous decision to risk trying to occupy Baghdad. The supply lines more than 350 miles deep into Mesopotamia were hopelessly tenuous and they finally snapped. The British lost a decisive battle near Ctesiphon on November 24, 1915, and of the eight thousand men who went into action, more than four thousand were killed or wounded in a single day.[45] The wounded were transported in punishing, springless wooden carts standing in for ambulances.[46] Townshend and the survivors retreated to Kut, where they endured a siege by Turkish forces led by Khalil Bey and a grueling battle of attrition for five arduous months from December 1915. With mounting daily losses and no hope of relief by another force diverted from France, Townshend finally surrendered on April 29, 1916, with his rump of three thousand British and six thousand Indian soldiers. The military historian A. J. Barker provides this grim assessment of the significance of Kut:

> In the whole history of the British Army there had never been a surrender like this; the nearest parallel was that of Cornwallis with 7,000 officers and men in the American War of Independence . . . Britain never recovered from the knock. The surrender of Kut completed what the failure of Gallipolli [sic] had begun; for the Empire it was the writing on the wall, to which, at Singapore a quarter of a century later, a metaphorical "finis" was added.[47]

By 1918, once the tide of the war had turned in other sectors, the British and Indian forces were able to conquer the *vilayets* (provinces) of Basra, Baghdad, and Mosul, thereby extending the imperial frontiers far beyond anything planned at the start of the war. But the catastrophe at Kut left deep psychological wounds and scarred British-Indian relations in significant ways. It was during the siege at Kut that Delhi lost to London control over war operations in Mesopotamia. Townshend, who seemed obsessed with the question of awards, honors, and promotions even during the height of the siege, wrote disparagingly of Indian soldiers to his new superior General Percy Lake on March 14, 1916: "Indian troops . . . [are] utterly unfitted for modern conditions of war under periods of great stress . . . in stress or siege they lose spirit quickly. The British soldier is simply splendid, the more trouble increases the more cheery he gets."[48] Faced with the shame of surrender in April 1916, he found a convenient scapegoat on whom to blame the defeat:

> The Indian troops throughout the siege have been dejected, spiritless, and pessimistic, and there were considerable numbers of desertions to the enemy and many cases of self-mutilation and malingering; there has been the difficulty of Indian Mohammedans not wishing to fight against their co-religionists—the Turks, no Mohammedan troops should have ever been sent to Mesopotamia if it were possible to send Sikhs, Gurkhas, or other Hindoo troops. In addition to all the above comes . . . the question of eating horse meat; . . . only by drastic measures have I been able to accomplish this *even after they had received permission by telegram from their religious leaders in India to eat horse flesh!* How easy would have been the defence of Kut had my division been an *all British one* instead of a composite one.

All this, Townshend hoped, would put an end to "the legends and fairy tales of the prowess of the Indian soldiers."[49]

Townshend's assessment notwithstanding, it was eventually

left to Indian soldiers—a number of Punjabi and Gurkha regiments in particular—to spearhead the entry into Baghdad on March 11, 1917, under the command of General Stanley Maude.[50] "Our armies do not come to your cities and lands as conquerors or enemies," the general declared on March 19, 1917, "but as liberators." Stanley Maude died of typhoid later that year and was spared the torment of facing the wrath of the Iraqi people during the great revolt of the summer of 1920. Indian soldiers were once more deployed against the insurgency, but on this occasion it was the brutal use of air power rather than the Indian infantry that decimated the rebels.[51] The revolt, however, ended the prospects of perpetuating direct alien rule. Furious debates ensued on the prospects of introducing elements of direct Indian administration in occupied Iraq.[52] Falling back on the well-worn British-Indian construct of indirect rule, the British installed Faisal on the throne and retained formidable informal influence on this Hashemite kingdom as well as the one in Jordan to the north.

Sovereignty Lost and Regained

If Indian soldiers were sent outside the colonial frontiers of India to extend and defend Britain's imperial frontiers, the anticolonial movement also drew from peoples beyond India's colonial frontiers. This is a powerful historical theme whose importance has not been grasped by political theorists and historians obsessed with the telos of territorial nationalism.[53] Perhaps the finest moment of the fusion of Indian territorial nationalism and extraterritorial Islamic universalism was represented by the noncooperation and Khilafat movement of 1919–1922, the first all-India mass agitation led by Mahatma Gandhi.[54] Gandhi was fully aware of the extraterritorial nature of the Muslim sentiment:

> Let Hindus not be frightened by Pan-Islamism. It is not—it need not be—anti-Indian or anti-Hindu. Mussalmans must wish well to every Mussalman state, and even assist any such state, if it is undeservedly in peril. And Hindus, if they are true friends of Mussalmans, cannot but share the latter's feelings. We must, therefore, co-operate with our Mussalman brethren in their attempt to save the Turkish empire in Europe from extinction.[55]

Within the Indian context, Gandhi supported the proposal of "Brother Shaukat Ali" that there should be three national slogans—*Allaho Akbar* (God is Great), *Bande Mataram* (I bow to you, Mother) or *Bharat Mataki Jai* (Victory to Mother India), and *Hindu-Mussalmanki Jai* (Victory to the Hindus and Muslims). Gandhi encouraged Hindus and Muslims to join in the first cry "in reverence and prayerfulness" since Hindus "may not fight shy of Arabic words, when their meaning is not only totally inoffensive but even ennobling." He expressed a preference for *Bande Mataram* over *Bharat Mataki Jai*, because "it would be a graceful recognition of the intellectual and emotional superiority of Bengal," a region that had coined this slogan. And since India could not be conceived without "the union of the Hindu and the Muslim heart," *Hindu-Mussalmanki Jai* was a cry to be ever remembered.[56]

One astute British commentator, F. W. Buckler, understood the basis of this fusion and in a seminal contemporary article published in 1922 advanced an insightful historical theory of sovereignty and frontiers. He persuasively argued the case for "the reality of what may be termed the *Respublica Moslemica,* obscured, in modern political jargon, by the hybrid word *Pan-Islamism.*" Even those who did not recognize the authority of the Sultan of Rum tended to respect his dignity. This was brought home to Buckler by an Indian officer who said: "sahib, in this cantonment there are two Christian churches—one Rumi *[sic]*, the other Angrez. You do not go to the Rumi Church, but would you like *your* Rum to fall into Muslim hands?"[57]

The desacralization and deportation in 1858 of the last Mughal emperor, Bahadur Shah Zafar, had "a far-reaching effect," necessitating the search for a Khalifa (caliph) beyond the borders of Hind. That year the aged Mughal sovereign was put on trial at the Red Fort of Delhi, the locus of Mughal imperial sovereignty, and sentenced to live out the remainder of his life in detention in Burma. Bahadur Shah died in a small wooden house in Rangoon on November 7, 1862. "A bamboo fence surrounds the grave for some considerable distance," the military officer in charge of the prisoner wrote in his diary, "and by the time the fence is worn out the grass will have again covered the spot and no vestige will remain to distinguish where the last of the Great Moguls rests."[58] It was not until 1934 that a small tomb was built on the site of the final resting place of the last Mughal emperor.

No historian has captured the critical importance of the 1858–1877 interregnum better than Buckler:

> The years 1858–77, the interregnum between the Mughal and the British Empires in India, coincided with the early years of the Young Turk Movement. The year 1877 marked, in fact, an epoch. Not merely does it mark the assumption of the title "Empress of India" by Queen Victoria and the amazing victories of Russia over Turkey; but about this time Saiyyid Jamal uddin visited Haidarabad, Deccan, and Tilak founded the Sivaji cult, not at Raigarh, the home of Sivaji's anti-Mughal and rebellious glory, but at Pratapgarh, with its associations of early loyalty to the Mughal. Here lies, perhaps, the clue to the easy union between the Hindu and Muslim opposition to-day in India.

Saiyyid Jamaluddin Al-Afghani, the Islamic universalist of the late nineteenth century par excellence, had argued in favor of Hindu-Muslim unity in India's anticolonial struggle. Balwantrao Gangadhar Tilak, the late-nineteenth- and early twentieth-century Indian nationalist, who enthused his followers by deploying popular Hindu symbols, was well versed in the history of the Mughal-Maratha accommodation and in the final year of his life blessed the green flag with the crescent that served as the banner of the Khilafat movement in India.

Buckler reminded his readers that the Mughal Empire was "established on the basis of toleration" and that Hindu support had been crucial in asserting independence from Persia in the age of Akbar (1556–1605). Shivaji, the Maratha leader, had been the Mughal emperor Aurangzeb's ally against the Muslim sovereign of Bijapur. Although Aurangzeb (1658–1707) alienated his allies in his later years, the second abolition of the *jizya* (the tax on non-Muslims that Akbar had first abolished and Aurangzeb had reinstated) in 1719 laid the groundwork for a lasting Mughal-Maratha alliance during the long eighteenth century. "Though Hindu by religion," Buckler ventured to suggest, "in politics they [the Marathas] were Mughal and consequently regarded the British assumption of Empire in 1877 as something approaching usurpation." The great revolt of 1857, triggered by "Dalhousie's indiscreet policy" that drove together Maratha and Muslim, had underscored the "reality" of the Mughal Empire. In the early 1920s the Hindu and Muslim peoples were once more in what the Englishman dubbed an "unnatural" alliance. "The triumph of British Oriental policy," Buckler concluded with scathing sarcasm, "has been to achieve the union of Muslim and Hindu in India, of East and West in the *Respublica Moslemica*—there only remains the removal of the schism of Shiah and Sunni in Islam! Up to date, it must be admitted, the 'non-violence' doctrine of Mr. Gandhi has done much to keep the movement in check, but the forces, so disturbed, cannot forever remain under control."[59]

The story of contested sovereignties and frontiers in the British Empire was to reach its final denouement during World

War II. As Indian anticolonialism gained strength, the pre-colonial Mughal Empire refused to die. A soldier, Lord Wavell, was the proconsul of India during the middle years of World War II. He firmly believed that for British India under threat of enemy attack, its imperial frontiers lay as far afield as Suez and Hong Kong, which had to be defended by Indian troops. One leading anti-imperialist, Subhas Chandra Bose, objected to this conceptualization, arguing that India had "no imaginary Wavellian frontiers," only "a national geographical boundary determined by Providence and nature."[60] Yet the only way Bose saw to resist British imperialism was to stimulate and harness a diasporic patriotism of Indian expatriates outside that national geographical boundary. It is no accident that the march of the expatriates toward Delhi, the capital of their homeland, began in Burma with a ceremonial parade and prayers on September 26, 1943, at the tomb of the last Mughal emperor, Bahadur Shah Zafar. Once the march to Delhi had been halted at Imphal, the defeated warriors and their leader gathered once more at Bahadur Shah's tomb on July 11, 1944. On that somber occasion Subhas Chandra Bose closed his speech with a couplet composed by Bahadur Shah after the collapse of the 1857 revolt:

> So long as ghazis are imbued with the spirit of faith
> The sword of Hindustan will reach London's throne.[61]

Current "empire talk" in the Anglo-American public sphere is conspicuously silent about colonialism, even while pondering the resemblances of the empire that cannot speak its name with the empire that showed no such bashfulness a hundred years ago. To break that silence on the present situation of the United States in the Middle East, and in the hope of preventing a simplistic reading of "empire" as having only to do with Britain's past global role, I have brought into the conversation the many varieties of imperial pasts. "America's cruise missiles," one critic of American empire writes, "are today's equivalent of the guns of the Royal Navy. The so-called 'Washington consensus' constrains lesser nations as tightly as the gold standard used to do."[62] An eloquent champion of U.S. empire implicitly laments that Americans are not more like the British used to be, especially when it comes to having the will to exercise imperial power: "The ideology of imperialism— the sense of the British mission to rule—was remarkable for its longevity. It can be discerned even in the Elizabethan period, before an empire had been acquired, and it did not really expire until the humiliation of the Suez Crisis. Many Americans, on the other hand, have always been reticent about their nation's global role."[63] Coyness is not a widely known American national trait. What then might be the reasons for this reticence?

There were key differences in both structure and ideology between precolonial and colonial empires—differences that have tended to be obscured by the easy contrast often drawn between empires and nations. If anything, modern colonial empires drew heavily from the model of European nation-states in their centralized structures and unitary ideologies of sovereignty, and they bequeathed these to postcolonial nation-states as poisoned legacies. Precolonial empires, by contrast, typically had looser, cascading political structures and espoused layered and shared sovereignty with lower-level leaders. The formalities of precolonial empire, unlike those of the colonial type, envisioned incorporation, not subordination, of lesser sovereigns, and this distinction was much more than a matter of rituals or political semantics.

"You can't compare empires let alone learn their lessons," Sheldon Pollock has noted wryly, "if you don't know what counts as empire, or if all that counts is whoever did as the Romans did." The "whoever" in modern times has generally been the British and lately, the Americans, whose type of empire has been characterized by "dynamic centralism, potent ethnicity, compulsory culture and aggressive religious universalism." The Indian history of "actually-existing empire" did not fit this paradigm and the Indian "imagination of empire" was even more radically different. The imperial idea in ancient India was based on a finite universalism that recognized multiple overlords conceived as *chakravartis*—those simultaneously turning the wheels of power across the geobody of Indian empire—a theme that was replicated across much of the eastern Indian Ocean. The coexistence of "universal polities and multiple Indias" was in "stark contrast" with "the Roman *imperium*, with its single *urbs* at the heart of the *orbis terrarum* and its frontier, often a very hard frontier." These were alternative visions of empire "beyond singularity, totality, ethnicity, and theodicy."[64]

While Pollock draws his examples from the period before 1000 C.E., his comments about the imagination and reality of empires have an even stronger resonance across the Indian Ocean rim in the period from 1000 to 1800, with the Mughal and Ottoman Empires being simply the most dramatic examples. Nor is this a matter of Indian or Indian Ocean exceptionalism: in the long and varied history of empires, it may well be that the reality of the British Empire and the dream of an American empire, which draw their shared genealogy from Rome, may prove to be the true exceptions. Empires in the precolonial Indian Ocean arena often knew how to share power and divide sovereignty and, in so doing, were able to accommodate religious and ethnic differences. This alternative imperial concept was never absent from anticolonial thought, even as it strenuously contested the assumptions and beliefs buttressing colonial empires. Yet the historical experience of subjecthood under modern, Western, colonial empires in general and the British Empire in particular is so raw and recent that it may have, sadly, delegitimized the very idea of empire shorn of all its nuances and creative possibilities. The sea change in sovereignty in the Indian Ocean arena ought to go some way toward explaining why the American empire refuses to speak its name.

3

Flows of Capitalists,
Laborers, and Commodities

India was clearly the economic prize driving the transformations in sovereignty in the Red Sea, the Arabian Sea, and the Persian Gulf. As far as the Middle East was concerned, the British interest until the discovery of oil was primarily strategic.[1] Yet in the late nineteenth century and the first three decades of the twentieth century, the trading and financial links of Persia, Iraq, and the various Gulf states with British India were also quite strong. Indian finance was of critical importance to the pearl economy of the Gulf, and the Oman-Zanzibar political connection had facilitated India's economic links across the Arabian Sea with East Africa since well before the formal colonial conquest of that continent in the last three decades of the nineteenth century. During this period, too, early Indian involvement in the ivory and slave trade on the East African coast was replaced with a new, and a relatively more benign, engagement with the cloves export economy of Zanzibar. Interregional trade and finance in the paracolonial setting of the western Indian Ocean exhibited some features that were different from the patterns on the eastern side, which bore clearer imprints of the priorities of British and other European colonial states of Southeast Asia. Indian intermediary capital was deployed in the form of credit to Burmese peasants to open up the rice frontier of Burma in the late nineteenth and early twentieth centuries and was made available as loans to migrant laborers on the rubber plantations of Malaya.

In the hundred years from the 1830s to the 1930s, nearly thirty million Indians traveled overseas and some twenty-four million returned.[2] It is most accurate to understand flows of people of this kind as constituting a kind of circular migration instead of an emigration. Of the considerable number of Indians engaged in the process of circular migration during the one-hundred-year span, roughly 5 percent (or one and a half million) are estimated to have been engaged in commercial enterprises.[3]

Histories of modern processes of economic globalization have tended to concentrate on the role of European and American capitalists. Yet there was no dearth of Asian capitalists with supralocal, if not global, ambitions. There were, for example, two networks of traders from Sind in colonial India whose business operations had a global scope. The land-based network of financiers and bankers from Shikarpur, which stretched northward through Kandahar to Central Asia and Iran, had roots going back to the Durrani empire of the eighteenth century. The sea-based network of Sindwork traders and merchants of Hyderabad, by contrast, forged its eventual worldwide web by initially taking advantage of the British colonial link between Sind and Bombay and then across the western Indian ocean between Bombay and Egypt. Indeed, an impressive array of evidence has been adduced to show how "South Asian merchant networks could operate with a certain degree of independence *vis-à-vis* European capital, although not in opposition to it."[4]

The general drift of this argument broadly echoes the important thesis put forward by Rajat Kanta Ray on the role of Asian capitalists during the era of European colonialism in the Indian Ocean arena.[5] It is necessary, however, to note clearly the important difference between the global and interregional roles of Indian capital. In terms of sheer geographical dispersion of Indian merchants and financiers, it may be tempting to align their story seamlessly with contemporary preoccupations about ties between the global and the local.[6] Yet between the global and local milieus of influence and activity lay the overland and oceanic interregional arenas, which were the key spheres of operation of even the Sind traders despite their presence as far afield as Panama. So far as the large majority of Asian capitalists were concerned, Ray convincingly portrays "an encounter between a global system of credit and trade centred on Europe and an Indian Ocean financial nexus dealing in negotiable credit instruments on principles that had evolved independently of those of the Western banks."[7] Only one Baghdadi Jewish mercantile family, the Sassoons, who had established themselves in Bombay in the 1830s, were able to penetrate the echelons of high finance in London from the mid-1850s onward. Most Indian, Chinese, and Baghdadi Jewish capitalists could at best aspire to dominate the bazaar economy of the Indian Ocean interregional arena that stretched from the East African coast to the shores of Southeast Asia.

The Indian intermediary capitalists tended to be drawn from a number of communities in particular regions and localities of India. Capital and community, far from being in an antagonistic relationship, as is often supposed in studies of global capitalism, were intimately bound. In the western Indian Ocean the Bhatias and Memons of Kutch and the Bohras and Khojas from elsewhere in Gujarat came to the fore in three contiguous zones—the Gulf with its primary base in Muscat, the Red Sea radiating out of the British outpost in Aden, and East Africa, having its economic node on the bustling island of Zanzibar. The rise of Gujarati capitalists occurred in partnership with the Arabs from the turn of the nineteenth century and preceded the European penetration of Africa. By contrast, the expansion of the Nattukottai Chettiar capitalists of Tamil Nadu in the eastern Indian Ocean was much more closely enmeshed with European colonial conquest. Here too there were three primary zones—Ceylon, Burma, and the Malay peninsula—that came under British colonial rule, even though Chettiar economic activities extended to French Indochina, the Dutch East Indies, the U.S. colony of the Philippines, and the formally independent Thailand.

In addition to these significant flows of Indian intermediary capital, India was the source of some of the largest circular migrations of labor in the modern world. The abolition of slavery gave rise to insistent demands for Indian indentured labor from the 1830s onward. The pernicious recruitment patterns, the horrors on the sea voyages, and the dismal working and living conditions on the plantations led some historians to believe that indenture and its associated forms of labor were no better than "a new system of slavery."[8] Aspects of this view have been effectively called into question. The depiction of women migrants, for example, as a "sorry sisterhood" of "single broken creatures" has been shown to be "simply a parody of the colonial discourse" on the social ills afflicting Indian society.[9] Yet there seem to be no reasonable grounds for accepting an opposing claim that Indian indentured labor migration was more akin to the movement of free white labor to the dominions than it was to the journey of African slaves to the New World.[10] Mortality rates on oceanic journeys were much higher for indentured Indian laborers than for free white labor but lower compared to those for African slaves.[11] The prospect of real freedom following the term of the indenture contract was also severely constrained. In an effort to keep workers tied to the plantation system, the planters executed a "strategy of threatening the livelihoods of the ex-indentured market gardeners and hawkers, and organizing a new migrant stream to diminish the bargaining power of the existing plantation workforce."[12]

As with the movement of Indian capital, it is necessary to probe how significant the Indian Ocean interregional arena was at a time when migrant Indian labor traveled as far as the Atlantic and the Pacific. Within the Indian Ocean arena streams of colonially regulated Indian laborers were exported in the century spanning the 1830s to the 1930s. In particular, these countries received approximately the following numbers of workers: Ceylon, 2,321,000; Malaya, 1,911,000; Burma, 1,164,000;

Mauritius, 455,000; Natal, 153,000; Réunion, 75,000; and East Africa, 39,500. The corresponding numbers of Indian laborers migrating to the Atlantic and Pacific worlds during this period were: British Guiana, 239,000; Trinidad, 150,000; Jamaica, 39,000; other British West Indies, 11,000; French Caribbean, 79,000; Dutch Guiana, 35,000; and Fiji, 61,000. There was a circular quality to Indian labor flows, especially in the Indian Ocean arena. Mauritius, for example, received some 455,000 Indian indentured laborers between 1834 and the end of indenture early in the twentieth century, of whom as many as 157,000 returned to India. There were undoubtedly certain analogies, if not global uniformities, of forms of labor in the plantation complex worldwide.[13] Yet not only did much larger numbers of Indian laborers migrate and circulate in Indian Ocean rim countries, but the movements of Indian indentured workers in this zone also followed patterns of family and kin group recruitment that were different from those of laborers who went to the Atlantic or the Pacific. In this respect indentured labor on the sugar plantations of Mauritius resembled what has been called *sardari* (overseer-led) or *kangani* (sponsored) migration; that is, it was based on precapitalist forms of loyalty and reciprocity that coexisted with the capitalist contract. Marina Carter shows the "the Mauritian experience of Indian colonization" to be linked "more closely with inter-Asian migrations than with the Caribbean or Fiji."[14]

The Indian Ocean arena was connected, therefore, by specialized flows of intermediary capital and migrant labor in the age of global empire. To these were added streams of Indian professional people and service groups seeking opportunities in colonies other than their own. These finely tuned networks of interregional specialization drew on earlier ties but were effectively forged during the nineteenth century. They were utterly indispensable to the working of global colonial capitalism and yet acutely vulnerable to its periodic downturns, especially the world depression of the 1930s.

Until the mid-nineteenth century, it may have been possible to advance for the eastern Indian Ocean a simple demographic typology of densely populated and sparsely populated zones.[15] The rise of plantations and mines dramatically unsettled that dichotomy. They drew their labor from the long-settled, thickly populated agrarian regions, which were reinvigorated through this escape-hatch of migration. Large contingents of Tamil labor, for instance, moved to the tea plantations of Ceylon and the rubber plantations of Malaya. But the new concentrations of population also needed new sources of food, which the old rice bowls of Bengal, Tamil Nadu, Java, and northern Vietnam were in no position to supply. This spurred the opening of the rice frontiers of the Irrawaddy delta in Lower Burma, the Chao Phraya delta in Thailand, and the Mekong delta in southern Vietnam—a process largely financed by overseas Chinese and Indian capitalists. The triad of old agrarian zones, new plantations and mines, and newer rice frontiers linked by specialized flows of labor and capital remained in place from the mid-nineteenth century until the crisis of the depression decade arrested or reversed most of these flows.

The significance of these interregional ties in the modern history of the Indian Ocean arena and the ways in which they unraveled in the 1930s can be best captured not with an exhaustive history, but with a series of micro-histories. These "slices" of history have to strike a balance: they must avoid an exclusive obsession with the particular that leaves the whole out of view as well as sidestep an all-encompassing meta-narrative on networks of capital and labor that is insensitive to actual life experiences. By bringing together the histories of mobile peoples and some of the commodities with which their fortunes were linked, the larger history will be more richly, and truly, narrated.

The Pearl and Oil Connection:
India and the Middle East

Ample evidence of British and Indian economic interests came to light during Curzon's primarily strategic exercise in the Gulf in 1903. During the viceroy's visit to Bahrain on November 26 and 27, 1903, the Hindu traders there presented him with a written petition. They had as early as 1864 opened trade relations with Qatif and "did large business there." But in 1895 one of them had been attacked, his right hand cut off, and pearls worth forty thousand rupees taken from him. Since Arab and Persian traders were now competing with the Hindu traders in Bahrain, the Hindus wanted to seek or renew other fields of operation and were "anxious to share in the growing trade of Qatif and Qatar." For this they needed the viceroy to appoint British officers or extend the protection of the British political agent in Bahrain to as yet unrepresented ports.[16]

The apparently obscure story of the trials and triumphs of Hindu traders in Qatif figures rather prominently in the British archives of that period. This was largely because prior to 1914 the Gulf had formed an uncertain frontier between the British and Ottoman Empires. Indian merchants and Arab customs agents were used by the two sides as pawns to probe for small advantages along this long, ill-defined border. The Indians and Arabs too sought special assistance from their respective imperial masters. In the 1880s Hindu merchants supplied Qatifis with rice, coffee, sugar, and cloth. Several Indians from Kutch, Veraval, and Porbandar on the Gujarat coast advanced money and came in Indian boats to purchase Qatifi dry dates. But then came the violence and the threats of further violence in 1895. In Qatar, too, Indian *banias* (traders) had until 1885 carried on a lucrative trade selling rice, cloth, coffee, sugar, and spices and buying pearls—that is, until their lives were threatened.

In 1903 the British political resident in the Persian Gulf and the consul in Basra not only took up with the administrators of Al-Hasa the question of the security of Indian traders, but also alleged overcharges of customs duties on dates being transferred from Qatif to Kutch. In 1905 the British found the export trade of Qatif to be in the hands of two local merchants, Mansur bin Juma Pasha and Ali bin Faras, to whom for the past dozen years the customs of Al-Hasa province had also been farmed out. The British claimed that the Porte, the government of the Ottoman Empire, believed in "periodic bleeding of two monopolist buyers [rather] than profits through free trade." Anxious to get a foothold in this sector of the Ottoman-British frontier, the British officers made much of the offers made by Indian *banias* to pay the expenses for the appointment of more British officers in that region. They also tried desperately to track down the elusive Indian merchant Seth Tekchand Dwarkadass to get him to substantiate his claims of harassment and overcharging of duties at Qatif. Tekchand, who styled himself a pearl merchant and customs agent of Bahrain and Thatta (Sind), was away in Bombay and said his only proof was entries in his own account books, which he had conveniently left behind in Karachi. Tekchand eventually arrived in Bahrain in 1907 with his account books, which showed that the excess customs charge on the boiled dates he had bought from forty-nine Qatif residents in 1903 was even greater than what had been reported before.

As part of its post-1908 reforms, the Turkish government abolished the system of farming out the duty of collecting customs in Hasa and Qatif, thereby curtailing extortion and fraud. The more level playing field was a boon for British Indian commercial interests. Seth Chatamal Tarachand, for example, who was a member of the leading Hindu firm of Bahrain, Messrs. Gangaram Tikamdas and Company, went to Qatif in 1910 where he did a brisk business and was treated very well. Although Bin Saud's takeover of Qatif in 1913 led to speculation and uncertainty about trade in and around the city, Indian traders did not seem to be deterred. Even old Tekchand sought permission from the British to do business there.[17]

At Muscat, Curzon had found in 1903 that there were no fewer than 1,300 British Indian subjects, most of whom had originally come "from the opposite shores of Sind and Kathiawar." Muscat's trade was "not only for the most part with India," but it was "largely in Indian hands." A deputation of more than thirty British Indian subjects and traders residing in Bandar 'Abbās told Curzon that Indian merchants had "penetrated into the furthest towns of Central Persia." The viceroy acknowledged that Bandar 'Abbās was indeed "a very important outpost . . . of Indian trade."[18] In addition to underlining British political and military supremacy, Curzon's cruise through the Gulf triggered the compilation of far better economic statistics than before of India's trade—data that encompassed not just its trade with the smaller Gulf sheikhdoms, but also its exchanges with the much larger economies of Persia and what was soon to become Iraq.

A detailed investigation of the foreign trade of three ports—Bahrain, Bandar 'Abbās, and Büshehr—for 1905 and 1906 revealed that the United Kingdom and India had the lion's share. They supplied 43 percent and 50 percent of Bahrain's imports and took 63 percent and 62 percent of its exports in 1905 and 1906, respectively. They also provided 73 percent and 56 percent of the imports of Bandar 'Abbās and acquired 82 percent and 82 percent of its exports in those years. And they supplied 65 percent and 70 percent of the imports of Büshehr and purchased 53 percent and 54 percent of its exports. For Persian trade as a whole there was stiffer competition from Russia, which commanded 57 percent of the share, compared to 13 percent for the United Kingdom and 8.5 percent for India in 1906–1907. The British and Indian figures, however, are probably underestimates because a large quantity of goods from these countries reached Persia via "Asiatic Turkey," which was credited with the export.[19]

In the period before World War I, British and Indian commercial interests had eyed Russian, German, and Turkish rivals with suspicion. After the war, too, the establishment of economic autonomy in Persia was seen to "impair" British influence in that country. The situation was counterbalanced, however, by the "extinction of Turkish sovereignty in all the regions of the Persian Gulf and ascendancy of British influence in Iraq." In addition, developments in the oilfields of Persia weighed in on the British side of the scale, and the danger posed by the German *Drang nach Osten* (drive toward the east) was deemed to be over. Given the well-established British influence in Baghdad, a railway line from there to Haifa was considered, in order to develop "the trade between the Middle East and India on the one hand and Central Europe and the Mediterranean countries on the other." What was more, Britain and India had by the early 1920s turned the tables on Russia regarding trade with Persia. In 1913–1914 only 21 percent of Persia's trade was with the British Empire, including India, while Russia commanded the lion's share, 60 percent. Ten years later, in 1923–1924, it was the British Empire that had cornered 57 percent of Persia's trade, leaving Russia with a mere 18 percent.[20]

The mid-1920s marked the high point of Indo-Gulf trading links. The British Empire and British India supplied between 60 percent and 70 percent of the imports of Persia in the period 1925–1927, while in the same three years the United Kingdom and India consistently supplied well over 50 percent of the imports of Iraq. Muscat's trade during these years was "almost wholly with India." The chief imports from India were rice, cotton goods, and coffee; the main exports were dates and dry sardines. India accounted for the bulk of imports into Kuwait and Bahrain and was also one of their most important export markets.[21]

The onset of the Great Depression sundered these Indo-Gulf trading ties on both the Persian and Arab sides of the ocean. The year 1929 was "a black one in the annals of southern Persia." Persian exports of carpets, gums, and boats dropped precipitously. So far as imports were concerned, "the piece-goods trade of Bushire, Shīrāz and Isfahan passed almost wholly over to Moscow." Indeed, "so cheap, so attractive and so fastly dyed [were] the Russian cottons" that the British products had been "rivalled in quality and defeated in price." Moreover, the Russians obtained a temporary monopoly on the sugar trade. Trade in Bandar 'Abbās had gone into "a steady decline," as it had in Lingah. As for the import trade of Karman in piece-goods and sugar, 45 percent was reported to be in the hands of Hindus, 35 percent in the control of Russians, and the remainder was dealt with by Parsi and Persian traders—even though only "a few years ago Hindus held 75 percent of the trade." In Trucial Oman, too, the pearl merchants were badly hit. One of the victims was the pearler Mohammed bin Ahmad Dalmuk, who because he had not received his money to equip his fleet had been "obliged to raise about Rs 200,000 from a Hindu merchant [obviously not a very far-sighted one!] at an interest rate of 36 percent." In Bahrain, merchants were believed to have sold not even half of their pearl catch of the year. Most pearlers in Kuwait were saddled with a catch of 1929 that remained "entirely unsold."

The big firms in Europe had "neither sent their representatives to the Gulf nor showed any inclination to buy."[22]

The year 1930 turned out to be as bad, if not worse. But unlike the collapse in prices elsewhere in agrarian Asia, domestic prices rose in Persia, partly because like China its currency—the *kran*—was based on the silver rather than the more pervasive gold standard, and partly because Persian policy led traders to take losses on exports in order to get certificates for obtaining sterling (and they then tried to make up these losses by hiking the prices of import goods). The Russians, resorting to a barter system, made rapid strides in the markets of southern Persia, while the Japanese waited in the wings. The "lately success" of the Japanese in the Arab coast markets was achieved "almost entirely at the expense of British and Indian interests." In Oman, pearl prices were 50 percent below the previous year's level, causing much "distress" and leaving *nakhodas* (boat captains) "unable to even pay for food supplied to their divers." In Bahrain, pearls fetched only 30 percent of their 1929 value and there was "next to no buying." In the midst of all this doom and gloom a "traffic in women from Malabar to Bahrain" came to light. Some were "repatriated," others "found husbands."[23]

In the good old days of the 1920s, the big merchants or their representatives would arrive in the Gulf and buy pearls worth at least £2 million annually in Bahrain alone. There were some five hundred diving boats registered in Bahrain, and fifteen thousand of Bahrain's inhabitants earned their livelihood by diving for pearls. Another fifteen thousand divers were engaged in the pearl industry off the coasts of Qatar and

Trucial Oman, while Kuwait employed approximately another five thousand men. The chief buyers were the continental pearl merchants Messrs. Rosenthal, Habib, and Pack, of Paris and Bombay, and Messrs. Mohammad Ali Zainal and Bienenfeld, of Paris, along with a couple of Indian and Persian merchants. They usually arrived just after the opening of the main diving season—the *ghaus*—and left one or two weeks after its close, their pockets bulging with pearls. The pearls would be "polished and graded in Bombay and then taken to Paris and London for sale to English and American buyers." Zainal alone had taken £600,000 worth in pearls to Paris at the end of the 1927 season.[24] Times had changed. The arrival at Bahrain of Victor Rosenthal and other reputed Paris dealers in September 1930 raised hopes. But when they departed having bought virtually nothing, "matters looked bad indeed." The 1930 pearl season in Kuwait was a complete failure. By year's end there was "the spectacle of wealthy pearl merchants, so poor that they could not pay nakhodas or divers their shares of the previous season's catch, even though they had safes full of pearls."[25]

The year 1931 brought more of the same gloom to the economy of southern Persia. The prospects for British and Indian commercial interests looked "dreary." The British political resident predicted, somewhat rashly, that Russia as a competitor had "come to stay," that its position was "assured by treaty," and that "being actuated by political rather than commercial motive" it could not "be opposed by the usual methods of commercial rivalry." In Bandar 'Abbās, all but two of the Hindu firms of long standing shuttered their operations in

June 1931. Carpets from Karman were exported in high volume but at prices so low that merchants recorded inflated prices to obtain the certificates they needed to finance imports. In Oman a further fall in pearl prices meant that the "poorer classes were reduced to the brink of starvation," while the merchants and boat captains defaulted on their obligations. In Bahrain the state of the pearling economy was even worse than the previous year. Had it not been for "a persistent demand from India for the cheaper grade of pearls," the Bahrain economy would have ground to a halt. The "surprising demand" from India was attributed to "money not spent on better class textiles owing to boycott [during the civil disobedience movement] being expended on pearls." Proceeds from gold sales after the devaluation of September 1931 may also have been partially channeled into investment in pearls. It was estimated that two-thirds of the pearling capital in Bahrain had "disappeared into the sea" over the previous three years. Qatif and Qatar were "ruined." In Kuwait pearl merchants refused to advance pay to the families of divers and haulers, provoking their refusal to go out to sea. Eventually, the sheikh coaxed and cajoled the merchants to offer something to the families and ordered the ring-leaders of recalcitrant divers "to be flogged and cast into prison."[26]

In the clouds of "widespread economic depression," silver linings appeared in 1932 in the form of a new civil air route and the growth of oil interests. In addition to being the civilian route to India, the airline and airfield infrastructure was, as the political resident noted, also "a strategical one." But the sea lanes were still important for commerce and war alike. The

Japanese deployed the usual methods of commercial rivalry to outdo both the British and the Russians. The cotton piece-goods market of southern Persia was "flooded with cheap Japanese goods of a design suitable to Persian tastes." The Russians, who had a couple of years earlier driven both Lancashire and Indian goods from the market, now met their nemesis in the Japanese, with whom they could not compete in price. The Japanese business was conducted "primarily through buying agents in Bombay where goods [were] trans-shipped to British Indian Steam Navigation Company's boats." The usual terms were 20 percent payment at the time of the order and the balance upon shipment of the goods. The Japanese allowed no credit, but offered attractive discounts between 10 percent and 40 percent. Faced with the Japanese onslaught, the venerable firm of Messrs. Zieglers had been un-able to recover the cost of importing "one of their oldest and most stable lines, a white shirting made especially for them." In Bandar 'Abbās, one of the two Hindu firms that had sur-vived until 1931 closed down and the remaining one planned to shut its doors after realizing irrecoverable losses. The im-port of tea, which was "almost entirely Indian," had "fallen considerably." With luxury goods having disappeared, observ-ers toward the end of the year reported the "deadness" of the Shīrāz bazaar; even "casual visitors were struck by the empti-ness of them and the forlorn look of the neglected shops."[27]

The situation on the Arab side of the Gulf was, if any-thing, even bleaker. The depression had "ruined" many local merchants and petty traders in Muscat. "Suffering and acute want among the lower classes," it was reported from Kuwait, "was a new and pathetic feature, and showed itself in the form of gangs of beggars who . . . roam[ed] the town"—this despite "a fair demand for second and third class pearls in India as well as pearls of large and perfect quality."[28] In Bahrain, where Japanese goods were beginning to make a spectacular entry, 31 percent of the imports were transacted by Hindu firms and another 7 percent by other Indian firms, a total of 38 percent for purely Indian firms. The bulk of the remaining trade either emanated from or was imported through Calcutta or Bombay. Although the pearl trade as a whole had declined, the British political agent corrected a misconception aired in a publication by the government of India that the trade had gravitated toward Europe and Indian interests had waned. In fact, the largest purchaser in 1932 was a Marwari named Gandmall Gashimal, who had bought twenty *lakhs'* (two million rupees') worth of pearls. The only purchaser that year who sent any pearls to Europe was Sol Pack, who had bought a paltry amount. The "entire remainder of the season's catch," it was reported, would "gravitate to Bombay in the normal way, where they will be drilled, polished, prepared and sold to the pearl buyers of Europe." Drilling of pearls was "an Indian monopoly except for one Parisian firm, Messrs. Bienenfeld."[29]

During 1932 there also was a rare instance of divers' resistance, put down by a small contingent of "Indian sepoys." Even in the best of times, the divers' lot had been unenviable. They typically received advances or loans known as *salaf* from *nakhodas,* who in turn raised capital from larger land-based merchants. It was the land merchants, the capitalists, who made the biggest profits. Hardly any of the divers operating within the *salafieh* system earned more than was necessary for bare subsistence. Often the better the diver, the greater was his debt because he was loaned more money "to put him into debt and bind him permanently to his Nakhuda." Some of the worst horrors to which the divers were subjected had been mitigated somewhat by a set of reforms enacted in 1924, but their condition continued to be bad enough.[30]

On May 25, 1932, a divers' agitation in Bahrain for better *salaf* triggered a conflict. When some of the leaders of the movement were arrested, their followers stormed the police station at Manama and freed them. A confrontation ensued between some 1,500 divers armed with clubs and sticks, a company of Indian sepoys (soldiers for hire), and some local policemen equipped with guns and live ammunition. The British political agent suggested to the political adviser, Charles Belgrave, that the sepoys should rush the right flank of the crowd and take some prisoners. Belgrave "unfortunately knew no Hindustani" and could only communicate with the sepoys through one or two noncommissioned officers who knew Arabic. "This disability," the agent commented, "also made itself felt later." In the confusion there were bursts of fire, probably from the local policemen. The rioters eventually yielded "after some determined scrimmaging" by the sepoys, and "a number of men fled into the sea." A "running fight now continued along the sea road" and "the rioters were gradually forced into the sea, except a few who were captured." Although the divers "strewed the sea for a mile," some had found "three jolly boats" and set sail in them for Muharraq. Two launches and the agency motorboat set out in hot pursuit.

At Muharraq, Belgrave's men captured some of the rioters but "the majority disappeared into the town by the shortest possible route and the assembled crowds gave [the pursuers] no assistance." It was then found, according to the resident, that "at some stage or another not known two divers were killed and another was found wounded in the chest." Some three or four more wounded were discovered later and there were "doubtless others who prefer[red] not to disclose themselves for fear of punishment."[31] A German journalist reported, however, that five dead men and six hopelessly wounded men were brought out of the water. He also counted over thirty wounded returned to Manama, with three dead and many other wounded taken to Muharraq.[32]

That night, another incident with the divers was to polarize Arab royalty in support of the British and "business as usual." While returning from Manama, Sheikh Abdullah, brother of the ruler Sheikh Hamad, had encountered two boatloads of divers and ordered them to stop. Instead, "they jeered at him and lifting up their clothes shook their membra virile at him," which apparently was "the highest insult" and set Abdullah "seething with rage." The "jolly boats" were traveling at high speed because of the wind and were past him in a minute. The next morning, congratulatory letters arrived from Sheikh Hamad for Belgrave. Orders were also issued that a house used for divers' meetings "be burnt to the ground" and that divers refusing to accept *salaf* be hauled before the government. The agent was "surprised at this energetic action" on the ruler's part. It appeared that "what really roused him was the insult offered to his brother." His attendant told Belgrave that had anyone done such a thing to him "he would have cut him down with his sword, no matter who it was or where it was." The agent thought it "odd that so curious an incident should be required to fire his resolution."[33] Thus not only did Indian financiers provide solid backing to merchants and boat captains during the profit-making decades of the pearl economy, but also Indian "sepoys" were deployed at its moment of crisis to snuff out an unusual protest by the hapless pearl divers.

During the years 1933 to 1935 the economy of the Gulf continued to be depressed. There were no more than marginal improvements in the value of exports and prices, and ordinary people continued to be distressingly poor.[34] In early 1935 a comprehensive report by F. H. Gamble, *Economic Conditions in the Gulf,* was published by the Department of Overseas Trade in London and received a fair amount of British media attention. According to the report, in Iran trade had been hampered "by restrictions, notably the quota system and the obligation for importers to obtain export certificates before they could procure import certificates." On both sides of the Gulf "money had been scarce," the primary cause on the Arab side being the collapse in the pearl trade. Japan had carried out a "successful economic penetration" of Gulf markets at the expense of British commerce. The main Japanese commodities were piece-goods, chinaware, glassware, and haberdashery. In addition, Japan had competed with cement and matches and "even undercut Indian rice in Bahrain and Kuwait." Russian trade, too, had receded in the face of the Japanese advance, especially once Iran had objected to Russia's trading methods and charged them with dumping. Japanese competition had "affected both the United Kingdom and India severely in the piece-goods market," with "both countries losing ground heavily."[35] The magnitude of this phenomenon can be seen in Bahrain trade reports for this period.[36]

The straitened economic circumstances of the depression decade stoked anti-Indian sentiment in many parts of the Middle East. Although there were no anti-Indian uprisings on the scale of what happened in Burma, resentment against intermediary Indian capitalists ran deep. In 1935 Aden was taken out of the jurisdiction of India's government, much to the chagrin of the over seven thousand Indians living there.[37] And at the triumphal moment of the Mesopotamian campaign in March 1917, it had been decided "to exclude Indians from employment in the local administration" and to put on hold the question of wider Indian immigration. The government of India responded in April 1917 that "any restriction of free Indian immigration for trade and other purposes into Iraq would cause bitter and legitimate resentment" and urged that if it had to occur, some "definite field" for Indian expansion be provided elsewhere, preferably East Africa. In the end, Indian immigration into Iraq was permitted due to the Iraqi need for labor in the postwar period.

Indian labor played a part in the rebuilding of Iraq until the onset of the depression.[38] In 1936 Indians were "being driven out of Iran and Iraq" and were "keen to try their luck in Kuwait." The pressure to leave had not come up before because it was "only recently that exclusion of Indians" had become "a serious part of the policy of Iran and Iraq." But they were not welcomed by Kuwaitis, either. Indeed, Kuwait's ruler wished to "keep out prosperous Indians desirous of setting up as merchants" because he was afraid that "much of the profit that the Indians would make they would remit home."[39] Urged by an Indian friend in Iraq, the poet Rabindranath Tagore, who had made a very successful visit to Iran and Iraq in 1932, made a futile plea to make the Iraqis change their exclusionary policies.[40]

It was only in the late 1930s that a rising oil economy began to offset the effects of the collapse in the commodities trade and the tightening of credit flows by creating a new sort of market for South Asian products, skills, and labor. The oil factor made the fundamental difference in the stories of interregional linkages between South and Southeast Asia, and South Asia and the Middle East, in both the eastern and western zones of the Indian Ocean. As early as 1935, Gamble had reported that "the loss of prosperity occasioned by the decline in the Bahrain pearl industry" had to some extent been alleviated by the high-wage employment given to many residents. The Bahrain Petroleum Company, a subsidiary of the Standard Oil Company of California, had made its first shipment of 25,000 barrels in June 1934.[41] That same year, the sheikh of Kuwait signed an oil concession with an Anglo-American conglomerate. On the eve of World War II, Alan Villiers found Al-Kuwait "to be composed of some eight thousand houses and . . . perhaps 70,000 or 80,000 people. Its roads were unmade (except for a brief mile or so running to the Sheikh's town palace, at the eastern end): its narrow streets a windy, sanded maze, threading in and out among the low-walled houses and the roofed bazaars." But, he noted, "half the sheikhdom swam upon a vast underground lake of oil."[42] On November 16, 1939, the political agent of Kuwait wrote that the town and its hinterland had "been at a subsistence level since time immemorial" but was now going through the throes of "a fundamental change." He continued: "As this port has always looked to India as its natural market both for buying and selling, it follows that now its importance to India is greater than ever before and is likely to become still more so."[43]

Responding to a statement by the Indian government that Indian interests in the Persian Gulf had declined and were still waning, the political resident maintained in 1938 that it was true for the Persian side but not for the Arabian side. In addition to the importance to India of the new air route and oil, he pointed to "an increasing market for Indian products and a small but potentially increasing field of employment for Indians." Developments in the oilfields of Bahrain, Hasa, Kuwait, and Qatar suggested the likelihood of "important new markets" in the next two to three years, "possibly supplemented later by 'oil-begotten' markets on the Trucial Coast and in Muscat." He foresaw a "fair amount of scope in the oilfields for Indians with some mechanical training." On April 21, 1938, he also shot off an enthusiastic letter to the master of Corpus Christi College, his alma mater, seeking help to "get first class Cambridge men into this American oil company."[44]

By September 1939 it was believed that "a very substantial expansion in employment and trade, particularly in Bahrain and Kuwait, had taken place."[45] Once all the facts and figures had been collected from the political adviser, Bahrain Petroleum Company (Bapco), PCL, Eastern Bank, Gray MacKenzie, Mission, Imperial Airways, and Cable and Wireless Ltd., the value of the Arab side of the Gulf to India was found to be "startling." From employment of various sorts in this Arabian part of the Gulf, except through sources related to the government of India, Indian nationals earned roughly 1.35 million rupees a year. (This included 200,000 rupees in wages for Indians of the oil company in Hasa, which fell "very much within the Bahrain orbit.") Indian merchants in Bahrain proper earned 1.0 to 1.2 million rupees annually, and Indian nationals living in or on the border of Bahrain earned roughly 2.5 million rupees a year.

These figures did not include in any way profits made in India on exports to the area. Exports to Bahrain alone from India had risen from 4.2 million rupees in 1933–1934 to 6.4 million rupees in 1938–1939. (The figure reached 7 million rupees in 1937–1938, but this spike was due in part to a rather favorable flow of precious metals.) These figures did not take into account the value of exports to the Trucial Coast or the goods reexported from Dubai and other Trucial Coast ports from India to Iran.

The estimates of earnings for Bahrain seemed to be substantiated by the volume of remittances to India through the bank and the post office. From January 1938 to September 1939, the Eastern Bank had remitted to India just over 10 million rupees, and money orders issued by the post office to India averaged well over 400,000 rupees a year. The number of British Indians registered with the political agency in Bahrain increased from 450 in 1930 to 1,550 in 1938. The number was likely to increase. Oil prospects in Qatar looked promising, while there were bound to be new oil developments along the Trucial Coast at war's end. These developments translated into increased opportunities for the employment of Indians.[46] Soon after independence and partition, 215 shops in Manama bazaars were owned by South Asians, of whom 119 were Pakistani and 96 Indian.[47]

The economic ruptures caused by the depression between South and Southeast Asia, as we shall see, took decades to repair fully. Indo-Gulf links of commerce and commodities suffered in the first half of the depression decade until the black gold began to forge new kinds of connections. On the placid waters of the Gulf, the era of the depression came to an end with at least a tiny wave of prosperity visible in the distance.

The Cloves Connection: India and East Africa

Growing up on the Gujarat coast, Nanji Kalidas Mehta had "heard the call of the sea" since his early childhood. When he was fourteen years old his family decided to send him to Madagascar with an older cousin. In late December 1900, Mehta boarded a dhow (a country craft) in Bombay. A journey by steamship from Bombay to Zanzibar would have cost thirty-five rupees and the Zanzibar-Majunga sector another eighty. The fare on the dhow *Phool-bhabhi* ("Sister-in-law Flower"), with its heavy sails and hundred-ton capacity, was a mere ten rupees for the entire journey from Bombay to Majunga via Zanzibar. Both *Phool-bhabhi* and its captain, Megha, came from Kutch. Megha determined the ship's position at night by gazing at the stars, even though he used the mariners' compass during the day. He also calculated distance on a slate by observing the reflected rays of the sun at noon with the help of large glasses. In twenty-six days *Phool-bhabhi* crossed 2,400 miles, making landfall at Mombasa on January 17, 2001. Mehta marveled at the sight: the "crystal-clear blue waters of Kilindini harbour touched the fringe of the rocky shore," behind which "rose the jade green foliage of cocopalms and mango groves." Mombasa at the turn of the century had a population of about 1,600 Indian traders—four hundred Hindus and 1,200 Muslims of the Bohra, Khoja, and Memon communities. The presence of Arabs, Syrians, Goans, and Europeans "lent an international colour to the cosmopolitan city." The harbor, the railway line from Mombasa to Kampala, and the government offices were being built by Indian indentured laborers. "Indian laws, Indian currency and Indian postal stamps were in use," Mehta writes in his memoirs, "and Mombasa almost looked like the counterpart of a big and flourishing Indian city."[48]

After a fortnight in Mombasa and having replenished its provisions, the dhow set sail once more. With a favorable tailwind, the boat covered the 120 miles to Zanzibar in a day. Zanzibar and Pemba together stretched 720 square miles and Mehta recounted that "these clusters of islands grew cloves which [were] supplied to the whole world." There was a time when ships used to come straight from Mandavi, the oldest port of Kutch, to collect ivory and spices for the Indian market. "It is said," Mehta writes, "that a hundred years before my visit, Zanzibar was a great centre of slave trade." Now the Bhatia merchants from Kutch dominated the Zanzibar market and "flags of eighty-four nations fluttered on ships in its world famous harbour." Sheth Ibji Shivji had collected the customs revenues for the Sultan until 1885 and another prosperous Indian merchant, Sheth Jetha Ladha Odadarwala, traded there. Some seven thousand Indians lived in Zanzibar at that time and the island was linked to India by a fortnightly steamer service. Mehta described Zanzibar as "one of the most beautiful islands in the world"—"a huge emerald set in a vast blue ring of the sea."[49]

Exemplifying the Indian penchant for circular migration, this was just the first of forty-five trips that Mehta would make between India and East Africa. On this first occasion, he left Zanzibar after twelve days, made a hazardous journey to Majunga where he learned the techniques of trade, and then returned to India. But he was soon back a second time accompanying some Bhatia traders from Karachi to Lamu and Mombasa, and worked for a while at the shop of Keshavji Anandji in Zanzibar. Mehta's ambition was to go to South Africa. But having failed to get a permit, he decided to move toward Kenya and Uganda, where he rose to become one of the leading Indian merchants and industrialists of East Africa.[50] Mehta was following the path pioneered by the Khoja merchant Allidina Visram, who had migrated from Kutch in 1863 as a twelve-year-old. In 1906, approximately the time Mehta arrived to trade in East Africa, an Indian association was established in Nairobi with Visram as president.

Merchants had certainly preceded laborers on the journey from India to Africa. Between 1895 and 1914 nearly 39,000 indentured laborers were taken from India to Kenya and

Uganda along with more than ten thousand voluntary migrants. By the 1930s there were over a hundred thousand Indians in East Africa. Since only about a fifth of indentured laborers stayed on in East Africa after their contracts expired, a considerable proportion of this number was made up of Indian traders, professionals, and service groups.[51] By the twentieth century many families in East Africa could trace their origins to both precolonial and colonial roots. One family, for instance, was descended on the one side from a saffron trader of the Kashmir valley who sailed in dhows from Bombay to the Middle East and East Africa with his parcels of saffron and brought back cloves from Zanzibar. On one of his voyages he decided to settle down in Zanzibar. He made one more trip back to India to marry a Kashmiri woman and bring her home to East Africa. On the other side of this family tree were two brothers whose father had left the vale of Kashmir for Punjab to escape the oppression of the Dogra maharaja and who had themselves migrated from Punjab as part of the colonial stream of the late-nineteenth and early twentieth centuries. Shams-ud-Deen initially joined the railway service in Kenya before making a mark in Kenyan politics, while Qamar-ud-Deen signed up for the police force in Zanzibar.[52]

Between 1820 and 1870, Gujarati merchants from the west coast of India had made their fortunes in Zanzibar through mostly dubious means. They were, for example, the chief financiers of the extensive slaving operations of the Imam of Muscat. By the mid-nineteenth century, however, they had turned to more legitimate forms of trade as well. In 1860 Lt. Col. C. P. Rigby found between five and six thousand Indian residents in the Zanzibar territories and the number was "annually increasing." They included Hindu Bhatias from Kutch and Jamnagar as well as Muslim Khojas and Bohras from Kutch, Surat, and Bombay. They were "gradually acquiring all the wealth and property of the island." "The Banians [Bhatias] never bring their families or females from India," Rigby wrote, "and always look forward to a return to their own country after having acquired a competence, but the Khojas and Bohras bring their wives and children, and become permanent settlers."[53] In 1873 Bartle Frere, a former governor of Bombay, was sent out to Zanzibar to finally stamp out the trade in slaves. But the 1873 antislavery mission must not lead us into any naive assumptions about British altruism. Frere had intricate financial ties with the shipping magnate William Mackinnon, one of the prime movers behind the British colonial empire in East Africa, whose British India Steam Navigation Company had received lucrative official favors in the 1860s, while Frere was governor of Bombay.[54] Frere reported calculations by John Kirk, the British consul in Zanzibar, that Indian capital invested in Zanzibar alone amounted to £1,600,000. A single Indian firm based in Zanzibar had £434,000 invested in East Africa, of which about £60,000 had been advanced in a variety of ways to the sultan of Zanzibar and his family. Frere summed up what he saw in 1873:

In a word, throughout the Zanzibar coastline with numerous large and fertile islands, all banking and mercantile business passes through Indian hands. Hardly a loan can be negotiated, a mortgage effected or a bill cashed without Indian agency; not an import cargo can be distributed nor an export cargo collected of which almost every bale does not go through Indian hands. The Europeans, Americans, Arabs or Swahilis may trade and profit but only as an occasional link in the chain between producer and consumer of which the Indian trader is the one invariable and most important link of all.[55]

While Frere could not "acquit any portion of the Indian community of indirect connection with the slave trade," he found "the more respectable Indian houses in Zanzibar" keen to see an end to it. They realized that its continuation hampered all other trade and postponed "the full development of the unrivalled commercial capabilities of the coast."[56]

As the slave trade died out in the last decades of the nineteenth century, cloves emerged as the most valuable item of international trade in Zanzibar. Along with nutmeg and mace, cloves had long been part of the romance of the European spice trade with Southeast Asia. First introduced in Zanzibar in 1818, cloves were "planted in picturesque bands streaking the red argillaceous hills and growing into a fairly tall, bushy and thick-foliaged tree, somewhat resembling a laurel."[57] Cloves were locally used as a condiment and medicine. Poor women wore them as ornaments in the form of necklaces and earrings. But the profits came from exports to the world market. By the close of the nineteenth century, Zanzibar and Pemba supplied 90 percent of the world demand for cloves. Indian merchants almost entirely financed its production. Clove stems were utilized in Europe as a mordant for dyeing silks. Low-grade cloves were required in the industrial markets of Europe and America, where they went into the manufacture of vanillin. Medium-quality cloves were exported to the Dutch East Indies, where they were consumed in cigarettes. The spice markets of India, meanwhile, demanded cloves of the very highest quality from Zanzibar.

From 1895 to 1929 the world prices of cloves were generally on a healthy upward trend. Indians, who dominated an interlinked product and credit market, made handsome profits, as they did farther south in colonial Mozambique, where they controlled the cashew economy. When Winston Churchill visited East Africa as undersecretary of state for the colonies in 1907–1908, he paid a rare tribute to Indians in this region:

> It was a Sikh soldier who bore an honourable part in the conquest and pacification of these East African countries. It is the Indian trader who, penetrating and maintaining himself in all sorts of places to which no White man would go or in which no White man who would earn a living, has more than anyone else developed the early beginnings of trade and opened up the first slender means of communication. It was by Indian labour that the one vital railway on which everything else depends was constructed. It is the Indian banker who supplies perhaps the largest part of the capital yet available to business and enterprise and to whom the White settlers have not hesitated to recur for financial aid. The Indian was here long before the first British official.[58]

It was one thing to win accolades for their subimperial role from their colonial masters and be tolerated by African colonial subjects while times were good, but quite another to withstand discrimination from above and resistance from below when times were bad. As elsewhere in the Indian Ocean arena, the onset of the Great Depression spelled trouble for Indian intermediary capitalists.

When K. P. S. Menon, a civil servant from colonial India, visited Zanzibar in 1934, he found the "Indian community in a state of panic."[59] Clove prices had collapsed: from 15.08 rupees per frasila (about thirty-five pounds) in 1929–1930 to 6.18 rupees per frasila in 1933–1934 in Zanzibar, and 14.36 to 5.66 rupees over the same period in Pemba. In the name of coming to the aid of distressed primary producers, the Zanzibar protectorate had issued a battery of decrees on the subject of agricultural credit and marketing.[60] Menon's criticisms of these measures and the protectorate's rebuttal provide fascinating insights into the strains imposed by faltering interregional links between India and East Africa. The laws had put severe restrictions on the alienation of land from Swahilis and Arabs to Indians. Menon complained that the legislation imported "the racial virus into this island." He would not have objected so strenuously if the law had restricted the sale of land from agriculturists to nonagriculturists, as had been the case in the Punjab since the turn of the century. Some Indians, Menon claimed, were settled agriculturists. He had even met one of them in Pemba, "an octogenarian" who told him that "the last occasion on which he was in India was when he underwent the ceremony of circumcision."[61] The Zanzibar authorities countered saying that "the Protectorate's problem" was "essentially a racial one" and that the laws were "necessitated by the 'racial characteristics of the Arabs and Africans' who needed to be 'protected against themselves.'" Surely the colonial government had to guard against the "prospect of an urban Indian oligarchy monopolizing the plantations and managing them through a dependent, indebted and spiritless tenantry of Arabs and Swahilis." Just in case the colonial discourse on race failed to clinch the argument, clove estates were described as analogous to gardens or orchards, making any Indian precedents on alienation of agricultural land irrelevant to the issue at hand.[62]

Menon conceded the existence of indebtedness, which was in desperate need of a solution. But he claimed that Indians had "not shown any inclination to dispossess the Arabs or the natives of the land." This was undoubtedly true in decades of good prices, during which the Indians were satisfied with the interest on the debt and the product. Menon was able to produce figures from 1922 to buttress his claim. These showed that Indians formed only 1.72 percent of the total plantation owners and possessed a mere 4 percent of the plantations and 5.08 percent of the trees.[63] The Zanzibar government was armed with more up-to-date statistics, however, and presented convincing recent evidence of massive alienation of clove and coconut plantations from Swahilis and Arabs to Indians. In Zanzibar 1.9 million rupees' worth of property was shown to have passed into Indian hands between

1926 and 1933. During the same period, Indians had made a net gain of a quarter of a million clove trees and 35,000 coconut trees in Pemba, which suggested an increase of Indian ownership from the 5 percent claimed by Menon to 17.5 percent in eight years.[64]

While the Zanzibar government had the more recent facts and figures, Menon was on target in criticizing that government's attempt to create a European monopoly in the marketing of cloves by squeezing out "middlemen." The Clove Growers' Association established by one of the decrees was a complete misnomer; it did not have any clove growers as members. It was composed of three officials, a banker, and one C. A. Bartlett, "formerly a partner of Messrs. Grazebrook-Bartlett & Co., which used to compete, not too successfully, with Indian exporters in the clove trade." The Zanzibar government's lame defense of Bartlett's experience notwithstanding, Menon was probably not exaggerating when he charged the Clove Growers' Association as striking "Indian traders as a Leviathan, brushing them aside, casting them adrift and trampling upon that freedom of trade which they had enjoyed for generations."[65] The tussle between the Zanzibar government and the Indian traders dragged on through the depression decade. On June 11, 1937, the *Indian Opinion*, a Natal paper founded by Gandhi, expressed solidarity with the Indians in Zanzibar: "We [the South African Indians] are not the only ones faced with the danger of being driven out of the Union or having to accept the status of helots . . . the colonial officer . . . is quite obviously intent upon making Zanzibar a white man's country. Indians in South Africa offer whole-hearted sympathy to their distressed brethren in Zanzibar and their moral support in their struggle for justice."[66]

South Asian migrants in various occupations became the targets of conflicts sparked by economic and ethnic grievances during the 1930s. During the Afro-Shīrāzi riots of 1936, triggered by a dispute over the grading of copra, Qamar-ud-Deen, the Kashmiri police officer in Zanzibar, was following the European Chief Inspector in an attempt to quell the disturbances. He "saw a man pull out a dagger to stab the European and stepped out to stop him—and was killed in his stead." This individual tragedy contributed to the broader pattern of circular migration in the western Indian ocean. Qamar-ud-Deen's widow left Africa with their children to return to Bombay and after the partition of the subcontinent moved to Lahore in Pakistan.[67]

Despite their difficulties in Zanzibar and elsewhere in East Africa, Indians were on the whole able to eventually ride out the crisis of the depression. This was partly because Indians had by then expanded their zone of operations from Zanzibar to Mozambique in the south and to Mombasa and Kampala in the north. The Indian "dukawalla" had penetrated deep into the continent and was the mainstay of the retail trade in consumer goods, whether of European, Indian, or Japanese origin. But the economic crisis of the 1930s had brought grim forebodings of the possibility of sharp conflicts along racial lines. This prejudice was to become a characteristic feature of the more bigoted forms of postcolonial nationalisms in Africa, reaching its climax in Idi Amin's expulsion of Asians from Uganda in 1972.

The Rice and Rubber Connection:
India and Southeast Asia

In May 1916, on the first stop of his voyage to the United States, Rabindranath Tagore observed a distinctly Indian character in the Burmese capital:

> The streets are straight, wide and clean, the houses spick and span; Madrasis, Punjabis and Gujaratis are wandering about in the streets and on the river banks. In the midst of all this if somewhere suddenly one spots Burmese men or women dressed in colorful silk, one imagines that they are the foreigners . . . the city of Rangoon is not a city of Burma, it appears to stand in opposition to the entire country.[68]

The Bengali poet had set off on this long voyage from Calcutta on May 3, 1916, aboard the Japanese ship *Tosamaru*. Being primarily a cargo vessel, it had just a few cabins for passengers. But there were plenty of deck passengers, mostly "Madrasis." These Tamils of south India, both Hindu and Muslim, moved in large numbers to Southeast Asia in the late nineteenth and early twentieth centuries as traders and laborers. Traveling on this route, Tagore encountered a mighty storm in the Bay of Bengal that left no dividing line between the clouds and the waves. Someone seemed to have opened the blue lid of the ocean and countless demons had emerged from below wrapped in grey coils of smoke, as in the Arabian nights, and were shooting up to the sky. After four days at sea the appearance of birds in the sky signaled that land was near. If the ocean was the domain of dance, its shores heralded a realm of music. As the ship moved up the Irrawaddy toward Rangoon, Tagore observed the row of kerosene-oil factories with tall chimneys along its banks, commenting that it looked as if Burma was lying on its back and smoking a cigar. Closer to the city, the long line of jetties seemed to him to be clinging to the body of Burma like so many hideous, giant, iron leeches. Other than the Shwedagon temple, Tagore did not find anything in the city that was distinctively Burmese. He lamented the cruelty of the goddess of commerce. "This city has not grown like a tree from the soil of the country," he wrote. "I have seen Rangoon, but it is mere visual acquaintance, there is no recognition of Burma in this seeing."[69]

The wealthiest of the "Madrasis" whom Tagore would have seen on the streets of Rangoon were the Nattukottai Chettiars, also known as Nakarattars, of the Ramnad district and the Pudukottai princely state of Tamil Nadu. "Displaced from the credit markets of Madras," writes David Rudner, "and displaced from British investment and exchange markets throughout greater British India, the Nakarattars found a new niche in servicing the credit needs of the indigenous Southeast Asians and migrant Indians who fought with each other and with the British in a race to produce agrarian commodities for the European export market."[70] Having made their initial overseas foray by following the British imperial flag into Ceylon and the Straits Settlements in the 1820s and 1830s, they carved out their largest zone of operations in Burma following the colonial conquest of Lower Burma in 1852. The opening of the Suez Canal in 1869 dramatically expanded the European rice market and provided a major incentive to further colonize the rice frontier of the Irrawaddy delta from the 1870s onward. The area under rice cultivation in Lower Burma increased from 600,000 acres in 1852 and just over 1,100,000 acres in 1872 to more than eight million acres by the 1930s.[71] The Nattukottai Chettiars of south India led the financing of this economic transformation. "Without their support," the Burma Provincial Banking Enquiry Committee reported in 1929–1930, "the internal and external trade of the country would break down and the rice crop could not even be produced."[72]

In the 1890s the Nattukottai Chettiar community numbered about ten thousand, and by the early 1920s it had grown to about forty thousand. Besides a couple of hundred Chettiars who had bought into landed estates in Madras by the close of the nineteenth century, most members of this community were engaged in trade and finance either on their own or as agents of their caste patrons. Circular migration from south India to Southeast Asia was very much the pattern, with young Chettiar apprentices typically sent out across the Bay of Bengal for three-year terms. Kinship networks and marriage alliances were integral to their capitalist enterprise, even as they taught the intricacies of double-entry bookkeeping to their children from the age of eight. Religion, too, was as important as local origin and caste in cementing the sodalities that characterized their business organization. Even the name

Nakarattars referred to the structuring of the community into nine *nakarams* (towns) with a *kovil* (temple) presiding over each. "A Chettiar temple is always established," the Burma Provincial Banking Enquiry Committee noted, "wherever a few Chettiars are doing business." In Rangoon the temple was managed by representatives of the four oldest Chettiar firms. It was located in a building on Mogul Street between Dalhousie Street and Merchant Street. The temple and the six rooms below it constituted "the real Chettiar Exchange; that is to say the place where gossip is exchanged every morning before the main business of the day begins, and a general body of opinion as to the financial situation and appropriate measures is developed."[73]

In the 1920s there were some 1,650 Chettiar banking firms in Burma: 1,443 in Lower Burma (including 360 in Rangoon), 195 in Upper Burma, and 12 in the Shan states.[74] In 1896 the total assets of the Chettiars had been estimated at 100 million rupees, which had increased eightfold by 1929.[75] The capital they deployed all across the eastern Indian Ocean rim was considerably larger. In Burma alone this was estimated to be around 750 million rupees, of which 535 million constituted their own capital, 115 million were received as deposits from Chettiars, and 100 million were borrowed from non-Chettiar sources. In Upper Burma, 10 million rupees went into the agricultural sector and 30 million into trade. In Lower Burma, agriculture attracted the much larger share—450 to 500 million rupees, compared to 210 to 260 million rupees for trade. While Burma was the most important field of their operations, the Chettiars were also thought to have working capital of 250 million rupees circulating in the Federated Malay States and the Straits Settlements, 140 million rupees in Ceylon, 50 million rupees in Cochin-China, and 10 million rupees in Madras, amounting to a grand total of 1.2 billion rupees.[76]

In the Malay zone the Chettiars began their operation in the 1820s by selling cotton piece-goods from the Coromandel coast. But the real breakthrough for Tamil capital in the Straits came with a waft of fragrant smoke and some notoriety, albeit not as sordid as the Gujarati involvement in the slave trade of East Africa. In the middle decades of the nineteenth century, the Chettiars worked hand in glove with branches of various European exchange banks to finance the opium trade from India.

By the turn of the twentieth century, however, the financial opportunities came from the rapid expansion of rubber plantations and tin mines to meet the rising demand from the industrial West. The acreage under rubber increased tenfold from a mere five thousand acres in 1900 to over half a million acres within a decade and had crossed the three-million-acre mark by the 1930s. The Nattukottai Chettiars made large loans secured by mortgages on rubber plantations during the first three decades of the twentieth century.[77]

Capitalists formed just one strand of the movement of Indians across the eastern Indian Ocean in the late nineteenth and early twentieth centuries. According to demographer Kingsley Davis's calculation, some 2,600,000 Indians participated in circular migration to Burma between 1852 and 1937.[78] More than 60 percent of those who emigrated from India to Burma in the late nineteenth century were from Madras, and over 25 percent were from Bengal. A very large number in the post-1870 period were low-caste Tamil and Telegu laborers, which altered the religious composition of the immigrant population. In 1872 there had been roughly the same number of Hindus and Muslims, but by 1901 Hindus formed 67 percent and Muslims 31 percent of the Indian population in the Burma delta. The migrant laborers tended to stay in Burma from one to four years. Most resided in urban areas, especially the capital city of Rangoon, even though the proportion of agricultural to industrial workers increased over time. Yet within the urban population the ratio continued to tilt in favor of Indians compared to the Burmese. In Rangoon, Indians made up just over a quarter of the population in 1872, but more than half by 1901. The number of Indians in Lower Burma was found to be 297,000 at the time of the census of 1901 and rose to 583,000 in 1931. Most were laborers in the docks or the rice mills.[79] In Malaya, Kernial Singh Sandhu estimates the total figure of Indian labor immigration between 1844 and 1941 to have been 2,700,000, of which 1,900,000 fell in the regulated and 800,000 in the unregulated category. The average number of Indian laborers annually going to Malaya rose from 15,000 in the 1890s to about 90,000 in the 1920s. A smaller, but significant, increase took place in the number of nonlabor migrants (from some 6,000 per year in the 1890s to 16,000 annually in the 1920s). The ratio of male migrants to female ones was approximately 9:1.[80] Among the nonlaborers were capitalists, professionals, and service providers.

The interdependence that was forged between India and Southeast Asia was finely balanced, and with the onset of the depression "the structure of interdependence quickly fell apart."[81]

Migrant Indians, Chinese, and Javanese had formed at least 10 percent of the working population in the eastern Indian Ocean during the first three decades of the twentieth century. The world depression either reversed or arrested these demographic flows. In 1929, as many as 346,000 Indians had entered Burma while 294,000 had left; in 1930 a smaller number of 301,000 arrived and a larger number of 314,000 departed. In 1931 the number of Indian emigrants exceeded the number of immigrants by 22,000. Although positive figures of net immigration were recorded once more from 1932 to 1938, the economics and politics of the depression era had made the condition of Indians in Burma tenuous.[82] The patterns of migration to Malaya tell a similar story. In the 138 years from 1790 to 1927, the number of Indian departures exceeded arrivals in only two years—1914 and 1921. From 1928 to 1938 there was a net emigration, the gap being especially large in the early years of the depression. In 1930, 1931, and 1932 the numbers of Indians leaving exceeded those arriving by 66,079, 69,661, and 57,535, respectively.[83]

As elsewhere in the Indian Ocean arena, the depression caused a catastrophic collapse in the prices of agricultural commodity exports and a dramatic shrinkage in the availability of credit. With the free fall in rice and rubber prices in Burma and Malaya, Indian financiers and moneylenders were unable to recover their debts. "Without the assistance of the Chettiar banking system," Harcourt Butler, the governor of Burma, had claimed in December 1927, "Burma would never have achieved the wonderful advance of the last 25 to 30 years." By 1929–1930, however, the perspective of a Karen witness deposing before the Burma Provincial Banking Enquiry Committee was very different:

> Chettiar banks are fiery dragons that parch every land that has the misfortune of coming under their wicked creeping . . . They are a hard-hearted lot that will wring out every drop of blood from the victims without compunction for the sake of their own interest . . . the swindling, cheating, deception and oppression of the Chettiars in the country, particularly among the ignorant folks, are well-known and these are, to a large extent, responsible for the present impoverishment in the land.[84]

Thuriya, a Burmese newspaper, reported on February 19, 1930, that Chettiars were buying up agricultural land from peasant debtors and having the land cultivated by tenants with no rights to it. The Nattukottai Chettiars' Association denied the charge in a letter to the newspaper on March 7, 1930, claiming that its members "had no desire to own paddy-land." The group pointed out that during a temporary depression in 1890, land had passed into Chettiar hands but had been sold off after a year or two, as soon as prosperity had returned. The banking committee members were divided among themselves on this question. The majority agreed with the newspaper that the Chettiars were of late showing a penchant to "seize land more readily" when loans were in arrears. The minority were persuaded by the Chettiar argument that the recent downturn may have caused "a temporary increase" in land alienation—one that did not indicate "a general change in policy."[85]

It is not difficult to see why the banking committee members were in disagreement. The Chettiars were typically uninterested in taking over land so long as their debts were serviced. They were even generally able to offer Burmese peasants more favorable rates of interest than other moneylenders while keeping them enmeshed in a cycle of debt. They made their profits by dominating an interlinked credit and product market and the profits were huge when rice prices soared worldwide. The years 1852 to 1902 had represented an "era of symbiosis" between Indian creditors and Burmese peasant debtors, albeit a skewed and unequal one. The two decades from 1908 to 1930, by contrast, could be seen with the benefit of hindsight as the period of a "closing rice frontier" preceding the decade of lengthy and unprecedented social and economic crises between 1931 and 1941. The tendency of the Chettiars to grab agricultural lands in the 1930s proved to be much different from the "temporary" alienation of 1890. As the economy slid into a long and deep depression, Chettiars foreclosed on mortgages to recover what they could before getting out of the quagmire of the Irrawaddy delta. In 1930 the Chettiar moneylenders owned only 6 percent of the land occupied in Lower Burma and 19 percent of the land held by nonagriculturists; by 1938 the same figures were 25 percent and 50 percent, respectively.[86]

The immediate consequences of the depression in colonial Malaya were not very different from those in Burma. The fall in tin and rubber prices led to default on loans, foreclosure on mortgages, and "transfer of property to Nakarattar banking firms," which the colonial government sought to stem by enacting the "Small Holding (Restriction of Sale) Bill" of 1931.[87] Colonial economic policy attempted to segregate the subsistence-oriented rice economy—where Malays were granted "reserved" lands—from the export-oriented tin and rubber sectors, in which Europeans, Chinese, and Indians played dominant roles. Malaya, therefore, did not experience the large-scale alienation of rice lands of the sort that occurred in Burma. Rice, in any case, was the key export commodity in Burma, which it was not in Malaya.

During downward fluctuations in the export-oriented rubber economy in Malaya, the colonial rubber restriction schemes were typically designed to protect the interests of the larger European-owned rubber plantations, not those of the small-holding Indian rubber tappers. Rubber prices fell by 1932 to one-fortieth of the peak it had reached in 1925. Consequently, the number of Indian workers on the larger rubber plantations was halved from at least 206,000 in 1929 to 104,000 in 1932. Indeed, between 1930 and 1932 more than 190,000 unemployed Tamil laborers were repatriated home.[88] The slump also led to widespread Chinese unemployment as many people were thrown out of work in the tin mines. The colonial government attempted to thwart Chinese attempts to "squat" on land reserved for Malays. The reservations policy, while certainly protecting Malay peasants from suffering the fate of their Burmese counterparts, became "an agent of economic fossilization." The colonial government's cynical attempts to make the Chinese scapegoats for the Malays' economic woes made it "guilty of contributing to racial polarization and discord." "Looking back," Lim Teck Ghee concludes, "it might not be too unkind to regard the Japanese invasion of the Peninsula as a timely and a positive factor, notwithstanding its hardships, in the course of Malayan history."[89]

It was in Burma, however, that racial polarization and discord became most explosive during the depression decade. In addition to the gathering resentments of Burmese peasants against Chettiar moneylenders, increasing joblessness made the urban centers new battlegrounds between Burmese and immigrant Indian workers. On May 6, 1930, Telegu workers in Rangoon harbor went on strike to protest the arrest of Mahatma Gandhi in India and to demand better wages. The shipping firms decided initially to replace the striking workers with eager Burmese recruits, but after a few weeks they were generally more inclined to reinstate the Indians once they had resolved to return to work. On May 26, 1930, rioting broke out near the docks between crowds of Burmese and Telegu workers, which were, according to Michael Adas, "almost wholly expressions of communal hostility produced by economic competition." Burmese laborers "made numerous forays into the Indian quarters, where they burnt homes, looted shops, and killed Indians whenever they could find them." A week's violence left an official toll—almost certainly an underestimate—of 120 persons dead and 900 wounded. Simmering tension in Rangoon and other towns of Burma during the depression decade erupted once more in late July and early August of 1938. On this occasion 204 persons were killed, over a thousand were injured, and property worth more than two million rupees was destroyed.[90]

On December 22, 1930, the most spectacular of all the depression rebellions in the Indian Ocean arena broke out in the Tharrawaddy district of Lower Burma. It was led by Saya San, a charismatic monk who portrayed himself as both "the *Setkya-min* (the avenging king of Burman legend) and the *Buddha Yaza* (the divinely sent creator of a Buddhist utopia)."[91] The Saya San rebellion undoubtedly had a staunchly anticolonial character and was directed against British rule. The main unifying issue was the highly regressive and inflexible capitation tax that was due to the colonial government at the end of the calendar year. Yet with its strong Buddhist millenarian overtones, the movement was also directed against the migrant moneylenders from the land of the Buddha, who were seen as the immediate quill drivers of colonial oppression. Some of the worst attacks against Indians in the Burmese countryside simply took advantage of the general turmoil unleashed by the rebellion and were not orchestrated by its leaders. The promised millennium without colonial taxes would also be free of debts owed to the Chettiars.

The Saya San rebellion spread to twelve of the twenty districts of Burma. Five districts of Lower Burma—Hanthawaddy, Insein, Pegu, Pyapon, and Myaungmya—were home to especially large-scale attacks on Indians. Indian moneylenders were robbed and Indian shops looted. But migrants were not safe in Upper Burma either. In the Prome and Maubin districts Indian homesteads were attacked and, in a few instances, entire families were killed. If some Burmese nationalist leaders preferred to concentrate their fire on the British, others like U Saw were not of a mind to spare the Indians. In a pamphlet analyzing the Saya San rebellion in 1931, U Saw described the Indians as "birds of passage who have come to this land to exploit by fair means or foul in the fields of labour, industry and commerce."[92]

The rebellion that began in December 1930 continued until June 1932 as a series of loosely coordinated local revolts. It had massive popular support, even though the precise targets of rebel anger varied according to the particular circumstances of the various districts. Before it was finally crushed, 9,000 rebels had been imprisoned, 3,000 killed or badly wounded, and 350 executed. Saya San himself was hanged in 1937 after a lengthy trial at which he was defended by the nationalist leader Ba Maw.

If Indian moneylenders were attacked by the rebels, Indian soldiers played the crucial role in putting down the rebellion as they had done in the late 1880s. Two divisions were specially brought from India to douse the flames of resistance. "The outcome was never in doubt," James C. Scott observes, "as poorly armed rebels, trusting in their amulets and tattoos, fell in waves before the Lewis guns of the British Indian Army."[93]

The Saya San rebellion in the countryside and the urban conflicts along lines of race contributed to the net emigration of Indians from Burma in the 1930s. Another exodus took place in December 1941 and early 1942 in advance of the Japanese sweep into Burma and their capture of Rangoon in March 1942. Perhaps 400,000 Indians attempted a perilous trek over land from Burma to India, among them the principal characters of Amitav Ghosh's historical novel *The Glass Palace*:

They found a boat that took them upriver, through Meiktila, past Mandalay to the tiny town of Mawlaik, on the Chindwin river. There they were confronted by a stupefying spectacle: some thirty thousand refugees were squatting along the river-bank, waiting to move on towards the densely forested mountain ranges that lay ahead. Ahead there were no roads, only tracks, rivers of mud, flowing through green tunnels of jungle.[94]

Yet for all those Indians who left, many more remained behind in Burma, where they would became players in one of the more fascinating dramas of diasporic patriotism that took place during World War II.

4

Waging War for King and Country

I am very glad that you are in India. For the people of India *[sic]* are very unlikely to see India again. The black pepper [Indian troops] has all been used up, and there is only a little of the red pepper [British troops] left. I have nothing more to say, for I cannot write more plainly.

—SEPOY HIRA SINGH, 41ST DOGRAS, K. I. HOSPITAL, BRIGHTON,
TO RANA SINGH, 55TH PUNJABIS, KOHAT, PUNJAB, JULY 9, 1915

In addition to capitalists and laborers, Indian soldiers formed an important population of South Asians who followed the British imperial flag across the globe and around the Indian Ocean rim. The sea change in sovereignty during the late nineteenth and early twentieth centuries may have been conceptualized by British proconsuls, but it was put into practice through the medium of Indian military personnel. Since "red pepper" was in short supply to meet the requirements of war, it was "black pepper" that was transported across the *kalapani* (black waters) to fulfill the imperial mission. Nearly sixty thousand Indian soldiers died fighting for the British Empire on the battlefields of Mesopotamia and France during World War I. During World War II, a significant segment of the British Indian Army joined members of some expatriate Indian communities in choosing to wage war against the British king-emperor. The migration of soldiers across oceans raises some of the same issues we encountered in our discussion of flows of capital and labor, in particular, the relevance of an interregional arena in the age of global empire. If Indian soldiers were to defend British imperial interests worldwide, did the Indian Ocean continue to have special significance for them? An answer can be found in the writings of Indian soldiers who fought for and against Britain in the Indian Ocean interregional arena and also, for comparative purposes, those who fought in Europe between 1914 and 1945. Without losing sight of the individuality of these texts and stories—which vary in terms of race, religious and linguistic community, class and rank, as well as gender—we can use them to explore commonalities in the experience of these South Asian men and women fighting overseas.

British rule in India was distinct from that of precolonial predecessors in that it featured a centralized colonial state with a monolithic concept of sovereignty. Its key institutional feature was one of the largest European-style standing armies in the world, which came into being during the Revolutionary and Napoleonic wars. At the close of Richard Colley Wellesley's governor-generalship of India in 1805, the strength of the English East India Company's armed forces stood at 155,000 men. In the early nineteenth century, the company's Bengal Army was deployed overseas in Ceylon, Java, and the Red Sea area. As a mercenary army, its loyalty was occasionally strained and sporadic mutinies took place. The refusal of some units to fight in Burma in 1852 led to the formal passage of the General Service Enlistment Act of 1856, which required recruits to serve abroad or, as many soldiers saw it, across the forbidding black waters.[1]

Following the quelling of the great 1857 revolt, when Indians rose up against the East India Company's rule, Britain's Indian Army was reorganized on the principles of a high European to Indian ratio, which did not fall short of 1:2 until the start of World War I. Next to what was seen as a grand counterpoise of a sufficient British force was the more insidious "counterpoise of natives against natives." In place of the caste peasantry of the Gangetic plain, the Crown raj now recruited from among new social groups, especially Sikhs, Gurkhas, Punjabi Muslims, and Pathans. They also organized the regiments in such a way that, as the secretary of state put it in 1862, "Sikh might fire into Hindu, Gurkha into either, without any scruple in case of need." By 1875 as many as half of the army's soldiers came from the Punjab alone. The new recruitment patterns of the colonial masters were buttressed by an elaborate, if spurious, anthropological theory of martial castes and races.[2]

During the high noon of colonialism in the late nineteenth century, the Indian Army protected Britain's far-flung imperial interests worldwide, but with a special emphasis on the belt that stretched from North Africa to East Asia. It helped put down the Mahdi uprisings of 1885–1886 and 1896 in the

Sudan and the Boxer Rebellion of 1899–1900 in China. Indian troops were used in Britain's intervention in Egypt in 1882, which triggered the European rivalries culminating in the partition of Africa. Closer to the subcontinent, the British Indian Army was used in the Afghan war of the late 1870s and early 1880s, for the final conquest of Burma and the crushing of guerilla resistance there in the late 1880s, to impose British influence in Tibet in 1902–1903, and to bolster British influence in the Persian Gulf region in the early twentieth century.

With the outbreak of war in 1914, the strict 1:2 ratio of British and Indian troops in the army could no longer be maintained. A new policy of large-scale recruitment resulted in the expansion of the army to 1.2 million men by war's end. More than 350,000 men were induced to join up in the Punjab alone. Even Gandhi lent a helping hand to the recruitment efforts upon his return from South Africa, hoping that Indian participation would induce the British to grant concessions to the nationalist cause at war's end. The Indian troops supplied the cannon fodder for General Townshend's ill-fated Mesopotamian campaign of 1915, which ended in the ignominious surrender at Kut in April 1916. Punjabi and Gurkha regiments were at the forefront of the columns that marched into Baghdad in March 1917 commanded by General Stanley Maude. Indian infantry brigades also saw action in the battlefields of France.

While historians have speculated on the extent to which Indians were coaxed, cajoled, or coerced into fighting for Britain, rarely has the spotlight been turned on the motives and experiences of Indian soldiers who fought in the Middle Eastern and European theaters of the Great War as expressed in their own words. These texts, relating both immediate and remembered experiences, help clarify the tension between the interregional and global roles played by Indian military personnel in the history of Britain's empire.

Subaltern Letters and Colonial Censors

"This is not a war," wrote Luddar Singh of the 41st Dogras, nursing his wounds in Barton Hospital, to Rijha Singh in Palempur, Kangra, on July 8, 1915. "It is a Mahabharat or the end of the world. When the whole world is being destroyed and ravaged, and all the houses devastated, who can call it a war? But what can we do? It is the will of the Almighty."[3] The sense of awe and fatalistic resignation in the midst of unprecedented death and destruction is just one among a range of moods captured in the hundreds of volumes of soldiers' letters compiled by the Censor of Indian Mails during the war. On the face of it, they represent a unique collection of primary materials offering a glimpse into the minds of Indian subalterns (in the literal, military sense of the word). Yet since historians can only find them dressed in the standardized uniforms of colonial order, they too need to be read between the lines, if not against the grain. To begin with, the materials present the usual problems associated with a loss of meaning in translation. Written mostly in Urdu, Hindi, or Gurmukhi, they were rendered into English for the benefit of military intelligence. The identities of the writers were fixed according to predetermined colonial categories. Each translated letter begins with the heading "Punjabi Mahomedan," "Sikh," "Pathan," "Dogra," or "Hindustani Mahomedan." Some of the attitudes reported through the colonial filter took the form, therefore, of self-fulfilling prophecies or uncomfortable deviations from expected norms.

The soldiers knew, of course, that whatever they wrote had to pass under the strict eyes of the censoring officer. "If I were to write about the war in a letter," commented Nur Muhammad of the 129th Baluchis on July 26, 1915, "my letter would not reach you. So we do not write about the war, because they open our letters in many places and read them and if they see anything about the war in them, they tear them up." But he then decided to take a chance and added, "Do not be anxious about them [the Indian prisoners]. They are very comfortable, in fact they are many degrees better off than we are."[4] In a similar vein Risaldar Hidayat Ali Khan wrote, "I have written four letters to you about our relation Umrao Ali Khan. I do not know why they do not reach you. He has been captured. He is in the Turkish camp. At the moment he is in Baghdad but not in confinement. All he does is to teach the Turkish Officers Urdu. He is perfectly well. Do not be anxious about him. When peace is declared he will return."[5] The odds are that this letter too did not reach its destination. Lance Naik Sherafuddin of the 40th Pathans was rather more creative in his attempt to beat the censors: "I cannot write the state of things that is going on here. You know it yourself, and if you have a great desire to see the tamasha take a head of Indian corn, and after wetting it, parch it in front of a furnace, and sit down and watch well how many of the grains burst and how many do not." The censoring officer added helpfully in parentheses: "But very few of the grains will remain and this is intended to symbolize the loss of life at the front."[6]

If life in the trenches was too nerve-racking and a sojourn at a military hospital barely tolerable, Indian soldiers knew how to enjoy the lights of Paris. Jamadar Ghulla Singh was quite disconsolate at being transferred from France to Mesopotamia. "We are in the greatest discomfort," he complained, "for it is bitterly cold and the mud is deep . . . Give my *salaams* to the 'bit of my heart' and tell her how I am suffering and give her this letter in French."[7] The more orthodox were not so delighted at the transgressions across lines of race, religion, and gender. Badshah Khan, an Afridi Pathan, was left "beseeching the welfare of all Mussulmans." He had seen "some who did not even keep the fast." "The Punjabis," he wrote indignantly, "do not keep it at all. They are dishonest rogues. When they are in the trenches they call upon the name of God, when they are at rest then it is 'Banju Madam,' 'Bonsowar Madam' [sic]."[8]

Santa Singh sounded distinctly gloomy when he wrote from Mesopotamia on January 26, 1917, to his best friend Ujagar Singh stationed in France: "You are in a better country than we are."[9] But Badan Singh, writing just two days later, proved that individual predilections mattered, however much colonial discourse might prefer the straitjacket of communitarian categories. He was much impressed by "Arabia"; the people there he thought were a "fine race." "Their language," he remarked, "is very strange. They are a fine-looking people too—finer looking than the people of any other country."[10]

Iran had the added advantage of being a stretch removed from the actual fighting and received some very positive reviews from Indian soldiers on visits. "Ispihan nisfi Jahan" (Isfahan is half the world) was all that Mahmud Khan needed to say on seeing that great city.[11] "The pay is excellent," gloated another officer attached to the Karman Rifles, "and the 'aram' [comfort] is not to be expressed in words."[12] For the more spiritually inclined, there was pride and joy in seeing some of the shared cultural symbols of Iran and India. As Lance Dafadar Mahomed Khan of the 15th Lancers wrote from Shīrāz to Dafadar Mahomed Khan of the 18th Lancers posted in France on December 16, 1917: "I was very lucky; when marching from Isfahan to Shiraz I saw Rustam's picture and that of King Darius on a mountainside. I also saw Jamshed's shrine and that of Tamas and many other interesting relics 2500 years old. I also saw the throne of Solomon and the fort of Bairam. I was fortunate enough to see more holy places when I got to Shiraz, the shrine of Sheikh Sadi the poet, of Hafiz and of Shah Chiragh and relics of many others of our holy men."[13] He also wrote feelingly of the "awful famine" sweeping the country.

Although the horrors of war and famine were much starker in Europe and the Middle East, the Indian soldiers' blind spot appeared to be the African continent—this despite the perception that France was distinctly foreign while East Africa lay within the outer limits of Hind. The racial prejudice exhibited toward Africa and Africans seems to have been pervasive among the officers and the ranks. Naik Firoz Khan's comment on Somaliland was not atypical: "You have asked for the latest news from this country. There is no news at all. The country is jungly and desolate and the people are savages."[14] In Syed Asghar Ali's letter from British East Africa to Abdul Jabbar Khan in France the bitterness ran deeper: "You amuse yourselves no doubt with the fairies but here there is not even a female ghost. Jungle and desert all around and no sleep to be got at nights . . . One ought never to say a word and this is what 'Martial Law' means."[15]

Apart from a few small-scale mutinies and rather more numerous instances of disaffection, the British were able on the whole to retain the loyalty of their fighting men from India during World War I. But a certain weary disenchantment seemed to take a toll once the war had entered its fourth year. Between 35 percent and 50 percent of wounds were found to be "on left hand and foot, probably self inflicted."[16] Night blindness in the 3rd Brahmans was discovered by the eye specialist to be a "self-induced disease by croton seeds."[17] "If I had known at the time that I should have to undergo so many trials," wrote Abdul Rauf Khan of the 2nd Combined Field Ambulance in Mesopotamia on February 19, 1917, "I would probably not have taken so much trouble to qualify at the examination. This war will never end, tell me then, what am I to do."[18]

Yet it was also in 1917 that Kazi Nazrul Islam, a Bengali eighteen-year-old, gave up his studies to join a newly formed "Double Company," later renamed the 49th Bengalee Regiment of Britain's Indian Army. The Bengalis were in the colonial view a quintessentially nonmartial race, but wartime pragmatism dictated the need for an experiment in the form of a

"Double Company." The Bengalee Regiment was first dispatched to Nowshera in the North-West Frontier Province and then stationed in Karachi until it was demobilized in early 1920. Havildar Quarter-Master Nazrul Islam spent his Karachi days perfecting his Persian and trying his hand at translating the Rubaiyat stanzas of the poet Hafiz. During 1919 he also composed a few poems and songs and wrote two stories that were published in the *Bangiya Muslim Sahitya Patrika* (Bengali Muslim Literary Magazine).

The graphic depiction of death in the trenches of Verdun in "Hena" might easily mislead the reader into believing that Nazrul was a direct participant in the war. In fact, the young havildar (sepoy sergeant) did not travel west of Karachi. Even though he did not cross the Indian Ocean, his literary imagination knew no bounds. His novella *Byathar Dan (The Gift of Pain)* begins as a straightforward, if counterintuitive, telling of the story of a love triangle involving an ill-fated lover (Dara), a noble but fallible beloved (Bedoura), and an initially wicked, but later repentant, seducer (Saif-ul-mulk). The story takes an unexpected turn when both Saif and Dara offer their services to a "liberation army" fighting "against exploitation on behalf of the oppressed citizenry of the world."[19] Saif observes Dara fight fearlessly in the battlefield until he is severely wounded. The commander-in-chief of the "liberation army" then eulogizes the blinded Dara: "It is not our custom to award 'Victoria Crosses' and 'Military Crosses' because it is hardly possible to give prizes to ourselves for our own work. The prize of our valour and sacrifice is the good of the citizens of this world . . . 'Khuda is undoubtedly great and he rewards those who perform good deeds'—isn't that the message of your holy Qu'ran?"[20]

A havildar's dream about heroism in "a liberation army" might suggest that there is nothing artificial in fictional narrative. As Paul Ricoeur has hinted in his *Time and Narrative*, fictional narrative has "a capacity to represent a deeper insight into the human experience of temporality than does either its historical or mythical counterpart." That does not, however, obviate the need to construct a historical narrative to which falls the task of representing "a reality that presents itself to human consciousness . . . the enigma of being in time."[21] If historians drawing on narrative theory have begun to lose their fear of trespassing across the borders of fictional and historical narrative, the role of poetry in conveying the enigma of feeling in time has been neither sufficiently theorized or historicized.

In May 1920 a picture of the Shatt-al-Arab adorned the frontispiece of the magazine *Muslim Bharat*. Inside was printed Kazi Nazrul Islam's celebrated poem, which opened with the stirring lines:

> Shatt-al-Arab, Shatt-al-Arab, sacred are your ancient
> shores.
> The blood of martyrs and the brave have been shed
> here by Arab heroes.[22]

The last stanza, the farewell message of a Bengali soldier to Iraq, expresses grief for the common loss of independence of his own motherland and of Iraq, "the land of martyrs." In

October 1921 appeared Nazrul's tour de force "Kamal Pasha," lauded by one critic as "perhaps the greatest literary ballad in Bengali." Meant to be declaimed rather than read silently in cold print, the poem "recreates the fervour of the war years" and "enshrines the sympathy which Kamal Pasha's efforts to throw off the invaders who were trying to carve up Turkey evoked."[23] No exercise in realist prose could come close to evoking the same depth of feeling of that historical moment. Nazrul never fully explained why during World War I he had enlisted in the British Indian Army. There is little evidence to sustain the popular myth that he had sought military training as preparation for active participation in an armed struggle for independence. Perhaps there was no more to it than his desire, as he reportedly told a friend, to forsake the university to see the universe. Be that as it may, by way of literary excursions in the trenches of France, the gardens of Iran, the coastline of Iraq, and the battlefields of Mesopotamia, Soviet Central Asia, and Turkey, he eventually found his way to becoming the revolutionary poet-laureate of Bengal.

A year and a half after Nazrul departed from the port city of Karachi, the Khilafat Conference met there on July 9, 1921. On the charge of making seditious speeches at that meeting, six Muslims and one Hindu were put on trial. They had all urged Muslim soldiers not to fight for Britain in the Middle East. The legal contest—the king-emperor versus Mohamed Ali and six others—generated texts that form a class of their own in the history of movement and memory. At one level the Muslim defendants acknowledged none other than Allah's sovereignty over the entire universe. In the name of Islamic universalism they also acknowledged the authority of the Sultan-Khalifa over the community of believers, which was perfectly compatible with the commitment they shared with their Hindu compatriots to the cause of the Indian nation.[24] Since British sovereignty over India was for the moment a political reality, the defendants merely sought to be able to practice their respective faiths without let or hindrance. Lack of opportunity to do so would compel Muslims to perform *hijrat*—that is, migrate to a territory where they could freely practice their religion.

Staged in a court of colonial law, the defendants' case, of necessity, took the form of an interrogation of power in which the memory of past British promises and present British perfidy loomed large. Mohamed Ali took two long days to address the jury. He did not hope to sway them in order to be found not guilty. His greatest success was in trying the patience of the British judge, whose many attempts to rule his lengthy treatises on religious law irrelevant proved utterly futile. The judge exercised his power to sentence Mohamed Ali to two years in prison, but the defendant had successfully communicated his argument to his audience of Islamic universalists and Indian anticolonialists and, in the process, made the colonial masters squirm. Mohamed Ali reminded the court of Victoria's Proclamation in 1858 that none would be "molested or disquieted by reason of their religion, faith or observances," a promise reaffirmed by two subsequent British sovereigns. In summing up his defense, Mohamed Ali skillfully wove together in his text multiple strands of resistance:

The Sepoys' Mutiny after which the Queen's Proclamation was issued had originated with greased cartridges in which cow's and swine's grease was believed to be mixed. But Islamic law . . . not only permits a Muslim to take swine's flesh if he is, in case of refusal, threatened with death; but lays it down that he would die a sinner if he refused it; but, if he is threatened with death unless he slay another Muslim, *he must refuse.* He may in like circumstances even recant Islam, if he continues to be a believer at heart but *he must not slay a Muslim.* And yet a Government which is so tender as to ask soldiers before enlistment whether they object to vaccination or re-vaccination, would compel a Muslim to do something worse than apostatize or eat pork. If there is any value in the boast of toleration and in the Proclamations of three sovereigns, then we have performed a religious and legal duty in calling upon Muslim soldiers in these circumstances to withdraw from the army, and are neither sinners nor criminals.[25]

Troubled Loyalty: King or Country?

Despite the best efforts of individuals like Mohamed Ali, the British were by and large successful in keeping their Indian Army insulated from the swirling currents of anticolonial nationalism until well into World War II. It was not until November 1945 that a Muslim officer along with two of his Hindu and Sikh comrades were put on trial, not for withdrawing from the army but for actually waging war against the king-emperor. They were part of an approximately 43,000-strong Indian National Army that had been raised in Southeast Asia to fight against the British.[26] It was an armed movement that elicited overwhelming support from the over two million Indians living at the time in Southeast Asia.

At his Red Fort court-martial of November 1945, Shah Nawaz Khan, an officer of the Indian National Army, addressed the president and members of the "honourable court," whose legality he refused to accept. He clearly meant to scale the ramparts of the fortress and reach a much wider audience among the Indian public. "I am going to lay before you," he stated, "very frankly, the considerations and motives that have impelled me from the day of my surrender in Singapore on February 15, 1942, to the day of my capture by the British forces at Pegu on May 16, 1945." Shah Nawaz was born to a family of Janjua Rajputs in Rawalpindi. His father had been the leader of the Janjua clan and served in the Indian Army for thirty years. During the two world wars, all able-bodied men of his extended family had enlisted, and in 1945 there were more than eighty of them serving as officers in the Indian Army. "I was brought up in an atmosphere," he related to the court, "which was purely military and up to the time of my meeting with Netaji Subhas Chandra Bose at Singapore in July 1943, I was politically almost uneducated. I was brought up to see India through the eyes of a young British officer, and all that I was interested in was soldiering and sport."[27]

On January 16, 1942, Shah Nawaz sailed from Bombay and joined his battalion in Singapore on January 29. He took part in the battle of Singapore on February 13, 14, and 15, until he was ordered to surrender. On the night of February 15–16, 1942, the "black pepper" was sorted out from the "red pepper." All Indians, including the king's commissioned officers, were asked to gather at Farrer Park on February 17, while the British officers and other ranks were to assemble at Changi. Shah Nawaz felt that that they were being left in the lurch and bristled "at being handed over like cattle by the British."[28] He remained for the moment one of the small minority of non-volunteers who did not respond to the invitation of Major Fujiwara and Captain Mohan Singh to join a national army.[29] Shah Nawaz divided his wartime role into three distinct phases. From February 15, 1942, until the end of May 1942, "the element of traditional loyalty to the King triumphed" and he refused to join the Indian National Army (INA). From June 1942 to July 1943 he chose in the interests of his men to volunteer for the INA, having determined "to sabotage it from within the moment [he] felt it would submit to Japanese exploitation." And from July 1943 to May 1945 he became "fully convinced that it was a genuine army of liberation."[30]

The first INA formed in 1942 in fact disintegrated because of differences with the Japanese. Shah Nawaz agreed to join the second INA in February 1943 on being assured that Netaji Subhas Chandra Bose, a former president of the Indian National Congress, would come to lead it. "When Netaji arrived in Singapore," he stated, "I watched him very keenly . . . I heard a number of his public speeches, which had a profound effect on me. It will not be wrong to say that I was hypnotized by his personality and his speeches. He placed the true picture of India before us and for the first time in my life I saw India, through the eyes of an Indian." Apart from the strength of character of his leader, Shah Nawaz was impressed by the enthusiasm of Indian expatriates in Southeast Asia who "became 'Fakirs' for the sake of their country." The mental conflict between loyalty to the raj, to which his family owed their material well-being, and the new consciousness of the "injustice" of colonial rule was eventually resolved in "the greatest and most difficult decision" of his life. "I decided," he told the court, "to sacrifice my everything—my life, my home, my family and its traditions. I made up my mind to fight even against my brother if he stood in my way, and in the actual fighting that followed in 1944, we actually fought against each other. He was wounded . . . the question before me was the King or the country. I decided to be loyal to my country and gave my word of honour to my Netaji that I would sacrifice myself for her sake."[31]

Shah Nawaz then pointed out that "the INA was raised, organized, trained and led in the field entirely by the Indians." He fought "a straightforward and honourable fight on the battlefield, against most overwhelming odds." During the military operations he along with his soldiers had "marched over 3000 miles in Burma." No mercenary army in his view could have "faced the hardships as the I.N.A. did." Having fought for the liberation of his motherland under a duly constituted Provisional Government of Free India, he had "committed no offence" for which he could be tried "by a court martial or by any other court." Indeed, the court's sentence of deportation for life could not be implemented and the Red Fort three were released by the commander-in-chief Claude Auchinleck in an atmosphere of intense public pressure.[32]

One of the defense witnesses at the Red Fort trial was S. A. Ayer, who in November 1940 had traveled to Bangkok as a Reuters special correspondent and in October 1943 had become minister of publicity and propaganda in the Provisional Government of Free India. Soon after the end of the war, in August 1945, he was in Japan. The world had collapsed around him with the death of his leader, Subhas Chandra Bose, in an airplane crash on August 18. As he "sat on a bench under the tall trees in the Omiya Park [Tokyo], day after day, with the Bible in hand, [he] read and re-read the Acts." "I prayed," he wrote, "for the strength of Peter and I prayed for an opportunity to bear humble and truthful testimony to Netaji's miraculous achievements." His prayer was answered. He was flown from Tokyo to Delhi and gave evidence at the Red Fort trial. Ever since the fulfillment of his prayer at Omiya Park, he had wanted to write about Netaji in East Asia, in a book that he considered "a purely personal tribute from a disciple to his Master."[33]

As he put the finishing touches to his book in 1951, Ayer felt that the passage of five years since the Red Fort trial had been valuable in gaining "the right perspective." He did not wish his book to be "a mere lifeless narration which sounded like something distant and unrelated to the realities of present-day India." "I worship Netaji," Ayer made clear in his preface without the slightest hint of embarrassment.[34] What he proceeded to deliver was a most vivid, and beautifully written, nonlinear narrative of Netaji and the Indian independence movement in Southeast Asia between 1943 and 1945. He also delicately documented his personal impressions of the relationships, diplomatic and cultural, of Indians with the Burmese, Thais, and Japanese. In terms of a natural literary flair, evocation of atmosphere, and eye for detail, Ayer's book stands in a class of its own among all the participants' narratives of that struggle. Not meant to be a critical biography, it had an emotional fervor balanced by an honest portrayal of failures and disappointments as well as a healthy dose of wit and wry, occasionally self-deprecating, humor.

Ayer chose to foreground in his narrative the "historic retreat" of Netaji and the INA from Burma to Thailand in early 1945, once the tide of the war had turned against them. Chased by enemy planes, Netaji, senior military officers and civilian officials, and nearly a hundred young women of the Rani of Jhansi Regiment made a twenty-three-day trek back from Rangoon to Bangkok. "Standing there in the open, in the bright moonlight, with fires and explosions in the distance, and no definite news of the position of the enemy was a peculiar sensation . . . We were literally living every moment of our life in those hours. We continued our march through the burning villages of Pegu."[35] Pages of breathtakingly evocative, thick description are punctuated in Ayer's book by short, reflective paragraphs: "Not only daylight; we dreaded the moonlight too, only a little less. We felt comparatively safe on pitch dark nights . . . rather primitive, do you think? Well, quite so. Otherwise, how can shelters dug 20 or 30 feet underground have such a fascination for man? How else can the sun and moon be objects of horror?"[36]

It is truly remarkable that the retreating column managed to cross the Sittang River without being decimated on that moonlit night. "We were asked to get ready," Ayer continues his story, "for the trek from Sittang to Moulmein en route to Bangkok. Major General Zaman Kiani was asked to take charge of the party. He ordered us to fall in and gave us instructions as to how our party, including Netaji, should march and how air-raid alarm would be given and how we should immediately disperse on either side of the road and take cover."[37]

"Such was his spirit of discipline," General Mohammad Zaman Kiani informs us, "that, to better arrange the march of the column and deal with related problems, he [Netaji] put me in complete charge and also put himself under my command for the duration of the march."[38] Between the participant narratives provided by Ayer and Kiani lies the great temporal and spatial divide of the partition of the subcontinent. Yet what is striking given the historic rupture of 1947 is the extent to which the two texts resonate with each other both in spirit and essential details. Kiani, commander of the 1st Division of the INA, describes his book as a "personal account of that movement known as the INA or Indian National Army, being written from memory after over thirty five years of the events it relates." His motive for writing his memoirs was simple. He felt "it would not be edifying in the least" for him "to die without leaving a record of [his] knowledge of this movement, which was both intimate and extensive."[39]

In 1931 Zaman Kiani had faced a career choice—to either go to the Olympic hockey trials being held in Calcutta or appear in the examination for admission into the new military academy at Dehra Dun. He passed the examination but the medical officer ruled him out from being admitted to the first term of the academy. The medical officer was a Hindu and the next man to be selected was a Sikh. This enraged all the Muslims of the battalion, who believed "the whole thing had been manoeuvred with a communal bias." Fortunately Zaman was later selected and joined the academy in its second term, which started six months later. "Little did I then realize," writes Kiani, "that in time to come, in a revolutionary movement . . . I would be one of the strongest advocates of inter-communal unity and harmony for the purpose of fighting against the foreign rule of our country."[40] In 1943 Kiani was one of the Muslim officers flanking Subhas Chandra Bose at a "national demonstration" and fund-raiser at the Chettiar temple in Singapore. Bose had refused to set foot in the temple unless his colleagues belonging to all castes and communities could come with him.[41] "When we came to the temple," Abid Hasan has written, "I found it filled to capacity with the uniforms of the I.N.A. officers and men and the black caps of the South Indian Muslims glaringly evident."[42]

Between 1943 and 1945 Kiani was the most senior field commander of a very different army from the one he had joined early in life. When Abid Hasan, a civilian, volunteered to go to the front, he found himself in a unit that contained Baluchis, Assamese, Kashmiris, Malayalis, Pathans, Sikhs, and Gujaratis. "No one had asked us," he writes, "to cease to be a Tamilian or Dogra, Punjabi Muslim or Bengali Brahmin, a Sikh or an Adivasi. We were all that and perhaps fiercely more so than before, but these matters became personal affairs." When their Netaji came to see the retreating men from Imphal at Mandalay, the "Sikhs oiled their beards, the Punjabi Muslims, Dogras and Rajputs twirled their moustaches and we the indiscriminates put on as good a face as we could manage."[43]

The fight did not end until the British forces landed in Singapore on August 25, 1945. Kiani received a message late that afternoon asking him to report to the general officer commanding (GOC) of the 5th Division aboard a British ship in Singapore harbor. His principal staff officers wanted to accompany him. The other commanders, especially those of the Heavy Gun Battalion and the AFV Battalion, resolved to let the senior officers negotiate the surrender of the INA forces, but promised that if the British tried to detain them at the first meeting "the Gun Battalion would open fire on the British beach-head soon after sun-set while the AFV Battalion would make a dash for [their] rescue." Such an eventuality did not arise. Kiani was handed a cyclostyled sheet of paper on behalf of the Supreme Allied Commander, South East Asia Command, on what was expected of the commander of the INA troops, and after the GOC had unobtrusively managed to peek at this strange soldier, he was allowed to return to camp. [44]

In 1947 Mohammad Zaman Kiani did not have much of a real choice. "Those of us whose homes were in the territories comprising Pakistan," he writes, "now acquired a new nationality and we geared ourselves loyally to fulfill our obligations as citizens of the new country and the state."[45] S. A. Ayer mentions in his 1951 book "a very unsporting taunt," "a hit below the belt," by certain circles in India that some INA officers were "fighting on the side of Pakistan against us." He replied by asking the question: "Who created Pakistan? Not the INA, anyway . . . and the convention of the INA held in Kanpur officially enjoined upon the nationals of Pakistan to be loyal subjects of their State. There was no other honourable course."[46] Kiani reports that it was "an uphill task" to be "rehabilitated" in Pakistan. They had all been cashiered or dismissed from the army by the British, and the postcolonial Pakistani Army was initially under British command. Also, "the Pakistani political leadership, with the exception of the Quaid-e-Azam Mohammed Ali Jinnah . . . still seemed overawed by the British and looked up to them for matters of guidance in most matters, particularly those of defence." The "stigma of dismissal" was eventually removed in 1949 "after the services of most of the officers had been made use of for liberating Azad Kashmir."[47] Kiani himself was later appointed political agent in Gilgit. An appendix in his book reproduces facsimiles of two documents on facing pages. The first, an order dated August 16, 1945, signed by Subhas Chandra Bose, head of state, provisional government of Azad Hind, reads: "During my absence from Syonan [Singapore], Major General M. Z. Kiani will represent the Provisional Government of Azad Hind." The second is a letter to Kiani dated September 26, 1958, in which General Mohammad Ayub Khan writes: "I think the people of Gilgit area should consider themselves lucky to have a man like you in looking after their interests."[48]

The final chapter of Kiani's book is entitled "Brief Sketches of Important Personalities." There are altogether fourteen such personalities, with the last named "The Unknown Soldier of the INA":

> He may have been an ex-P.O.W., who took up a rifle once again after having been put through the shame of surrender, he may have been a petty trader from Burma, a shop-keeper from Thailand, or a labourer from Malaya, who came hundreds of miles, marching on foot, or crammed in goods trains with little or no amenities. But, he took up a rifle for a cause which he held sacred and dear. He came at the call of his leaders and particularly of one of the greatest leaders of his country, who himself was always prepared to face all the dangers and also go through all the hardships that his men were to face. He gave his all and his remains now lie mingled with the earth in the desolate Kabaw Valley of Burma or the forbidding hills and jungles on the border of India, where he kissed the earth of his country when he first set his foot on its soil and gave his life.[49]

Might it have been useful to have a "participant narrative" to unravel the consciousness of "a true INA subaltern"? A testimonial text, perhaps, of a laborer turned soldier? A few transcriptions of such narratives do exist.[50] Yet if "the prose of counter-insurgency" of the colonial masters produces inversions of the indices of insurgency and develops an antagonism between itself and its subject, testimonial literature on its own cannot uncover the consciousness of the subaltern subject.[51] A testimonial, whether as collected fragment or published commodity, becomes part of a master narrative even while contesting its dominance. The need to stay "off the dangerous hook of claiming to establish the truth-knowledge of the subaltern" has led to a focus on how a discourse varies from the ideal subaltern position and a strategic maneuver to understand the subaltern consciousness through difference.[52] This point of entry into nationalist thought has paid some rich intellectual dividends, but is inherently limited by its focus on middle-class culture and consciousness and its corresponding neglect of action and event.[53] Such an approach to the history of ideas has also privileged territorial nationalism, finding its telos in the centralized nation-state and glossing over the extraterritorial or supraterritorial dimensions of anticolonialism. Participant narratives of the movements of "dominant" as well as "true" subalterns can only be made to yield their full range of meaning and historical value by creating a dynamic intertextuality across spatial boundaries of colonies and nation-states and across temporal thresholds of great displacements, such as the 1947 partition.

The fusion of memory and imagination is seldom the domain of the historian; instead, artists, novelists, and filmmakers often take the lead. On the occasion of the fiftieth anniversary of independence, Indian public television showed on its national network *Pahela Aadmi* (The First Man), an old black-and-white Hindi film made in Bombay soon after war's end by the well-known director Bimal Roy and the INA soldier turned actor-director Nazir Ahmed. It is a love story between the son of an Indian doctor in Burma swept away by patriotic zeal and his conservative neighbor's daughter, neither of whom has ever seen India. The father sends his son to the Indo-Burma front, where he succeeds in blowing up a strategic bridge and becomes the first man to plant the flag of freedom on Indian soil. He is wounded in the action and dies in the base hospital run by his father. The young woman hears the news while caring for the other injured soldiers. The last scene shows her with the Rani of Jhansi Regiment, not in retreat, but marching resolutely toward India. Significantly, the regiment's leader had at one time said: "We shall not repent even if the advance of our revolutionary army to attain independence of our homeland is completely defeated . . . Even if the whole army becomes only spirit we will not stop advancing towards our homeland!"[54] This mentality is not easily understandable in terms of colonial rationality and demands to be retold in new modes of historical narrative.

From Mesopotamia to Malaya the Indian Ocean interregional arena formed a crucial spatial venue for Indian soldiers to rethink their identities and loyalties. The stark choice between the global British Empire and the territorial Indian nation with rigid borders was not necessarily the only one available to them. Lurking in the background of the rival claims of king and country, the complex and yet not fully understood phenomenon of a diasporic patriotism confronted the soldiers.

5

Expatriate Patriots

Anticolonial Imagination and Action

> As though to warn us of the coming real storm on land, a terrible gale
> overtook us, whilst we were only four days from Natal. December is a
> summer month of monsoon in the Southern hemisphere, and gales, great
> and small, are, therefore, quite common in the Southern sea at that
> season. The gale in which we were caught was so violent and prolonged
> that the passengers became alarmed. It was a solemn scene. All became
> one in face of the common danger. They forgot their differences
> and began to think of the one and only God—Musalmans, Hindus,
> Christians and all.
>
> —MOHANDAS K. GANDHI, *AN AUTOBIOGRAPHY*

If a storm at sea in December 1896 reminded Indians of various religious faiths of their common humanity, various storms
on land at overseas destinations contributed to a sense of Indian-ness among a people fractured by religion, language, local origin, caste, and class. The depths of an inchoate, yet
intense, patriotism that gripped Indian expatriates at critical
moments of their history are not easy to fathom. It is a delicate task to retrieve sentiments and emotions—as difficult as

lifting a precious cargo of a shipwreck from the ocean bed—
for which appropriate tools have to be used. Those who have
railed against any unitary notion of an Indian diaspora, emphasizing instead the primary loyalties shaped by local origin,
have been naturally puzzled and discomforted by the appearance of a diasporic patriotism. Used to dealing with the rational calculations of merchants' account books and colonial political economy, they have tried unsuccessfully to attribute
awkward political choices made by Indian migrants to short-
term, interest-driven assessments of benefits and costs, safety
and risk.[1] Others less viscerally opposed to the concept of the
nation intermediating the levels of the local and global have
noted how Indians have tended to discover their Indian-ness
after leaving the shores of India. Yet such investigations of
the relationship between nation and migration have generally
stressed the aspect of an externally imparted Indian identity
whenever and wherever expatriates have encountered the racial bigotry of hostile states or economic vested interests.[2]
Discreetly kept out of view have been the ways in which Indians of various religious, linguistic, local, caste, or class backgrounds may have—as historical subjects in their own right—
juggled their multiple identities in a diasporic public sphere.

Can we devise an approach to address the issue of patriotism among expatriates without resurrecting the monolith of
the Indian nation? It is possible if we keep in mind the key
distinction between the diverse forms of precolonial patriotism and the unitary overtones of modern territorial nationalism. Precolonial patriotism connoted a link between land and
people without the land being too closely delimited. Love for

regional homelands, often termed *watan* or *desh* in Indian languages, drew on both the affective bonds informed by the languages of devotional religion and rational doctrines about legitimacy and good governance. The concept of space in precolonial patriotism could be simultaneously finite and infinite, restrictive and expansive. The name Hindustan for India could, for instance, refer to the north Indian Gangetic plain or to the whole of the subcontinent, which itself has fuzzy boundaries.[3] Modern Indian nationalism, far from being exclusively derived from discourses on the European territorial nation-state, drew significantly on elements of this legacy of patriotism and kept it alive through continual, creative innovation. Forms of patriotism that celebrated memorialized homelands were extendable and transportable by migrant communities, whose circular movements in the Indian Ocean arena meant they never really lost touch with their points of departure. The imaginary homeland of Gujarat, quite as much as Gujaratis, could in a sense travel to Africa, or Tamil Nadu to Southeast Asia, and back again.

In the late nineteenth and early twentieth centuries, the Indian nation was actively evolving, with a variety of individuals, linguistic groups, and religious communities seeking to help imagine it into being. There were both rooted as well as mobile aspects of this "nation in formation," even though only the rooted ones have been emphasized by theorists of the nation as "imagined community." Benedict Anderson and those who followed in his wake tracked the global dispersal, replication, and piracy of the nation-state form from the west to the east, leaving out of their account the multiple meanings of nationhood and alternative frameworks of states that were imagined in the colonized world of Asia and Africa.[4] Anti-colonialism in the Indian Ocean arena was nourished by many regional patriotisms, competing versions of Indian nationalism, and extraterritorial affinities of religiously informed universalisms. It is all too easy to identify the vertical and horizontal splits in the Indian diaspora in the Indian Ocean arena and beyond. Yet it is the very fractured nature of migrant communities that on occasion made them rise to the challenge of crafting an "Indian" anticolonial politics that was based on a creative accommodation of differences rather than the imposition of singular uniformity. Globalism and nationalism were not antithetical in this kind of anticolonial project.

The histories of patriotism among expatriates were marked by an interplay of nationalism and universalism in their normative thought and political practice. This process is exemplified in two key moments and locations associated with the life histories of two iconic figures of Indian anticolonialism. The first is Mahatma Gandhi's South African phase, which clarified his own conception of Indian nationality and its constituent parts. This period was in important ways the formative stage of Gandhi's emergence as leader of the nationalist movement in India from 1919 onward. The conceptualization of Gandhian nationalism in South Africa was of critical importance to Indian history. The second is Subhas Chandra Bose's Southeast Asian phase between 1943 and 1945, during the turmoil of World War II. This was the climactic stage in the life of a leader who had made his political debut in Gandhi's noncooperation and Khilafat movement in 1921. In what ways did the Indian communities of South Africa and Southeast Asia shape or define Indian nationality? It is impossible to fully comprehend Indian nationalism, sense of self, and mission without knowing the experiences of those who operated in the wide Indian Ocean arena. The oceanic dimension of anticolonialism may go some way in freeing the study of nationalism from its land-locked state.

Satyagraha in South Africa

On November 29, 1896, Mohandas Karamchand Gandhi embarked on his second voyage to South Africa on board the steamship *Courland* with his wife, two sons, and a nephew. The *Courland* had been recently bought by Dada Abdullah, whose firm Gandhi had represented as a lawyer in a commercial dispute in 1893–1894. (Gandhi and his family were offered free passage by his erstwhile clients.) Another steamship, *Naderi*, sailed from Bombay for Durban on the same day. Together the two ships carried about eight hundred passengers, approximately half of whom were bound for the Transvaal. After weathering a "terrible gale" off the coast of Natal, the two ships cast anchor in the port of Durban on December 18, 1896, and hoisted the yellow flag. A short period of quarantine for incoming ships was normal practice and, since there had been plague in Bombay, some additional precautions were to be expected. It soon became clear, however, that the threat of disease was a mere pretext for trying "to coerce the passengers into returning to India." A group of white residents of Durban charged that while in India, Gandhi had "'indulged in unmerited condemnation of the Natal whites' and had brought the two shiploads of passengers with a view to 'swamping Natal with Indians.'" While his detractors tried their tactics of intimidation, Gandhi kept himself busy boosting the morale of the passengers and lecturing the captain and his officers on "Western civilization," which, he argued, unlike "the Eastern" was "predominantly based on force." Once he disembarked, he was surrounded by a group of belligerent white youths who pelted him with "stones, brickbats and rotten eggs," "snatched away" his turban, and battered and kicked him. With "bruises all over" and an abrasion, he was somehow escorted to the home of a wealthy Parsi merchant of Durban. The youths now surrounded the house and demanded that Gandhi be delivered to them. While the police superintendent kept the ruffians amused by singing the tune "Hang old Gandhi on the sour apple tree," the future Mahatma escaped in disguise through a neighboring shop. He later gave a statement to the police that he did not wish his assailants to be prosecuted, thereby scoring a moral victory.[5]

Whatever else Gandhi may have been guilty of, he had not induced the two shiploads of Indians to come to Natal. The first shiploads of Indian indentured laborers had been brought in 1860 to work on the sugar plantations. Between 1860 and the end of indentured immigration in 1911, the colonial government of India recorded 152,184 laborers leaving Madras and Calcutta by sea for Natal. According to their contracts, these Indians were entitled to a free return passage after serving one five-year term as indentured labor and another five years as "free" labor. Until 1890 ex-indentured workers could

5.1. Indians arriving in Natal. Museum Africa, Johannesburg.

choose to receive a plot of land in Natal instead of a free return passage to India. Just over half of the Indian indentured laborers ended up remaining in the colony after the expiration of their contracts. This ex-indentured population of Indians spawned another category of Indians known as the "colonial-born" or simply "colonials," many of whom migrated north from Natal to the Transvaal in the last decades of the nineteenth century. In East Africa the Indian merchants had preceded the arrival of indentured laborers, but in South Africa the sequence was the reverse. From the mid-1870s merchant immigrants began to come in the wake of the sizeable indentured workforce. They were commonly referred to as the "passengers" because they paid for their own passage, unlike the indentured workers who were shipped under contract.[6] Aboobaker Amod is thought to be the first Indian trader to have arrived in 1875 as an ordinary immigrant and set up shop in Durban. An owner of ships and considerable property, he showed the way to other Indian merchants by branching out from Natal to the Transvaal. The pioneer spent no more than a decade in South Africa; he died on a visit to India in 1886 when he was only thirty-six years old.[7]

It was at the call of one of the leading Indian merchant firms of Natal and the Transvaal—Dada Abdullah and Company—that Gandhi came on his first sojourn to South Africa in 1893. He was all set to return to India after settling the company's case when a law designed to severely restrict the electoral franchise of Indians in Natal made him change his plans. Gandhi read in the *Natal Mercury* an article supporting a new franchise bill in June 1894: "The Asiatic comes of a race impregnated with an effete civilization, with not an atom of knowledge of the principles or traditions of representative government."[8] He immediately resolved to stay in Natal and agitate against the new legislation through the constitutional methods of prayers and petitions being used back in India by the Indian National Congress. The agitation, Gandhi claimed, "infused new life into the community" and engendered the conviction that "the community was one and indivisible." A new organization called the Natal Indian Congress was established on August 22, 1894, with leading merchant Abdullah

Haji Adam as president and Gandhi as honorary secretary. Gandhi was aware that the name "congress" was "in bad odour with the Conservatives in England," but it was "the very life of India." Since it "savoured of cowardice to hesitate to adopt the name," Gandhi recommended to his fellow expatriates that the name "congress" be allowed to migrate from India to Natal.[9] Gandhi did not advocate the principle of "one Indian, one vote" and had no quarrel with a property qualification for the franchise. "What the Indians do and would protest against is colour distinction," he wrote in an appeal to every Briton in South Africa—"disqualification based on account of racial difference."[10] Despite the efforts of Gandhi and his peers, the franchise bill was passed into law in March 1896 after only slight modification by the Natal legislature.

Following the familiar pattern of circular migration of most Indians across the Indian Ocean, Gandhi left for India in June 1896 and returned with his wife and children to Natal in December 1896. He received a hostile reception from the white community. While in India, Gandhi had written a bestselling "Green Pamphlet" detailing the many facets of racial discrimination suffered by Indians in South Africa.

During the 1896 to 1906 decade, the merchant class continued to be Gandhi's principal political constituency both in Natal and in the Transvaal. Already during his first visit, a trembling and weeping Tamil man named Balasundaram, "in tattered clothes, head-gear in hand, two front teeth broken and his mouth bleeding," had brought home to Gandhi the abuse to which Indian indentured laborers were subject.[11] He wrote in his "Green Pamphlet" about the severe hardships caused by the three-pound poll tax imposed on ex-indentured laborers in 1895. But he did not as yet champion the laborers' cause in the manner in which he took up both legal and political briefs for the Indian merchants. Nor had he worked through in his mind at this stage a clear anti-imperialist stance. Even though his "personal sympathies" were with the Boers in the Anglo-Boer war of 1899–1902, his "loyalty to the British rule" drove him to participate on the British side in that war. Indeed, Gandhi raised an ambulance corps of about a thousand men (which had "the honour of carrying soldiers like General Woodgate") and won a war medal. The Zulu rebellion that followed was, as Gandhi could see, "no war but a man-hunt" by the British. Even though it was hard to "hear every morning reports of the soldiers' rifles exploding like crackers in innocent hamlets," he "swallowed the bitter draught" and once more set up an ambulance corps. Because his corps was entrusted with the task of nursing the wounded Zulus who were otherwise "uncared for," the work eased his conscience.[12] Away from the war front, Gandhi had significant organizational achievements. In 1903 he set up the British Indian Association in the Transvaal, which like its counterpart the Natal Indian Congress galvanized the Indian mercantile elite. The following year he launched a new paper, *Indian Opinion*, which became the premier organ of Indian political expression in South Africa. A skilled and tireless pamphleteer and columnist, Gandhi's exhortations to the Indian community appeared regularly in the editorial pages of this journal. Yet "despite the universalist ring of his ever increasing editorials on duty to the wider community, the public weal, public service, and so forth,

Gandhi was as yet no more a politician of the people than he had ever been."[13]

During the years of passive resistance, or *satyagraha*, from late 1906 to 1914, the politics of the Indian community became increasingly radicalized in terms of aims, methods, and social composition. The provocation came in the form of an "Asiatic registration" ordinance issued by the Transvaal government, which would have required all "Asiatics" in that territory to register and carry certificates bearing their fingerprints. Gandhi exhorted Indians to pledge not to submit to this compulsory registration. At a mass meeting in September 1906, three thousand Hindus, Muslims, and Christians took an oath to go to jail rather than register in this fashion. Haji Habib and H. O. Ally enthused the crowd of merchants, small traders, and hawkers with their oratory. Although the immediate issue at hand was the registration ordinance, Haji Habib's fiery speech in Gujarati did not fail to mention European designs against the Ottoman Empire. The organizational backbone for this popular mobilization was supplied by the Hamidia Islamic Society, a Muslim charitable organization formed in Johannesburg in July 1906.[14]

Undeterred by the Indian opposition, the Transvaal government introduced the ordinance in barely modified form as a bill in early 1907. The *satyagraha* campaign against it began in earnest in April 1907. A nominal prize was offered through *Indian Opinion* for an Indian name for the movement that could transcend the inadequacies of the English phrase "passive resistance." Maganlal Gandhi won the prize by coining the word *sadagraha* (with *sat* meaning truth, and *agraha* meaning firm resolve). But his more famous namesake changed it to the grammatically incorrect *satyagraha* to "make it clearer."[15]

One of Gandhi's first moves was to strike an alliance with the overseas Chinese in South Africa led by Leung Quinn of the Transvaal Chinese Association. The understanding did "not entail integration of the Chinese and Indian political communities," but it was based on mutual respect.[16] Nor was there any attempt to erase the religious differences among the Indian community and replace these with a discourse on secular uniformity. Religion as faith had always been part and parcel of Gandhi's political philosophy and the fount of his political inspiration. For his followers too he was prepared to hold up religion and honor as motivating principles underlying his *satyagraha*. In August 1907 Imam Abdul Kadir Bawazeer, a Konkani who had been a businessman in the Transvaal for over a decade, took over as chairman of the Hamidia Islamic Society. He was ably supported by Moulvi Syed Ahmed Mukhtiar, a new migrant, who preached at the Surti mosque in Johannesburg. The preacher told his audiences that they faced a choice between "the law and the faith." Among the Hindus much the same message was being conveyed by Ramsunder Pundit, also a new migrant, who helped build a temple and organized the religious organization Sanatan Veda Dharma Sabha. Gandhi himself invoked the blessings of Khuda-Ishvar, the hyphenated form of common terms for God among Hindus and Muslims, in support of the movement.[17]

The antiregistration drive proved remarkably successful. "The natural consequences of such legislation," Gandhi had warned, "would be segregation in locations and finally expul-

5.2. Gandhi, *third from left,* and Leung Quinn, *second from right,* 1908. Vithalbhai Jhaveri/GandhiServe.

sion from the country." By November 30, 1907—the government's deadline—only 511 out of some 13,000 "Asiatics" had submitted to compulsory registration. During the next two months, nearly two thousand Indians and Chinese were jailed in Johannesburg for violating the registration law. The way in which Gandhi's paper *Indian Opinion* reported on the arrests gives some insight into his strategy of forging unity based on a healthy respect for cultural differences. In an attempt to show how people of diverse religious, regional, linguistic, and caste backgrounds supported the movement, a typical update catalogued the following arrests: "4 Surti Mahomedans, 1 Memon Mahomedan, 2 Pathans, 3 Madrassis, 3 Bannias, 1 Lohana, 1 Brahman, 2 Desais, 1 Calcutta, 1 Parsi, 1 Punjabi, and 3 Chinese."[18]

On December 28, 1907, Gandhi himself was imprisoned for the first time along with Leung Quinn and a number of other leaders. Gandhi's reading habits in jail reflected the political philosophy that underpinned unity among religious faiths in the movement. He read the Gita at dawn, the Qu'ran at noon, and used the Bible to give lessons to a fellow Christian convict. As if to underscore the universalism in his thinking, books by Socrates, Plato, Bacon, Carlyle, Tolstoy, Huxley, and Ruskin were added to the mix.[19] Negotiations with General Smuts were conducted from jail and eventually Gandhi, Quinn, and Thambi Naidoo accepted a settlement by which they agreed to voluntary registration in return for a subsequent repeal of the law. Gandhi's compromise did not please his more radical followers, however; he was severely assaulted by an irate Pathan on his way to the registration office on February 10, 1908.[20]

Gandhi's critics had a point. Smuts did not repeal the registration act. Stung by this "breach of faith," the Transvaal Indians gathered on the grounds of the Hamidia mosque in Johannesburg on August 16, 1908, and burned some two thousand registration certificates. "The whole assembly rose to their feet," Gandhi wrote, "and made the place resound with the echoes of their continuous cheers during the burning process."[21] Yet Smuts had succeeded in disrupting the momentum of the movement and had engineered splits within it.

5.3. Gandhi recovers after an assault by irate followers, 1908. Vithalbhai Jhaveri/GandhiServe.

In Natal, too, divisions emerged in Indian politics as the colonial-born white-collar workers, dissatisfied with their representation in the merchant-dominated Natal Indian Congress, formed their own Natal Indian Patriotic Union with the Tamil leader P. S. Aiyar as president. This development might be seen as positive because it promised to broaden the social base of Indian politics.

More problematic was the prospect of conflict on religious lines. Religion in politics could be a double-edged sword. Harnessing religion as faith and cultivating respect for religious differences, as Gandhi did, strengthened mass movements and lent them an intensity that they otherwise might not have had. But others were tempted to appeal to religion as demarcating separate if not clashing identities, something that tended to happen whenever mass movements went off the boil. By April 1909 a Hindu religious figure, Swami Shankeranand, had imported the politics of communitarian bigotry from the Punjab to Natal.[22] He "favoured drawing a sharp line between Hindus and Muslims." Taking advantage of grievances among some Hindu traders and hawkers about lack of access to marketing facilities and the undue dominance of the Durban mosque market, Shankeranand successfully drove a wedge between the two religious communities. By playing the Hindu communitarian card in the politics of the rising colonial-born elite, he "retarded the process of unification" of the various segments and strata of the Indian community.[23]

It required a visit from an Indian leader of a very different outlook to breathe new life into Indian politics in South Africa. The arrival in October 1912 of Gopāl Krishna Gokhale, one of the leading lights of the Indian National Congress, reenergized the mercantile and colonial-born elites worried about issues of immigration and movement across provincial boundaries, and infused new hope in indentured workers suffering under the three-pound poll tax. The event also brought Gandhi out of temporary semiretirement. With Gandhi by his side, Gokhale made a triumphal tour of Natal, the Transvaal, and the Cape, where he was given enthusiastic receptions by large crowds of Indians.[24] While a few members of the elite complained that Gandhi was a little too possessive of Gokhale, the leader from India addressed a number of very large mass meetings organized by the merchants in the Durban area. Some ten thousand small cultivators and agricultural laborers gathered for him in Isipingo, another ten thousand mostly indentured laborers assembled on the Mount Edgecombe sugar estate, and a crowd of five thousand collected in Durban proper. This moderate leader of the Indian National Congress could hardly be expected to adopt a tone of flaming radicalism in South Africa. He made measured statements on doing what he could to redress the inequities faced by the merchants and laborers alike. Talks held by a leader of his stature with key figures in the South African administration also raised expectations that long-standing issues of concern would be seriously addressed. Overall, Gokhale's tour "served, inadvertently, as a significant step towards mass Indian mobilization." The comportment of Gandhi was altered as well. When he said farewell to Gokhale at Dar-es-Salaam on December 1, 1912, he "wore Indian dress for the first time in his adult life."[25]

The Indian Immigrants' Bill of 1913, which included various restrictions on domicile and interprovincial migration and a refusal to accord recognition to marriages conducted according to Indian rites, triggered the renewal of the *satyagraha* campaign. The lead was taken in May 1913 by the British Indian Association of the Transvaal whose president, Ahmed Mahomed Cachalia, worked closely with Gandhi to launch the movement. The Transvaal Indian Women's Association strongly endorsed the resolution to begin *satyagraha*. By June 1913, Gandhi had made up his mind to take up the cause of the indentured workers and included the repeal of the three-pound poll tax in his charter of demands. In 1913 more than 65 percent of the indentured laborers were serving second or subsequent terms of indenture, as tax debts and lack of employment opportunities forced them into a vicious cycle of indenture contracts with little prospect of freedom.[26]

The *satyagraha* began on a modest scale with a small number of men and women courting arrest by illegally crossing the Transvaal-Natal border in mid-September 1913. It expanded dramatically as soon as the indentured workers in the coal belt of northern Natal resorted to a strike on October 16, 1913. Gandhi at once sent experienced *satyagrahis* as well as new recruits among the Tamil-speaking Natal-born Indians to support the workers. Gandhi himself, along with Thambi Naidoo and C. R. Naidoo, addressed mass meetings of more than three thousand workers. Faced with an ultimatum from the mine owners that the workers' food rations would be withheld, Gandhi led a march of two hundred strikers and their dependents out of the mining compounds in Newcastle toward the Transvaal border on October 29, 1913. Over the next couple of days Thambi Naidoo led a second party of three hundred workers and their families, and another leader, Albert Christopher, headed a third column of 250. Within a few days some four thousand striking workers and their families, assisted by other colonial-born Indians and veteran *satyagrahis,* had marched into the Transvaal from Natal. Women passive resisters, mostly Tamil, played a significant role in the campaign and did not hesitate to go to jail.[27]

Gandhi and the coal miners ran the risk of being outmaneuvered by Smuts. But the success of the strike was "en-

5.4. Women resisters, mostly Tamil. "Golden Number" (a special edition) of *Indian Opinion*, 1914, reprinted in Uma Dhupelia-Mesthrie, *From Cane Fields to Freedom* (Cape Town: Kwela Books, 2000).

sured" when it spread to the coastal sugar plantations of southern Natal by November 7, 1913. The movement in these parts took on distinctly millenarian overtones inspired by a wide array of popular myth and rumor. One such rumor was that Gokhale was himself coming from India to abolish the hated tax and was bringing with him a regiment of soldiers. Others persuaded themselves that they were acting on Gandhi's orders. The rumor that unsettled the Natal authorities most was that Indians were calling the Africans to their side or that the Africans were contemplating lending support to the Indians.

The police responded to the strike with savage brutality, shooting dead a number of strikers. During the month of

November 1914, the strike "paralysed the Durban and Pietermaritzburg produce markets, closed down some of the sugar mills, and stripped many coastal hotels, restaurants and private residences of their domestics (although these were reluctant to come out), resulted in some 150 acres of cane being illegally burned, and had inconvenienced the coal industry, the N[atal] G[overnment] R[ailways], and other, smaller industries in coastal Natal." Gandhi was arrested on November 9, his close associates H. S. L. Polak and Herman Kallenbach the next day, and a host of other leaders and rank and file over the subsequent couple of weeks. The spread of violence and adverse publicity in India and Britain forced the South African administration to take some serious measures in response to the Indian demands.[28]

The government instituted the Justice W. H. Solomon commission of enquiry to look into the causes of the Natal strike and *satyagraha*. Gandhi did not take part in the proceedings of the commission because it had no Indian representation, but his views were indirectly taken into consideration. The recommendations of the commission presented to the union parliament in March 1914 formed the basis of the Indians' Relief Act of July 1914. The abolition of the three-pound tax of 1895 through this legislation was the crowning achievement of the *satyagraha* campaign. On the question of immigration, one wife and any minor children of a marriage by Indian rites were permitted to join husbands residing in South Africa. In addition, plural wives who had lived or were living in South Africa were able to stay. Some Muslims were unhappy with what Gandhi was able to achieve on this score. And full satisfaction was not obtained on the discriminatory aspects of trade license laws or the restrictions on the right of free interprovincial migration. Despite these shortcomings, Gandhi felt that the Indians' Relief Act of 1914 signified a successful conclusion of "the Passive Resistance struggle which commenced in the September of 1906" and constituted "the Magna Carta of our liberty in this land."[29] With the exception of some of the mercantile elite in Natal and the Transvaal, public opinion in South Africa, India, and Britain tended to agree with Gandhi's assessment.

Gandhi departed the shores of South Africa on July 18, 1914. "This subcontinent [South Africa] has become to me a sacred and dear land," he said in a parting message, "next only to my motherland."[30] He returned after two decades with his conception of Indian nationality deeply influenced by his overseas experience. Although he was the most famous person to have extended his regional homeland abroad and connected it back to a larger, extraterritorial conception of India, he was not alone in this endeavor. Although the activities of "East Africa Indians" may not have produced any flamboyant and charismatic personalities like South Africa's Gandhi, they too engaged in a process of "overseas homecoming." Narasimbhai Ishwarbhai Patel, a Gujarati patriot in East African exile between 1913 and 1932, was one such individual: he articulated through his letters and books an alternative to a territorially based conception of nationalism. Patel's Gujarat stretched far beyond its specific territorial location to East Africa, from where he continued to be dedicated to the idea of Indian anticolonialism.[31]

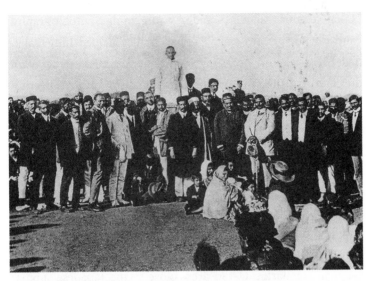

5.5. Farewell to Gandhi, Durban 1914. "Golden Number" (a special edition) of *Indian Opinion*, 1914, reprinted in Uma Dhupelia-Mesthrie, *From Cane Fields to Freedom* (Cape Town: Kwela Books, 2000).

Gandhi brought back from South Africa not just new techniques for struggle, but also an approach to the crafting of Indian unity that was respectful of internal cultural differences and yet was able to transcend them. He deployed this approach with great effect in achieving Hindu-Muslim unity in the Khilafat and noncooperation movement of 1919–1922, the first all-India mass movement against British rule under Gandhi's leadership. Despite the many compulsions of subcontinental politics during the next two decades and a half, he never wholly lost sight of this vision. It is a Gandhian legacy that has been obscured in histories written around the false binary between secular nationalism and religious communalism.

"I am a good sailor," Gandhi wrote in his autobiography, "and do not get sea-sick."[32] That quality helped him realize that there was no necessary contradiction between love for the land and the sea, territorial nationalism and extraterritorial universalism—which was often tinged with religious inspiration.

Azad Hind in Southeast Asia

On April 26, 1943, at approximately 25 degrees south latitude and 60 degrees east longitude in the Indian Ocean some four hundred nautical miles off the coast of Madagascar, the German submarine U-180 drew close to the Japanese submarine I-29 at a prearranged rendezvous point. "We put up a periscope," remembered Abid Hasan. "They put up their periscope. We knew which direction to look. And they knew which direction to look. So we could spot the periscopes. Then we came up a little, they came up a little, as already arranged and ultimately we both surfaced. But the sea at that time was very choppy."[33] The submarines sailed alongside each other for what seemed like an eternity. At dawn on April 28, even though the waves were still high, Hasan and the Indian leader Subhas Chandra Bose climbed down from the German submarine into a small rubber raft and transferred across to the Japanese submarine.

Their voyage had begun at Kiel harbor on February 8, 1943, and they had traveled north of Scotland, south through the Atlantic, and around the Cape of Good Hope into the Indian Ocean. On April 18 the U-180, commanded by Captain

5.6. Subhas Chandra Bose, *left*, and Abid Hasan during their submarine voyage, 1943. Netaji Research Bureau, Calcutta.

Werner Musenburg, had encountered and sunk the British merchant ship *Corbis*. This U-boat of the 9D type could travel at the speed of 18 knots on the surface and 7.3 to 7.7 knots when submerged. Conditions had been cramped inside the German submarine and the journey through enemy-infested waters difficult and dangerous, but the German crew had been very friendly and courteous to their two Indian guests. Yet as soon as Hasan and Bose boarded the Japanese submarine in the Indian Ocean, they felt "something akin to a home-coming," Hasan reminisced.[34] The flotilla commander, Captain Masao Teraoka, vacated his cabin for the Indian leader; the skipper of I-29, Juichi Izu, threw a party in celebration of the unique successful transshipment; and the cooks tried their best

5.7. Submarine to submarine transfer of Subhas Chandra Bose in the Indian Ocean, 1943. Netaji Research Bureau, Calcutta.

to prepare Indian meals with supplies they had acquired at their base in Penang. Traveling south of the Indian subcontinent, the Japanese submarine, more spacious than the German one, reached its destination, Sabang on the coast of Sumatra, on May 6, 1943. Subhas Chandra Bose autographed a photograph with the crew taken just prior to their disembarking: "It was a great pleasure to sail aboard this submarine . . . I believe this will mark a milestone in our fight for victory and peace."[35]

Subhas Chandra Bose, a top-ranking leader of the Indian independence movement and president of the Indian National Congress in 1938–1939, had undertaken this perilous sea voyage across half the globe in order to reach the large commu-

5.8. Subhas Chandra Bose with Japanese crew before disembarking from a Japanese submarine, Sabang, May 1943. Netaji Research Bureau, Calcutta.

nity of more than two million Indian expatriates in southeast Asia. A key participant in the Gandhian *satyagraha* campaigns since 1921, he had come to believe that an armed thrust from outside the subcontinent was necessary to finally dislodge the British from India. He had made a dramatic escape from India in early 1941 and made his way to Europe to gain access to Indian prisoners of war being held by Germany and Italy. The German invasion of the Soviet Union ruined his plans of leading an army of liberation into India from the northwest. But the Japanese sweep across Southeast Asia in early 1942 opened new possibilities for him at the other end of the globe. A conference of Indian patriots in Southeast Asia held at Bangkok on June 15, 1942, had invited him to come and lead them. At the time he had been able only to send them a message underscoring the need to "link up Indian nationalists all over the world," no less.[36] Now, a year later, he was at last among them. The largest number of Indians in Japanese-occupied Southeast Asia were to be found in the British colonies of Malaya and Burma, from where the colonial masters had been forced to make an ignominious retreat. Some 800,000 Indians were estimated to be living in Malaya and, even after the departure of 400,000 from Burma in the early months of 1942, nearly a million Indians remained in that country. Smaller but significant numbers of Indians resided in Indochina, the East Indies, and the Philippines. Among them were capitalists, big and small, as well as laborers, lawyers, doctors, and teachers. They were to form the civilian, social, and economic base of an Indian army of liberation.

On July 2, 1943, Subhas Chandra Bose arrived in the port

city of Singapore, once a bulwark of the British Empire. Two days later, at an enthusiastic representative assembly of Indians in Southeast Asia held in the Cathay theater, he accepted the leadership of the Indian Independence League from Rashbehari Bose, a namesake and old revolutionary in exile. The following day he took over as supreme commander of the Indian National Army. "Indians outside India," he thundered at a mass meeting in Singapore on July 9, 1943, "particularly, Indians in East Asia, are going to organize a fighting force which will be powerful enough to attack the British army of occupation in India. When we do so, a revolution will break out, not only among the civilian population at home, but also among the Indian Army, which is now standing under the British flag. When the British government is thus attacked from both sides—from inside India and from outside—it will collapse and the Indian people will then regain their liberty." He had already given his soldiers the slogan "On to Delhi," which was reminiscent of the 1857 rebellion in India. From the Indian civilians in Southeast Asia he called for "total mobilization for a total war." In return for such mobilization of men and women, money and resources, he promised "a real second front for the Indian struggle."[37]

There is little doubt that a large majority of Indian expatriates in southeast Asia responded with great emotional fervor to this patriotic call. At least eighteen thousand civilians, mostly Tamils from south India excluded by the British from their mythology of martial races, enlisted in the Indian National Army and trained for battle alongside professional soldiers from the northwestern regions of the subcontinent. Many

5.9. Indian National Army, Singapore, 1943. Netaji Research Bureau, Calcutta.

tens of thousands more joined the numerous local branches of the Indian Independence League, which provided support of various kinds.[38]

While traveling in the submarine, Subhas Chandra Bose had dictated a speech to Abid Hasan, which he planned to deliver to a women's regiment of the Indian National Army of his dreams. This regiment, named after the Rani of Jhansi (of 1857 fame), was formed and a thousand young women from Malaya and Burma—again mostly but not exclusively Tamils—volunteered and received parental permission to join. Its commanding officer, Lakshmi Swaminathan, was a medical doctor based in Singapore. Her mother had been active in the Indian National Congress in Madras and she could remember having seen Subhas Chandra Bose when she was a young girl at the annual session of the Congress in 1928.[39] The Tamil woman who rose to become the second-in-command of this regiment was, however, born in Malaya. Janaki Davar's father had come to Malaya from Tamil Nadu in 1911, worked in a law office for awhile, and eventually became the well-to-do owner of a dairy farm. In July 1943 the seventeen-year-old Janaki went to hear Subhas Chandra Bose speak at a rally in Kuala Lumpur. At the end of the meeting people came forward to "offer money, jewelry, anything they had, to the freedom cause." Janaki took off her earrings and put them in Bose's hands. Her parents learned of what she had done from a photograph on the front page of the local newspaper the next day. When Lakshmi Swaminathan came recruiting for her regiment, Janaki Davar persuaded her father to sign his consent on her application form. She then went with the regi-

5.10. The Ranis, mostly Tamil. Netaji Research Bureau, Calcutta.

ment to Burma in January 1944 and was one of the hundred women who retreated on foot with Subhas Chandra Bose from Burma to Thailand in May 1945.[40] "I remember a walk I had once," Abid Hasan writes of meeting Davar, "not far from Rangoon, with Capt. Thevar [Davar] of the Rani Jhansi Regiment. We went to a hillock and sat there looking at the ground around us. 'Doesn't the countryside remind you of home?' I inquired, adding, 'it looks so typically Indian.' 'I do not know,' she replied simply, 'I have never been to India.'"[41]

Having enthused Indians in various southeast Asian countries during a whirlwind tour, Subhas Chandra Bose proclaimed the formation of a provisional government of "Azad Hind" (Free India) in Singapore on October 21, 1943. "The Provisional Government is entitled to, and hereby claims," the proclamation said in an echo of its Irish predecessor, "the allegiance of every Indian. It guarantees religious liberty, as well as equal rights and equal opportunities to its citizens. It declares its firm resolve to pursue the happiness and prosperity of the whole nation equally and transcending all the differences cunningly fostered by an alien government in the past."[42] By June 1944, 230,000 Indians in Malaya alone had written oaths of allegiance to the provisional government.[43]

The Azad Hind movement was remarkably successful in bridging the differences of religious and linguistic communities, but it had some serious difficulties spanning class-based divisions. Initially, the poorer Indians seemed more generous with their contributions than did the richer Indian merchants and moneylenders. Evidence of Bose's exasperation with a few of the richer Indians comes through in his speeches. "When the INA is getting trained either to march to victory or to spill its last drop of blood on the way," he said to the Chettiars and other merchants on October 25, 1943, "the rich people are asking me whether total mobilization means 10 per cent or 5 per cent. I would ask these people who are speaking of percentage whether we can tell our soldiers to fight and spill only 10 per cent of their blood and save the rest."[44] It seems that the provisional government gratefully accepted 100 percent from the enthusiastic and settled for 10 percent from the reluctant. That proved sufficient for a successful fund-raising campaign assuring a flow of nearly two million Straits dollars a month by the close of 1943.[45]

The question of class was connected with issues of religion and caste. In the autumn of 1943 the high priests of the main

Chettiar temple in Singapore came to invite Subhas Chandra Bose to attend a religious festival. Bose refused on grounds that the temple barred entry not only to non-Hindus, but to members of the subordinate castes among the Hindus as well. The priests returned to re-invite him, having resolved to hold a "national demonstration" in the temple that would be open to all castes and communities. Abid Hasan accompanied his leader to this event. As Bose crossed the threshold of the innermost sanctuary, Hasan held back for a moment; the priests behind him, however, "gently but resolutely" pushed him in. Hasan could not remember the speech that Netaji, his revered leader, gave on that occasion. "The memory I retain," he wrote much later, "is one of an invigorating music as that of a symphony dedicated to the unity of the motherland and the common purpose of all Indians to be united in their efforts to establish their identity." It was the echo of that music that was to sustain him during the disastrous retreat from Imphal in late 1944.[46]

The provisional government took some conscious steps to inculcate this sense of unity. "Jai Hind" ("Victory to India") was chosen as the common greeting or salutation when Indians met one another. Hindustani, an admixture of Hindi and Urdu written in the Roman script, became the national language, even though instant translation into Tamil was made available at all public meetings. A Hindustani translation of a song by Rabindranath Tagore, "Jana Gana Mana," which aspired to a universalism beyond specific religions in seeking divine benediction for India, became the national anthem. A leaping tiger, reminiscent of Tipu Sultan of Mysore who had resisted the British in the late eighteenth century, was featured as the national emblem on the tricolor flag and uniforms. Three Urdu words—"Itmad" (faith), "Ittefaq" (unity), and "Kurbani" (sacrifice)—encapsulated the motto of these expatriate patriots.[47]

Once this overseas nationalism had constituted itself as a government in exile, it felt the need for land or territory as a mark of its legitimacy. Subhas Chandra Bose, carried away by the enthusiastic response of his audiences in September 1943, had rashly promised that the Indian National Army would be on Indian soil before the end of the year. There was no realistic prospect of the INA reaching the Indian mainland within that time frame. But the purpose that a few islands in the Atlantic served for Charles de Gaulle's Free French, a group of islands in the Bay of Bengal might do for Bose's Azad Hind. In late December of 1943 the provisional government managed to acquire de jure territorial jurisdiction over the Andaman and Nicobar islands while de facto military control remained in Japanese hands. These islands had symbolic importance for the Indians because generations of Indian revolutionaries had served long prison sentences in the Cellular Jail on Andaman island. On a flying visit before the year was out, Bose renamed Andaman as "Shaheed" (martyrs) and Nicobar as "Swaraj" (freedom).[48]

Any armed assault on British India from the northeast had to use Burma as its launching pad. In early January 1944 the headquarters of the provisional government were moved from Singapore to Rangoon by arrangement with the Burmese government headed by Ba Maw and Aung San. Subhas Chandra

Bose had already visited Burma on the occasion of the constitution of this independent government on August 1, 1943. "From 1925 to 1927," he stated then, "I used to gaze from the verandah of my cell in Mandalay prison on the palace of the last independent king of Burma and I used to wonder when Burma would be free once again. Today Burma is an independent state and I am breathing the atmosphere of that liberated country."[49] Burma had also been the venue of a romantic battle for freedom in Bengali literary imagination. A popular Bengali novelist, Sarat Chandra Chattopadhyay, had spent some time as a circular migrant in Burma and in 1926 published *Pather Dabi (The Road's Demand)*, which was promptly banned by the colonial government of India for inciting sedition. The most stirring passage in the novel occurs in a scene at Rangoon harbor where the police are waiting to apprehend a "Raj-Bidrohi," a rebel against the British king-emperor, who is expected to alight from an arriving ship. Apurba, one of the key characters, launches into an ode to Sabyasachi, the superhuman Bengali revolutionary:

> You have given your all for your country, that is why your country's boats cannot give you passage, you must swim across the river Padma; that is why the highways of your country are closed to you, you must climb over the peaks of forbidding hills and mountains; in some forgotten past it is for you that the first chains had been forged, prisons had been constructed thinking only of you—that is your glory! Who can dare ignore you! These countless guards, this huge armed force, they are

all meant just for you! You are able to bear the terrible weight of sorrow, that is why God has placed this heavy burden on your shoulders! Pioneer on the road to freedom! Anti-imperialist rebel of a subject nation! A hundred million tributes to you![50]

Needless to say, the fictional revolutionary slipped the police dragnet prepared for him at Rangoon harbor and the novelist's lines in his honor served both as anticipation and posthumous eulogy for a historical revolutionary in subsequent decades. There was another piece of history too in Rangoon that provided symbolic inspiration for India's expatriate patriots. This was the tomb of Bahadur Shah Zafar, the last Mughal emperor, who had died as a prisoner in exile. On September 26, 1943, a ceremonial parade and prayers were held at this site to signal the INA's determination to march to the Red Fort of Delhi. "We Indians, regardless of religious faiths, cherish the memory of Bahadur Shah," their leader said, "not because he was the man who gave the clarion call to his countrymen to fight the enemy from without, but because he was the man under whose flag fought Indians from all provinces, Indians professing different religious faiths, the man under whose sacred flag . . . freedom-loving Hindus, Muslims and Sikhs fought side by side in the war that has been dubbed by English historians as the sepoy mutiny, but which we Indians call the first war of independence." That spirit of dynamic unity, not listless uniformity, had to be emulated in "the last war of independence."[51]

If the interconnected history of India and Burma supplied

5.11. Subhas Chandra Bose with Ba Maw and other Burmese leaders, Rangoon, 1943. Netaji Research Bureau, Calcutta.

inspiring symbols for new battles, it was the source of formidable difficulties as well. The Burmese were proud of their sovereignty, which had been scorned in the nineteenth century and was now enmeshed in a complex process of recovery. The economic crisis of the depression decade had spawned intense racial conflict between Burmese and Indians, capitalists and laborers alike. Given that history of tension, Burmese and Indian anticolonial leaders and organizations must be given credit for keeping Indo-Burmese relations on an even keel during the tumultuous years of World War II. The Burmese permitted the Indians to use their territory as the springboard for their armed thrust into India; the Indians in turn were especially sensitive about the need to show respect for Burmese sovereignty. At Bahadur Shah's tomb in September 1943, the Indian leader handed over to the head of the Burmese government a *nazar* (respectful donation) of 250,000 rupees in the name of the last Mughal emperor as "a very small token of our love and admiration for Burma and all that Burma stands for."[52] But a certain imbalance remained. In 1944 the provisional government of Azad Hind based in Rangoon was better organized and better financed than the wartime government of Burma. When the Indian government in exile decided to set up a National Bank of Azad Hind in Rangoon on April 5, 1944, much to the chagrin of its Japanese ally, it was able to begin with a capital of ten million rupees contributed by just four Indians, with many others following with smaller contributions. An Indian millionaire in Rangoon, Habeeb Saheb, donated all his assets in return for a garland given to the Indian leader, and Shrimati Betai did much the same, earning thereby the decoration of "Sewak-i-Hind" or "Servant of India."[53] Altogether the Azad Hind bank was able to raise 200 million rupees from Malaya and Burma.[54]

By the time the bank was founded, the INA had crossed the Indo-Burma frontier alongside the Japanese forces. Having first seen action on the Arakan front in February 1944, the INA moved into northeastern India toward Imphal and Kohima on March 18, 1944. Care had been taken to project common cause with Indian freedom fighters at home. Three brigades of the first division of the INA had been named after Mahatma

Gandhi, Jawaharlal Nehru, and Maulana Azad, the preeminent leaders of the Indian National Congress. "Father of our Nation," Subhas Chandra Bose said in a special broadcast to Gandhi, "in this holy war for India's liberation, we ask for your blessings and good wishes."[55]

Elaborate plans were drawn up for civilian administration of territories in India that fell to the INA.[56] The promised march to Delhi was, however, halted in Imphal. The British and Britain's Indian Army with American air support were able to able to break the siege of Imphal after three-and-a-half tense months and beat back the Japanese forces and the INA from the outskirts of Kohima as well. Naga Sundaram, a Tamil civilian in Burma who had joined the field propaganda unit of the INA and fought in Imphal, has described how with supply lines cut the soldiers of the INA had to subsist on jungle grass and small fish caught in little streams with mosquito nets.[57] The military debacle in Imphal by July 1944 was followed by a harrowing retreat punctuated by a few determined rearguard actions by the INA in Burma during late 1944 and early 1945. The defeated rebels and their leader gathered once more at Bahadur Shah's tomb on the anniversary of his death, July 11, 1944. Their solace on this somber occasion, in addition to a Bahadur Shah couplet about a warrior's faith composed after the collapse of the 1857 revolt, was a well-known verse in English: "Freedom's battle once begun, bequeathed from bleeding sire to son, tho' baffled oft, is e'er won."[58]

"It was the battling with no hope along the Irrawaddy, not the battling with high hope about the Manipur basin," Peter Fay has plausibly argued, "that justified the freedom army and gave it in the end such moral leverage."[59] The hardships faced by the INA in retreat were immense. Abid Hasan met his Netaji at Mandalay in mid-1944 upon his return from Imphal. When asked to give a true description of what they had gone through, Hasan simply quoted a Japanese officer who had told him that the situation was "slightly not so very good." Yet the pride of this civilian-turned-soldier was undiminished even after the catastrophe on the battlefield:

> What a group we were and ours was but a unit among many of its kind in our army. I felt proud and I feel more proud today that I belonged to it. Baluchis were there among us and Assamese, Kashmiris and Malayalis, Pathans and Sikhs and Gujeratis, proud members of classes called the martial and those till then denied reputation for martial valour but who proved in battle that they could by their deeds claim equal honour. Every region in India was represented and every religion and every caste, mixed inseparably together not only in bigger formations but even in small platoons and sections, each unit being a living tribute to the unity of India. We had our different private faiths and we had our different languages but in our purpose and in our political belief we were a well-knit, determined and indivisible whole.[60]

If British general William Slim could gloat over turning "defeat into victory" in a military sense, the INA would not be denied a chance to return the compliment on a political plane.[61]

"What did you mean, you people," General Douglas Gracey

had asked Prem Sahgal upon Sahgal's capture at Mount Popa, "by going on fighting? We had armor, artillery. You chaps had nothing. But instead of surrendering, you fought. It was madness." Sahgal conceded it was madness, but of a deliberate, revolutionary sort.[62] Gracey was a calculating soldier and may be forgiven for failing to appreciate the method in the madness. Historians have no such excuses when they deploy the same blunt instruments used to analyze military or business strategy for unraveling the motivations of anticolonial rebels. The rebels' determination to fight against the odds was "neither light-hearted nor born of hurrah-patriotism."[63] It was a "grim resolve" based on a degree of political education imparted at the camps, perhaps at the cost of military training. But by early 1945 the weight of steel was decidedly against them in Burma.

March 1945 brought a further complication. Aung San, who had returned to Burma with the Japanese in early 1942 at the head of a Burmese nationalist force, now turned against his erstwhile ally. The tide of the war had turned and Burma's anticolonial rebels, who had taken advantage of an international war crisis to further their own cause, saw no good reason to continue to side with a new imperialist power instead of an older one. The Burmese resistance was taking place on Burmese soil. The Indians in Burma, however, were still expatriate patriots and did not have the luxury of switching sides midstream. The best they could do was to reach a truce with the Burmese, an understanding that was to hold fast despite the history of past racial conflicts.[64] During the remaining months of the war, the bulk of the Azad Hind movement relocated to Thailand and Malaya, leaving a small detachment in

Rangoon to maintain order during the transition to British authority. On VJ Day, August 15, 1945, Subhas Chandra Bose issued the following special message to the Indians in Southeast Asia:

> Sisters and brothers, a glorious chapter in the history of India's struggle for freedom has just come to a close and, in that chapter, the sons and daughters of India in East Asia will have an undying place. You set a shining example of patriotism and self-sacrifice by pouring out men, money and materials into the struggle for independence . . . I regret, more than you do, that your sufferings and sacrifices have not borne immediate fruit. But they have not gone in vain because they have ensured the emancipation of our Motherland and will serve as an undying inspiration to Indians all over the world. Posterity will bless your name, and will talk with pride about your offerings at the altar of India's freedom and about your positive achievements as well.

Urging his followers not to falter in their "faith in India's destiny," he ended with his conviction that "India shall be free and before long."[65]

All that remained was to build a martyrs' memorial on the coast of Singapore. Cyril John Stracey of the INA built it in record time, bearing the words of their motto—faith, unity, and sacrifice.[66] By the time the memorial was erected, Subhas Chandra Bose himself had perished in an air crash on August 18, 1945, so he was among the legion of martyrs being honored.

The British forces landed in Singapore soon afterward and blew up the monument with dynamite. But it proved easier to destroy this structure of brick and mortar than to erase the spirit of faith, unity, and sacrifice that it represented. The "triumph of the INA," as historian Peter Fay sees it, occurred in the winter of 1945 in the Red Fort of Delhi, where its soldiers were brought as prisoners but were hailed by the Indian public as heroes.[67] It was here that the veterans of an armed struggle for independence connected with Gandhi, the apostle of nonviolence. Forgetting his political differences with Bose in 1939, Gandhi now lauded him as a "prince among patriots." In his appraisal of the INA, Gandhi chose to emphasize the values for which he himself had fought in South Africa at the turn of the twentieth century and in India in the early 1920s. "Though the INA failed in their immediate objective," he wrote in the *Harijan* on April 14, 1946, "they have a lot to their credit of which they might well be proud. Greatest among these was to gather together under one banner men from all religions and races of India and to infuse into them the spirit of solidarity and oneness to the utter exclusion of all communal or parochial sentiment. It is an example which we should all emulate."[68]

How did this spirit of solidarity take hold among Indians overseas? One of the platoon lectures given to INA recruits, titled "Unity of India, Past and Present," provides some clues. "Once the Moghul rule was established," the recruits were told, "Hindus and Muslims lived as brothers." In more recent times Mahatma Gandhi was deemed largely responsible for uniting the masses of India in striving for a common cause.

5.12. Subhas Chandra Bose's last salute, Saigon, 1945. Netaji Research Bureau, Calcutta.

But the recruits even then were taught that Indians in Southeast Asia "should form one common blood brotherhood for the achievement of Purna Swaraj [complete independence] for India."[69] The discourse on unity sanctified by the fire of sacrificial patriotism, whether of Mahatma Gandhi or Netaji Subhas Chandra Bose, relied more heavily on the language of blood than on the language of rights, even though there was room for both in their formulations. In this respect Gandhi's call in 1942 that "rivers of blood" must flow to pay the "price of freedom" was not much different from Bose's similar exhortations in 1943. The false dichotomy between "good" civic nationalism and "bad" religious or ethnic nationalism in recent literature obfuscates the real challenges faced by anticolonial nationalism in dealing with internal differences. It requires no special insight to see that discourses on blood and lineage can and have degenerated into horrors of religious bigotry and ethnic hatred. What is less easily recognized is that the conceits of unitary, "civic" nationalism, which draw on discourses of rights, can and have caused a deep sense of alienation among those defined as minorities—a deeper rift, indeed, than that caused by the minority social groups' attachments to their particular cultural differences. Secular nationalism has slid rather easily into forms of religious or ethnic majoritarianism. When it came to uniting people of different backgrounds and faiths, exclusively rights-based discourses on secular uniformity have generally failed where discourses on blood sacrifice and blood brotherhood did not. Perhaps this success was easier to achieve in an overseas context where the obsession with land in territorial nationalisms did not loom large. In any event, the secret and intimate path to a cosmopolitan anticolonialism among expatriate patriots was forged only when they were able to combat religious prejudice without making religion the enemy of the nation. Once the tide of oceanic anticolonialism had receded after the heady winter of 1945–1946, the politics of territorial nationalism ensured the partition of the motherland on August 14–15, 1947.

6

Pilgrims' Progress under
Colonial Rules

Seest thou not that
The ships sail through
The Ocean by the grace
Of Allah?—That He may
Show you His Signs?
Verily in this are Signs
For all who constantly persevere
And give thanks.

—*SURAH LUQMAN*, VERSE 31

A child's inspired recitation of the later verses of the *Surah Luqman* of the Qu'ran, with its references to the ocean, ships, waves, and storms, was interpreted by Khwaja Hasan Nizami as a divine indication that he should visit the holy grave of the Prophet Muhammad in Medina.[1] So in 1911 he became one of the tens of thousands of Muslims who in the early twentieth century annually journeyed across the western Indian Ocean in search of the signs of Allah. Most pilgrims went on the hajj or *umrah* to Mecca and Medina, but some included visits to

6.1. Portrait of an Indian pilgrim, 1885, by Snouck Hurgronje.

several other holy cities and sites in West Asia and North Africa.[2] Muslim pilgrimages at this moment in history had to negotiate a formidable European colonial presence in the entire interregional arena, including well-entrenched British colonial rule in India and less formal pressures that contributed to changing political fortunes in the Hejaz. The hajj had been a key integrative element in the economy, religion, and culture of the Indian Ocean in the precolonial era. If anticolonial nationalism leaped beyond the frontiers of colonies to craft Indian Ocean networks of its own, religious universalism in the form of pilgrimage by sea had certainly not weakened as a bond across the ocean in the age of global empire.[3] Exploring the tension between the pilgrims' spiritual fervor and the rules of passage defined by colonial rationality, we circle around the center of the pilgrims' ultimate destination, Mecca, before reaching it.

Temporal sovereignty over Mecca and Medina in this period passed from the precolonial Ottoman Empire to a nominee of the colonial British Empire before being seized by the Saudi state in 1925. Both the British raj and the Saudi regime sought to exercise strict surveillance over the performance of the Muslim pilgrimage. In the process, a modernizing colonial state and an ultra-orthodox Islamic one caused rifts in the expressions of a religious universalism. Yet Muslim colonial subjects who undertook the pilgrimage could never be wholly subjected to the discipline of states. The hajj turned out to be a crucial Indian Ocean activity that was a vehicle for an anticolonial current that state boundaries could not contain. Religion, even more so than the idea of nation, proved adept at crossing seas.

The Itinerary of a Scholar-Pilgrim

Khwaja Hasan Nizami (1878–1955) was a Sufi mystic and a custodian of the famous shrine of Nizamuddin Auliya in

Delhi. Nizami's choices of holy sites to visit suggest an alternative mental map of sovereignty to that drawn by colonial frontiers in South and Southeast Asia and about to be extended to the Middle East as well. Nizami's mental map was centered on a sense of sacred geography. His departure from the premier colonial port city of Bombay, for example, had to be preceded by a visit to the oldest Sufi shrine in India, that of Khwaja Muinuddin Chishti in Ajmer. It was a meeting place for devotees from all over the subcontinent. There Nizami met Naubahr Husain, a Rasool Shahi fakir from Hyderabad, and exchanged mystical experiences with him before venturing out toward the final resting place of the Rasool, the Messenger of God.

While in Bombay, Nizami stayed at the Shahjahan Hotel, which he deemed a congenial place for Muslims. He spent his time in the company of Maulavi Yusuf Khatkhate as well as Maulana Shibli Nomani, an eminent Islamic scholar from Aligarh who was now in Bombay. Nomani had done a grand tour of West Asia and North Africa in the mid-1890s while researching his book *Heroes of Islam*. But it was on the advice of a Syrian friend that Nizami finalized his itinerary. He would go, first of all, to various tombs and shrines in Egypt, then on to Damascus and Jerusalem, and finally to Medina.[4]

On June 1, 1911, Nizami set out on his voyage aboard an Austrian ship. The way to forget material discomfort, the poor quality of the food, and seasickness was to turn to the Qu'ran. The undulating movement of the ship then felt akin to the Sufi breathing practice of *pas-e-anfas*.[5] Conversations with fellow passengers and the people he met at the ports of Aden and

Basra covered a wide array of subjects. With Rustamji he talked of the need for a ship owned by Indians to ply these waters. At Aden he was pleased to see that conditions seemed to have improved since Shibli Nomani's visit. The Somali children were no longer begging for alms, but came to sell their goods to the passengers, with whom they were able to converse in different languages. He was even more pleased to find an Urdu *madrasa* (school) in Aden. Back on board he chatted with a Hindu judge and his wife from Surat about the status of Indian women, Hindu and Muslim alike. Once away from India, he observed, there was no discrimination between Hindus and Muslims.

While visiting Basra he discussed with the British consul general the conditions of the Muslims in general and the Turks in particular. He regarded the British diplomat's poor opinion about Turkey's progress to be part of the general misinformation spread about the Turks. One day as the ship was passing through two mountains a fellow passenger, a German, told him that on the one side there was a mountain of one color while on the other side there was a mountain of two colors: the former was that of the Hejaz, where the Turks had no partner in government; the latter that of Egypt, where the British were running a condominium. Egypt was a country that had been turned into a British protectorate in 1882.[6] Nizami clearly preferred the temporal sovereignty of the Ottoman sultan-caliph to British domination.

During his sojourn in Egypt, Nizami encountered both openness and closure across cultures. Muhammad Shah Jilani, a Sindhi businessman in Cairo, took Nizami to meet an Egyptian Muslim deeply interested in Hindu mysticism. A dinner meeting with Syed Al-Bakari, a leading mystic of Egypt, provided an occasion for an exchange of views about Muslims of the world as far afield as China and India. It was a quiet time at the famous Al-Azhar University during a vacation, but Nizami was able to meet four Indian students studying there. A deeply emotional moment was the homage at the grave of Imam Husain, the martyr of Karbala. Nizami appreciated the pyramids, but could not help telling a wonderstruck Arab that the one thing older than "the oldest minarets" of the world was the earth itself. Sufism and the condition of Indian Muslims were the subjects of discussion with the editors of *Al-Liwa* as well as *Al-Manar,* a journal that was read widely in India. Nizami's brush with the Hindu merchants of Sind at their *sabha* (association) in Cairo, however, must have led him to reconsider his happy notion that Indians left their prejudices behind when they departed the shores of their homeland. After extending a warm welcome, his hosts treated him to the teachings of Krishna followed by a biography of Guru Gobind Singh that was very unflattering to the Muslim rulers. Upon hearing this tale, Nizami understood why it was so difficult to forge Hindu-Muslim unity in India. He tried to explain to the Sindhi Hindus that rebellion rather than religion was what determined the treatment of Guru Gobind Singh at the hands of the Muslims. He ventured to add that when Arjuna of the great Hindu epic the *Mahabharata* had thrown down his weapons on seeing his relatives arrayed against him on the battlefield, Krishna had told his disciple that the sword, wielded with a sense of duty, not hatred, would in fact purify his enemies and give them a chance at redemption. Yet Nizami well knew that his skillful use of the *Mahabharata* analogy stood little chance of lessening the ingrained animosity felt by his hosts toward Muslims.[7]

From Cairo, Nizami went north to the port city of Alexandria, where he visited the grave of a mystic and received the blessings of a hundred-year-old Sufi. His next stop via Port Said was the holy land of Palestine. In Jerusalem, Nizami stayed at the *takiya* (literally, seat) of Baba Farid Ganj Shakar (1173–1266), a legendary Sufi mystic of the Punjab. At a meeting of the Aunjuman-e-Ittehad, a religious association, unity proved elusive: although some Jews and Christians came, the Arabs stayed away from an organization dominated by the Turks. The contours of the sacred geography of tombs took Nizami to Beirut and Damascus, where he visited several schools and the graves of Bilal, the Prophet's African companion, and of the great Sufi intellectual Sheikh Ibn Arabi, exponent of the *wahdatul wujud* (unity of being) philosophy.[8]

Finally, Nizami set off for the Hejaz by train. As they approached Medina, the passengers were overjoyed. The streets of Medina were not especially clean, but Nizami preferred the Prophet's city to London or Paris. After the *isha* (night) prayer, the *muezzin* climbed up the minaret of the Prophet's mosque, recited some verses of the Qu'ran, and sent salutations to the Prophet. Nizami felt this practice ought to be adopted to inspire and unite Indian Muslims. He was disappointed to find that the four schools of Islamic jurisprudence—Hanafi, Shafi'i, Maliki, and Hanbali—performed their congregational prayers separately. But whatever the rival claims on the mosque, the green dome of the Prophet's tomb beckoned like the full moon. Mothers circumambulated their infants around the grave in an effort to earn the Prophet's blessings.

Nizami's long and passionate prayer at the grave of the Prophet reveals the depth of the sentiment of Muslim universalism in the face of the Western colonial onslaught. Nizami was not an inveterate opponent of British colonial rule in the manner of a Jamaluddin Al-Afghani, but Islam, he lamented at the Prophet's grave, was under siege. He had even seen foreign currency circulating in pure Medina. Since currency was the symbol of sovereignty, he wondered if Islamic sovereignty even over Medina had been lost:

> Sovereignty is slipping through our hands. We are subjugated in China, we are subjugated in Java, we are subjugated in Egypt, we are subjugated in Tatar and Bukhara, in India too we are in a state of subjection . . . Iran is facing a storm of turbulence, Morocco's throat has been slit, blood is flowing . . . I have just seen Egypt with my own eyes . . . in Afghanistan one notices a ray of hope in the realm of religion and politics. But it is sadly placed between two strangers. Conflict here, conflict there too . . . O Messenger of God, Christendom wields not just political sovereignty, it has also robbed us of our culture, dignity and good ethics.

Yet he allowed optimism to trump experience in his concluding words, there expressing the hope that both the awakened spirit of the Indian nation and the Muslim university with which he was associated at Aligarh would find fulfillment.[9]

In a conversation with the sheikh of Haram about the Khilafat and Turkey's role in it, Nizami tried to suggest ways in which the *ummah,* the world community of Islam, might seek to contend with the multiple challenges that beset it. The world's Muslims, he argued, respected the Turkish Khilafat, but that was of little use without some form of practical manifestation. He urged the Turks to establish a postal department for information about the Muslim predicament worldwide. He also felt that hajjis who came to Mecca should be administered an oath of allegiance by the *naib* or Sultan's representative and that a few hajjis should be authorized to administer similar oaths in their respective countries. Such an oath should not be seen to entail any interference in national and political affairs. It would simply swear obedience to Allah, the Prophet, and the Khalifa in acting on the commandments of the Muslim faith. The sheikh of Haram saw a couple of difficulties in this otherwise excellent scheme: first, the Muslim world was linguistically diverse, which made communication difficult; and second, foreign countries would say a dangerous conspiracy was being hatched against the infidels. Nizami replied that the problem of language could be solved by having the representative in Java explain matters to the Javanese Muslims, the one in Hindustan to the Indian Muslims, and so on. The charge of a conspiracy was more difficult to address. It could be rebutted with the claim that the Sultan-Khalifa was extending his extraterritorial sovereignty to religious affairs alone. But to be intimidated by such a charge could be catastrophic. "One day," Nizami warned, "you will have to give up your responsibility for haj because the foreign kings view even this with suspicion."[10]

Having exhorted the sheikh of Haram to uphold an alternative mode of sovereignty, Nizami was given a stern reminder of the temporal sovereignty of the British imperium on his return voyage. At Aden, twenty-two Indian Muslim prisoners boarded the ship. They had no food to eat, so Nizami asked the captain to give them food free of charge. His request was curtly refused. Fortunately, Nizami had initiated a few people at Aden into the Chishti *silsilah* (order) and had received some presents in return. These gifts could now pay for the subsistence of his unfortunate compatriots returning with him to a country enslaved.[11]

The Colonial Policing of the Hajj

It was not just that, as Nizami warned the sheikh of Haram, the European colonial powers viewed the performance of the hajj with suspicion. Of course, a watchful eye was kept on all those who might use the congregation at the annual pilgrimage for fomenting political subversion. But disorder was feared in all its forms. The dread of disease was one factor that contributed in a major way to the colonial regulation of the hajj. The obsession with sanitation in all its senses reached its peak exactly at the time that the communications revolution of the late nineteenth century made the oceanic voyage to the Hejaz a technical possibility for an ever larger number of the faithful within the Indian Ocean arena.

Steamships and cholera were bound in an intimate relationship. A key turning point was the cholera epidemic of 1865, which originated in Java and Singapore and spread from the Hejaz to North Africa and Europe. That year some 15,000 of the 90,000 pilgrims who came to Mecca died. Hajj in a time of cholera was subjected to more stringent means tests and quarantine barricades for those wishing to make it from colonial South and Southeast Asia.[12] From the late 1860s to 1896, the hajj from India consisted of carefully controlled flows of pilgrims from the three ports of Calcutta, Bombay, and Karachi. The outbreak of plague in 1896 led to the closure of Calcutta as a pilgrim port for thirty years. In 1908 hajj committees were set up at Bombay and Karachi by executive order. Because Bengal among all the Indian provinces typically supplied the largest contingent of pilgrims, hajj committees were also established at Calcutta and in Bengal by the government of India in 1913, but they acquired greater importance once the port of Calcutta had been reopened for pilgrim traffic in 1926. The commissioners of police of Bombay and Calcutta were the ex officio chairmen of the hajj committees of these two cities and also functioned as the executive heads of the pilgrim departments of the ports. Karachi provided a minor variation, with the collector of taxes being head of the pilgrim department, while the hajj committee elected its own chairman whose powers were mainly advisory. All three ports also had Muslim officers as "Protectors of Pilgrims"; these officers were appointed by the government "to assist" the commissioners of police.[13]

Such close surveillance of the Indian hajj from 1908 onward has reaped some unintended benefits in the form of a wealth of factual information (albeit tainted by a colonial rationality).[14] Between 1909 and 1928 (leaving out the years of World War I and 1925, a year of political upheaval in the Hejaz), the average annual number of hajj pilgrims sailing from Indian ports was more than 19,000, with the peak of 36,089 being reached in 1927.[15] The main factor determining the number of pilgrims, according to the "Haj Enquiry Committee Report" of 1929, was "the failure or success of the agricultural season in the principal Muslim districts." (This was indeed true if by "agricultural season" was meant not just climatic conditions, but the state of prices and credit.) The number of British Indian subjects was usually about two-thirds of the total, averaging approximately 13,000 per year over this period. Of these, "at least half" were "normally from Bengal and Assam, with the province contributing the next largest number being the Punjab."[16] In 1927, the year of the biggest hajj, 27,546 of the 36,089 pilgrims embarking from the three Indian ports were British Indian subjects, of whom 15,495 came from Bengal and 4,572 from the Punjab.[17] Women usually constituted about 20 percent of the Indian pilgrims.[18] Until the onset of the depression, the number of pilgrims from the Dutch East Indies was about double, and from British Malaya nearly half, the number of Indians. The Javanese and the Malays tended to spend several months in the Hejaz, while the Indians' visit was much more focused on the specific period of the hajj.

The journey of pilgrim ships to the Hejaz was governed by the relevant provisions of the International Sanitary Convention and the Indian Merchant Shipping Act. In 1913 Messrs. Turner Morrison and Company had six steamers servicing the hajj, the newest of which was twenty-five years old. In addition, the Arab Line had four steamers and the Khandwani Line two small steamers, all of which were equally old or older. By 1928 the Mogul Line of Messrs. Turner Morrison and Company had eight steamers specially designed for the accommodation of pilgrims. The oldest, *Dara* (4,922 tons), was built in 1915; the smallest, *Alavi* and *Jehangir* (3,566 tons), in 1924; and the largest, *Rahmani* (5,291 tons), in 1928. In addition, Messrs. Shustari and Company ran *Sultania* (4,397 tons) built in 1903, while the Nemazee Line, operated by its agent Mohamed Karim Khalili, had in service *Sarvestan* (7,714 tons), built in 1899, and *Arabestan* (5,029 tons) built in 1903.[19]

The "average Indian pilgrim," the Haj Enquiry Committee noted, came "from the poorer classes," this being "particularly the case with Bengal and Assam pilgrims who comprised about half of the Indian pilgrims proper." The pilgrimage from Java and the Malay states tended to operate "with greater smoothness," in the opinion of this committee, because the pilgrims from those countries were "fairly prosperous and nearly all of one class."[20] A Persian pilgrim on hajj in 1910–1911 had noted the wide class disparity of pilgrims from India:

Indian pilgrims are of a very mixed character. Some are rich to the point of prodigality, others have barely the wherewithal to stay alive. You see rich people who will pay several pounds for a flacon of perfume, pour it all out on their heads and walk off; or who will pay several rupees for a glass of Zamzam water which, if they waited a few moments, they could have had for nothing. On the other hand, there are wretches in a state of total privation, lying nearly nude along the road, seeking some relief in the shade of the bushes called mughilan, the only vegetation which abounds in these deserts. Passers-by give something to eat to these unfortunates who are at the mercy of the sun and the sand, and occasionally some generous person will take them with them to Mecca on their camels.[21]

The relatively poor from India continued to make the pilgrimage from India, braving political vicissitudes through the final years of Ottoman sovereignty over the holy places, the brief Hashemite interregnum in the wake of World War I, and the early years of "Wahabi" domination under Bin Saud. The pilgrim ships did not sail from India in 1916, 1917, and 1918, but the British managed to send eight thousand Muslim soldiers in batches of two thousand for the hajj in 1917, the second year that it was held under Hashemite auspices. The dislocation caused by the Saudi takeover in 1925 meant that few made it from India that year, but during the late 1920s the largest pilgrimages of the pre–World War II period occurred—before the 1930s depression made it impossible for even the most motivated among the poorer Muslims from Bengal, Java, and Malaya to travel across the seas.

The colonial perception of the pilgrimage as ordeal and the pilgrim as victim gives a very partial, loaded, and distorted picture of the journey to Mecca. Yet that perception needs to be analyzed, because it impinged directly on the conduct of the pilgrimage. Some of the hardships involved in making the pilgrimage were real enough and the vulnerabilities to fraud and exploitation numerous. These material difficulties are detailed in the official sources without providing any sense of the spiritual experience that managed to transcend them. The privileged traveling first or second class did not naturally have to endure the same torment as those who could afford no better than third class. The *muallim* or professional pilgrim-guides who scoured the Indian countryside in the months preceding the hajj were in the habit of underestimating the cost and overestimating the ease and comfort of the journey. The pilgrims were said to receive their "first shock" on an arduous railway journey to one of the ports. On arrival at the port they would be "met by a policeman or other representative of the Protector of Pilgrims." Accommodation would be found either in a *musafirkhana* (travelers' inn), in a pilgrim camp, or with friends. Bombay had "one very excellent *musafirkhana*," the Haji Sabu Siddiq Musafirkhana, and two others of lesser quality, which together could accommodate about 1,800 pilgrims. Karachi accommodation for about the same number consisted of a specially constructed camp and a couple of *musafirkhanas*. Calcutta had two or three *musafirkhanas* in the heart of the city, but they were not exclusively reserved for pilgrims.

A majority of pilgrims from Bengal continued to embark from Bombay, and as many as 85 percent returned to Bombay even after the port of Calcutta was reopened in 1926. The main task at the port was to obtain a pilgrim's pass and book a steamer ticket, which might take about a week. Before being given a ticket, the pilgrim had to have a pass prepared and be vaccinated. On the day of embarkation, each pilgrim had to undergo an individual medical inspection. In Calcutta this inspection was carried out under the open sky on the wharf at Outram Ghat, whereas Bombay and Karachi had "regular sheds set aside for the inspection of all deck passengers." In Karachi the pilgrim emerged from the disinfection shed with a hand rubber-stamped in crimson ink. In Bombay this system had been abandoned by the late 1920s "in view of the objections raised"; instead, a special medical certificate was attached to the pass and ticket. Finally, after "something like a free fight to secure accommodation on board" with heavy luggage, the pilgrims traveling third class laid claim to their "authorised rate of sixteen superficial feet per person."[22]

Jeddah, the port of destination, was about 2,362 miles by sea from Bombay. It was nearer from Karachi by 168 miles. The distance from Calcutta to Jeddah was as much as 4,009 miles. Traveling by the faster pilgrim ships in the late 1920s, the journey to Jeddah took nine days from Karachi, ten days from Bombay, and seventeen days from Calcutta, including the twenty-four hours' mandatory detention on the quarantine island of Kamaran. The "discomforts" of a pilgrim ship were compounded, if the official sources are to be believed, by the lack of a spirit of brotherhood that might have been expected on such an occasion. The Bengali pilgrim was supposed to live "almost in dread of his life, if he happen[ed] to be occupying a portion of the deck next to a party of Afghans or Persians."

He was "from the outset told to make himself as small as possible and to avoid being a nuisance." The only support from outside Bengal for the effort to keep Calcutta open as a pilgrim port came unexpectedly from Maulana Syed Sulaiman Nadvi of Azamgarh and Haji Rashid Ahmad Shah of Delhi, who testified before the Haj Enquiry Committee "that pilgrims from Bengal and Assam should be compelled to sail from Calcutta, whether they like it or not, and should not be allowed to mix with pilgrims from other parts of India." Faced with such regional prejudice, witnesses from Bengal like Maulana Syed Ismail Ghaznavi felt that each extra day on board the ship was "a penalty" to the hajji.[23]

The typical Indian pilgrim wanted "to spend as short a time as possible" in the Hejaz so long as he could be present at Mecca on the day of the hajj and visit Medina either before or afterward. The distance from Jeddah to Mecca of about forty-five miles required a two-day camel ride, while the much longer distance from Jeddah to Medina of 275 miles took nearly a fortnight on camelback. Once automobiles were introduced in 1926, the Jeddah-Mecca journey could be accomplished in three hours and the Jeddah-Medina one in two days. Not everyone, however, could afford the automobile, and camels continued to be the mainstay of desert transportation. Besides, the speed of automobile transport conflicted with the rhythm of the sea voyage across the Arabian Sea, leaving many pilgrims with long waits at Jeddah for the return journey by boat.[24]

The pilgrimage report of 1926 by the British agent and consul is a perfect example of the colonial view of the hajj.

This official considered it his duty "to note and examine the many and various forms of abuse to which the hapless pilgrims [were] subjected," a difficult task previously restricted "by considerations for the pilgrim," who was "looked upon as a helpless sort of individual suffering temporarily from a form of religious mania which caused him to resent official interference in any form." He was proud to report that Bin Saud had cooperated with the British Agency. One *mutawwif* (pilgrim guide) who had robbed thirty pilgrims had been "condemned to have both his hands cut off when apprehended" upon the agent's complaint. As consul he had refused visas to certain *mutawwifs* to prevent them from going to India to "collect victims for the following season." The "victims" themselves failed the consul's test of proper hygiene. The practice of allowing the pilgrims to cook their own food on board ships was "conducive to extreme filthiness" with "vegetables in a more or less advanced state of putridity" and cooking utensils in "a greasy and malodorous condition." Only when shipping companies were given the responsibility of supplying food, the official argued, would pilgrim ships become "less filthy and odoriferous." As soon as the quarantine flag was lowered, the ships of most of the lines were "overrun with a mass of great hulking negroes" employed by the dhowmen for their luggage-carrying business. The official, who had a penchant for order, not to mention racial stereotypes, wanted the shipping companies (for an addition of two rupees to the fare) to be in charge of transporting the pilgrims and their baggage ashore, thereby avoiding "the necessity of pilgrims opening their purses which [were] hidden in various odd corners of their bodies whilst in a crush of people either in the dhow or in the Customs House." The official also had concerns about the return journey, during which the poorer pilgrims had to suffer the whims of agents of shipping companies and "many actually died of starvation in the streets of Jeddah." The over-all death rate during the 1926 hajj had not been ascertained, but the hope was that it would "not exceed five per cent" and the deaths were at least partly attributed to "the will to die." The report recommended British agents for British pilgrim ships and taking away the agencies from "the ruthless and un-scrupulous Arabs to whom every form of vice and corruption where the pilgrims [were] concerned had been developed to such an extent as to be almost second nature." The British consul seemed especially irked by the agent of the Mogul and Nemazee lines, who was simultaneously governor of Jeddah, and described him as "most despotic and absurdly stupid and pig-headed in his official capacity if it in any way affect[ed] his private pocket." The three ways to end these various ills that afflicted the pilgrimage were the "adoption of the com-pulsory deposit system only [for return voyages], suitable passports with photographs [which British Indian authorities were too coy to ask of Muslims] and the appointment of hon-est, straightforward agents by the shipping companies."[25]

As mentioned earlier, during the 1926 pilgrimage a novel means of transport was introduced—the unpredictable auto-mobile, supplementing the ever reliable camel. About a thou-sand Indian pilgrims seized the opportunity of "alternately riding in and pushing the cars of the motor concession."[26] But the Indians were not impressed by the other novelty of the

1926 hajj, namely, ultra-orthodox Wahabi domination. The Saudis had destroyed the domes and cupolas of tombs revered by the Indian pilgrims, including that of Syedna Hamza, those of the Prophet's family in Medina, and the tomb of Khadija, the Prophet's wife and first convert to Islam, in Mecca.

The report on the 1926 pilgrimage lists at least seven types of religious restrictions imposed by the Saudis and an equal number of grievances against them. First and foremost was the restriction on offering prayers at the tombs. This was deeply resented by "the Persians who appear[ed] to be inveterate tomb worshippers and the Indians who were also inclined in that direction." Those who were "loudest in their condemnation of the local authorities were Indians," some of them leading lights of the Indian Muslim world who had come to attend the World Muslim Conference in Mecca. Among them were the Ali brothers, Mohamed and Shaukat; Maulana Suleiman Nadvi of the Indian Khilafatists; and Maulana Kefiatullah, president of the Indian Ulema Society. Guards were on duty at the cemeteries and holy shrines, and any wayward pilgrims were denounced as *mushriks* (idolaters) and *kafirs* (infidels) and beaten by these guards. But "an occasional lucky pilgrim would get in a surreptitious kiss or rub and so satisfy his conscience and become the envy of his fellows."[27]

A second grievance was that during Ramadan only a Wahabi *imam* was permitted to lead the prayers. This put off many pilgrims from going to the Holy Mosque and *mutawwifs* had to be sent after them to bring them along. Third, the abolition of the Milad-ul-Nabi reading in praise of the Prophet was lamented. Fourth, the erection of special pulpits near the Kaaba for Wahabi *ulema* to preach provoked other *ulema* to denounce the Wahabi tenets. Extra police had to be drafted to prevent the verbal duels from turning into physical fights. Among the debaters were Maulana Sanaullah, president of the Indian Hadith Society, and the celebrated Sheik Rashid Rida of Egypt, "who attacked the orthodox sects with great vehemence." Fifth, pilgrims were prevented from calling on the Prophet with the cry "Ya Rasool-Allah" (O, Messenger of God), which came naturally to Khwaja Hasan Nizami when he prayed at the Prophet's grave. Sixth, when the king's father and family arrived from Riyadh, the Mutaf (courtyard) around the Kaaba was "cleared of all pilgrims who were performing the *tawaf* (circumambulating the Kaaba seven times)." Such a rude interruption happening for "the first time in the history of Islam" caused great offense. Seventh, the ban on smoking was enforced, and although it may have seemed trivial, "much more was heard of this restriction from the common run of pilgrims than of all the others."[28]

Muslims of South and Southeast Asia were clearly ready to brave Wahabi restrictions to make their pilgrimage. The hajj of 1927 was "the largest since the war" and was "thought by many to have established the record of all times." A total of 132,109 pilgrims arrived by sea at Jeddah. Of these, 39,157 had embarked from the Dutch East Indies, 36,089 from India, 29,604 from British Malaya, and 18,876 from Egypt. Mortality was high, "roughly 8 percent for all pilgrims," ranging from 12 percent for those coming from Malaya, 10 percent for those leaving from the Dutch East Indies, and 6 percent for those embarking from India. The differences could probably be explained by the length of the journeys and the duration of the stays. The 1927 hajj was bigger in scale, but not so much in temper, from the pilgrimage of the previous year. There was no World Muslim Conference, however, and so the report recorded only one "notorious non-co-operationist" (read, anti-colonial activist), Abdul Kaser Kusuri, among the prominent pilgrims. The use of motor transport was expanded, but the cost of petrol was high and the camels in the Hejaz were "as yet shy of mechanically propelled vehicles," making it an uneasy marriage of two radically different modes of transportation. The *mutawwifs* continued to "cheat the living" and "rob the dead." They were "accused especially by Bengali pilgrims," more than fifteen thousand of whom had come on the hajj in 1927, "of playing on their ignorance and making extortionate charges for advice and fictitious services."[29]

By the time the Haj Enquiry Committee of 1929, chaired by H. B. Clayton, came out with its recommendation for elected hajj committees to help combat the influence of *muallims/mutawwifs*, a worldwide crisis was beginning to cast a long shadow on the economic capability of many devout Muslims to make the pilgrimage. The total number of pilgrims arriving in the Hejaz by sea declined from the high of 132,109 in 1927 to 100,767 in 1928, 88,538 in 1929, 84,821 in 1930, and then registered a very sharp drop to 39,346 in 1931. The number declined further to 29,065 in 1932 and 20,705 in 1933 before showing a slight revival to 25,291 in 1934. The collapse of agrarian prices and the crisis in rural credit were clearly factors causing Egypt, Java, and Bengal to have the most dramatic decline in the number of pilgrims between 1930 and

1931, but the populations of pilgrims from all areas dwindled.[30] The numbers tapered even further during 1932 and 1933, there being fewer pilgrims from the Dutch East Indies in 1932 for the first time than even the small numbers going from British India. The number of destitute pilgrims who had to be repatriated at government expense did not, however, go down. A few hundred continued every year to be a charge on the exchequer, much to the annoyance of colonial officialdom.

If an economic slump in the countries of origin dramatically reduced the number of pilgrims in 1931, conditions in the Hejaz were no better. The Hejazi market was overstocked and "the local merchants suffered severely from trade depression." A monetary crisis accompanied the downslide in trade, manifested in "a heavy depreciation of the local silver and nickel currency." The silver riyal, officially pegged at ten to the English gold pound, "broke away" and the nickel *halalas,* used for retail trade, "suffered a serious devaluation." The towns were filled with "numerous half-starved Bedouin" and the British Indian vice-consul drew "a pitiful picture of these famished and often naked unfortunates." In the midst of this economic gloom, Bin Saud gave his annual banquet. The guest list included several Indians and Egyptians. A tribute paid by an Egyptian to the Indian leader Shaukat Ali "elicited from His Majesty an angry denunciation of that personage." Shaukat Ali's fault seems to have been that he had spoken of the Jews as "our brethren," whereas Bin Saud "disclaimed all friendship with Jews and Christians alike." In this climate of intolerance, the hajj took on overtones of resistance to both Saudi orthodoxy and European imperialism. Among the notable personages who made the pilgrimage in 1931 was ex-king Amanullah of Afghanistan, with whom a number of "Indian political agitators" took the opportunity to "establish or renew contact."[31]

The numerical low-water mark of the hajj in the early twentieth century (excepting war years) was reached in 1933. A rebellion in the northern Hejaz in 1932 compounded the problems already caused by the economic depression across the Indian Ocean rim, which at this moment was most acute in the Dutch East Indies. Despite "every effort made by the Saudi Government to stimulate the flow of pilgrims overseas," the total number was down to a meager 20,705 in 1933 compared to 29,965 in 1932. The smaller pilgrimage resulted in a 1 percent lower mortality than the previous year (an estimated 0.8 percent for both Indians and others). The exchange value of the riyal fell to twenty-one riyals to the pound, but there were a few signs of optimism about the future. In February 1933 one S. A. K. Jeelani of Madras obtained a concession to build a railway from Mecca to Jeddah. The Iraq Petroleum Company and the Standard Oil Company of California competed for the petroleum concession in Hasa, which Standard Oil eventually won in May. Some Hyderabadi Indians floated a scheme to stimulate employment in the Hejaz by starting a textile industry. And the Saudi government was in negotiation with Messrs. Ibrahim Jewan Baksh of Calcutta to create a public electric supply in Mecca.[32]

In 1933 there were signs as well of a more tolerant religious policy on the part of the Saudis. Special consideration was shown to "notable Indian pilgrims," including Indian Shia Muslims, which suggested "a new desire to disarm Shia hostility to Wahhabi ascendancy." Among leading Indian anticolonial activists, "agitators of known importance" (in the colonial parlance) Hasrat Mohani of the Jamiat-ul Ulema-e-Hind and Ismail Surati came on the 1933 hajj. Some of the shrines that had been destroyed in the first flush of Saudi iconoclasm were being partly restored—although domes on the graves were not being rebuilt. And the Nejdi guards at the Prophet's tomb, who once strictly enforced the ban on kissing the rail, were "now very amenable to the influence of even the smallest tip and will positively encourage those in a position to cross their palms with silver riyals, even to the extent of discreetly withdrawing altogether while they perform their devotions."

But sporadic incidents of intolerance continued. Indian pilgrims who went to Jebel Nur were challenged by Nejdi guards and pelted with stones. A disciple of Mian Muhammad Taqi had a book snatched from him in the Haram at Mecca. The Sufi teacher Pir Seyyid Jamat Ali Shah, who had been threatened with expulsion, prayed by himself in Medina. Overall, visits to shrines other than the Kaaba were "still strongly discouraged." And soon after the pilgrimage, an elderly merchant of the Ahmediya community was ordered to leave the country after being charged with preaching heresy.[33]

In 1934 there was a welcome increase in the total number of overseas pilgrims to 25,291 from the 1933 low of 20,705, even though the numbers were not to rise again to their late 1920s level until after World War II.[34] Despite the increase in the number of pilgrims, economic depression was said to have "settled even more heavily over the Hejaz." The contraction of revenues, the stagnation of trade, the lack of spending power in the hands of pilgrims, and the nonpayment of salaries to government officials made for a dismal economic scenario. The Standard Oil Company of California "intervened with a timely loan of £35,000 gold (believed however to have found its way into the Privy Purse rather than the public exchequer)." Foreign creditors, including the British and Indian governments, still awaited settlement of their dues. The Hyderabad textile scheme of the previous year seemed to be "a ship sinking under the feet of numerous well-paid officers and an inconsiderable crew." A proposal by Nizamat Jung to build caravansaries on the Medina road "was left in abeyance." The tightening of the purse strings even extended to the weaving of the *kiswa* (cover) for the Kaaba. Unlike for earlier pilgrimages, Hejazis and domiciled Indians were employed for the task, rather than Indians brought from the subcontinent.[35]

There were, however, enough Indian pilgrims of note to evoke anxiety and interest among colonial officials. Among anticolonial activists, Muhammad Irfan, general secretary of the central Khilafat committee, and Akhtar Ali of the Lahore paper *Zamindar* were recorded as being present. The pilgrimage was also thought to be "probably the first to be attended by unveiled Indian ladies of modern outlook and idea," including the sisters of the nawab of Cambay; Begum

6.2. The tomb of one of the Prophet's wives, Maymunah, at Sarif on the Mecca-Medina Road, 1885, by Snouck Hurgronje.

Mahomedullah Jung, the educated wife of an Allahabad barrister; and Fatmah Begum, superintendent of the municipal girls' schools of Bombay, who served on the hajj committees on the pilgrim ships *Rizwani* and *Khusru*. A modern outlook was not incompatible with devotional practices. Begum Mahomedullah Jung, for example, "had secured the privilege of kissing daily the Holy Railings at Medina by payment of a regular gratuity to one of the Nejdi guards there," even though that did not save her "from receiving three blows of a cane from another guard." Her beating was unusual, however; by and large, the more liberal attitude toward non-Wahabis initiated in 1933 was continued. Many pilgrims visited the

"Ghar al Hara, Ghar al Thor," hitherto out of bounds. The payment of a few riyals to the Nejdi guard "enabled an educated Indian pilgrim to visit the tomb of the Lady Khadija the Great, by night." The committee of virtue now chastised "neither with whips nor scorpions," although no doubt there were a few exceptions. The community of Bihari Muslims from Patna in Jeddah had a mosque of their own and clearly went too far in celebrating the ceremony of "Milad-ul-Nabi" in praise of the Prophet. Two of their leaders were "summoned to the police station and seriously warned."[36]

The colonial reports, indispensable though they are in reconstructing the broad lineaments of the annual hajj, convey little of the spiritual fervor of the individual pilgrim or, indeed, of the collective experience of the faithful. Well-intentioned, if patronizing, calls by colonial officials (and cooperative Muslim notables) to "rationalize" aspects of the pilgrimage often proved both counterintuitive and counterproductive. At the urging of the Haj Enquiry Committee of 1929, for example, the Indian Merchant Shipping Act was amended to prevent pilgrims from taking their own food on board. It was in 1934 that "for the first time in the annals of the Indian pilgrimage" the system was introduced whereby shipping companies provided "compulsory food on board the pilgrim ships." The results were "vigorous protests and complaints . . . from pilgrims arriving by each ship" and from members of the committees of pilgrims. Some ships reported cases of "hunger strike, passive resistance and active opposition." Although the government of India was informed telegraphically of the need for remedial measures, similar "grievances were also aired in the homewardbound ships."[37] Colonial rationality had its limits in regulating even the most mundane aspect of a spiritual endeavor.

A Runaway Slave Returning to His Lord

Quoting these verses from the *Surah Al-Baqarah* and the *Surah Ali Imran* of the Qu'ran, Abdul Majid Daryabadi (1892–1977) began his book describing his experience of the hajj in 1929:

> The Hajj or Umrah
> In the service of Allah . . .
> For *Hajj*
> Are the months well-known.
> If any one undertakes
> That duty therein,
> Let there be no obscenity,
> Nor wickedness,
> Nor wrangling
> In the *Hajj*
> And whatever good
> Ye do (be sure)
> Allah knoweth it.
> And take a provision
> (With you) for the journey,
> But the best of Provisions
> Is right conduct.[38]

The first House (of worship)
Appointed for men
Was that at Bakka (Makkah)
Full of blessing
And of guidance
For all kinds of beings:
In it are Signs
Manifest; (for example),
The Station of Abraham;
Whoever enters it
Attains security;
Pilgrimage thereto is a duty
Men owe to Allah.[39]

The year 1929 was when the Haj Enquiry Committee—chaired by a British civil servant, H. B. Clayton, and consisting of nine Muslim notables who had made their peace with the colonial system—conducted their ponderous deliberations and came out with recommendations for the reform and rationalization of the pilgrimage from India. An intertextual reading of the colonial report and Daryabadi's literary masterpiece scales the distance between the externally imparted image of the pilgrim as victim and the innermost submission of the pilgrim as slave.

Immediately following quotations from the Qu'ran, Daryabadi cites a line from a hadith: "The greatest *jihad* is accepted *haj*." The pilgrimage, according to these traditions, swept away poverty and sin, just as the bellows removed impurity from gold, silver, and iron. Bad luck had deprived the author an opportunity in the past to visit the sublime place that was envied even by the sky, a place where the Prophet Abraham had proclaimed the oneness of Allah and where lay the footprints of the Prophet Muhammad. His negligent heart, wicked self, and evil mind had led him to believe that all the commandments regarding the hajj concerned others and not him. Daryabadi considered himself a sinner who, being a recipient of Allah's mercy, now had the chance to embark on the pilgrimage. His journey, this student of philosophy and rising star of the Urdu literary firmament made clear, was not for any academic purpose or research. He was a runaway slave returning to his Lord, a particle that had a desire to shine with the light of the sun.

Abdul Majid, along with his wife and mother-in-law, left his home village and headed for Bombay via Lucknow. At Lucknow railway station he was seen off by friends from his village and a large gathering of writers, scholars, and *ulema*. In Bombay he stayed at the office of the Khilafat Committee. The pilgrim ship *Akbar* took him from Bombay to Jeddah, and from there he chose to go first to Medina before performing the hajj at Mecca. The morning of April 11, 1929, he writes, was a blessed one because the biggest dream of his life was about to be realized: he, a sinner *ummati* (member of the community), would be fortunate enough to offer salutations to his affectionate and intercessor Prophet. Indian women called this month Zul Qadeh, an empty month, but Daryabadi felt it was hardly empty for someone who could visit the Prophet's grave. The previous night had been spent at Ber-e-Hisan preparing for an early morning departure for Medina. As Medina appeared in the distance, bathed in the refulgent morning light, the pilgrims saw at the end of the barren desert pleasant green hills greeting them, a sight that transformed the quality of the material and spiritual realms alike. The entire caravan was seized with the deep emotional fervor of devotional love. Even the "Nejdi" (dour) chauffeur for the moment became a "Wajdi" (someone entranced with sheer joy and delight). As for Daryabadi, he could not tell whether he was dreaming or awake.[40]

In Medina and Mecca, professional *muallims* or *muzawwirs* arranged accommodation for visitors, with each guide tending to specialize in a particular city or region of India. Some Indian philanthropists had built several *rebats* (inns) in Medina, such as Rebat-e-Tonk, Rebat-e-Bhopal, and Rebat-e-Hyderabad. Daryabadi's party stayed at the Rebat-e-Hyderabad and were looked after by Sheikh Jafar Dagistani, a polite and sociable *muzawwir*. In his chapter on the Prophet's abode, titled "Astana-e-Nubuwwat," Daryabadi addressed the tension between the tomb and the mosque, between Indian Muslim sensibility and Wahabi doctrine. He began this chapter by invoking verse 64 of the *Surah Al Nisa:*

> We sent not a Messenger,
> But to be obeyed, in accordance
> With the will of Allah.
> If they had only,
> When they were unjust
> To themselves,
> Come unto thee

And asked Allah's forgiveness,
And the Messenger had asked
Forgiveness for them,
They would have found
Allah indeed Oft-Returning,
Most Merciful.[41]

Having at the outset cited the authority of a Qu'ranic verse, Daryabadi dealt with the controversy over whether a pilgrim should make his *niyat* (intention, or prayer offering) at the grave of the Prophet or the mosque of the Prophet. The Wahabis held that the intention directed toward the Prophet's grave amounted to *shirk* (polytheism) and *bidaat* (unacceptable innovation). But Daryabadi did not agree. He drew on a commentary on the Qu'ran by Hafiz Ibn-e-Kathir, accepted even by Nejdi and Wahabi scholars, to highlight an incident narrated by Utbi. In this narrative, a bedouin comes to the Prophet's grave and after reciting the verse from *Surah Al Nisa* says: "I have come to you asking forgiveness for my wrong deeds. Therefore intercede with Allah for me." Utbi goes to sleep after the bedouin leaves and sees in a dream the Prophet, who tells him to convey the good news to the bedouin that Allah had indeed forgiven him.

In another sign of how seriously many pilgrims contemplated every aspect of their religious journey and experience, Daryabadi wrote of his concern with where he should pray when at Medina. Daryabadi wished to transcend a needless controversy by underscoring the importance of both the mosque—Allah's house where the Prophet had offered his *namaz* (prayer)—and the grave where, according to him, the Prophet was still alive. The Hanafi *ulema* were of the opinion that the intention should be made both to the mosque and the grave located within its precincts. Daryabadi quoted approvingly the views of those Muslim jurists, who regarded the space of the Prophet's grave as far better than other parts of the earth including even the Kaaba, the Arsh (throne), and the Kursi (chair). At one of the entrance doors to the mosque, Daryabadi came across Syed Ahmed Faizabadi, elder brother of the eminent Indian religious and political leader Maulana Husain Ahmed Madani. Faizabadi had migrated to Medina twenty-five years earlier and devoted his whole life to the service of the pilgrims. Daryabadi felt the company of such a pious person was a windfall for him as he stood looking with throbbing heart and trembling feet at the majestic sight of the mosque.

Once Daryabadi had reached the Prophet's grave, he found devotees uttering the *darood*, the incantation of peace, and salutations to the Prophet. They were saying: "Ya Rasool-Allah! (O, Messenger of God!) You have preached the message, discharged the assigned responsibility, admonished the *ummah*, removed the darkness and struggled in the way of Allah. We ask for your intercession and make you our mediator with Allah." The dome was echoing with these words. Everyone was heading toward the grave and was facing not the *kaaba* made of stone but the *kaaba* of their hearts and souls.[42]

While conveying a communal, pious atmosphere at Medina that was hardly ever reflected in the colonial reports, Daryabadi did confirm instances of conflict between Indian pilgrims and Nejdi guards. He writes:

> Around the Prophet's grave there are Saudi *sipahis*. Some of them are very harsh. They push the pilgrims and sometimes they flog them with their willow and club. They do not hesitate to even drag the women. Thus they seek to impose the "Nejdi Shariah" [conservative religious law]. But some of the *sipahis* are very mild and they neglect or overlook the violation of rules and regulations by the pilgrims. Some of them even take rupees and let the pilgrims do what they want.

Daryabadi had other grievances against the Saudis. The space between the Prophet's house and grave known as Rauza-e-Jannat was like a part of paradise where pilgrims felt deeply fortunate to say their *namaz*. But this sacred space was cleared every Friday for the Amir-e-Medina appointed by the sultan of Hejaz—an act that in Daryabadi's view clearly contravened the Islamic tenets of universal brotherhood and equality. The Nejdis had helped the cause of unity by appointing a single imam to lead the prayers at the Prophet's mosque instead of the four imams of the four schools of Islamic jurisprudence that Nizami had noted during his 1911 visit. Yet after the evening prayers, a government-appointed *ulema* stood up preaching Wahabi ideology. One evening, too, Daryabadi heard an official theologian say: "Those who take the soil of this place to their home and consider it sacred are sinners and they will not be forgiven by Allah." Bin Saud had also stopped the Turkish practice of bringing black eunuchs from Africa to serve as attendants at the Prophet's mosque, but many remained from earlier times. Daryabadi urged the pilgrims to make some offerings to these attendants, who had devoted themselves to the service of the Haramain.[43]

Like most Indian Muslims, Daryabadi was critical of the Saudi government's demolition of parts of sites sacred to Muslims. Upon receiving an invitation to meet Sultan Abdul Aziz at Medina as he traveled from Riyadh to Mecca, he prepared a memorandum on the subject and had it translated into Arabic. The sultan's attendants, however, made certain that the ruler was not disturbed by complainants. Daryabadi and his associates were reduced to sending the sultan a letter urging him to take a more liberal attitude toward historical monuments and to respect the sentiments of those who considered them sacred.

While deprecating the activities of the Saudi government, Daryabadi was concerned that Muslims should not fight among themselves. They should rather concentrate their energies on meeting the challenge posed by the Gog and Magog (the Western and Christian powers), who were successfully both having Islamic law amended by Muslim rulers and infusing the feeling of nationalism in Muslim minds. Like Nizami nearly two decades before, Daryabadi was also dismayed to find the markets of Medina full of Western products—even the prayer mats, as well as the beads and carpets used in prayer and reciting God's name, were imported. The Medina that Daryabadi saw was not the Medina of the Prophet and his companions, but a Medina of the twentieth century. One could not, as Daryabadi put it, expect to find spring in the autumn. Yet Medina was once the city of the Prophet and it was with a sense of wistfulness that Daryabadi departed from the modern incarnation of it.

On his way to Mecca, Daryabadi visited the mosque in Jeddah, where people of different countries and races presented an admirable picture of unity. He described the wearing of the *ihram*, the unstitched white cloth of the hajji, as the numbing of the self before approaching the center of Muslim faith and spirituality. The area around the Kaaba—called Haram, since all fighting and killing was *haram* (forbidden) in that space—reflected the greatness and majesty of Allah and the Prophet himself had walked here barefooted.[44] At this point in his narrative Daryabadi quoted a verse from the *Surah Al-Qasas* of the Qu'ran:

> Have We not
> Established for them a secure
> Sanctuary (Haram), to which are brought
> As tribute fruits of all kinds—
> A provision from Ourselves?[45]

In Daryabadi's opinion, the fruits of the country were now being sent to Europe. Yet even as he wrote, people from many countries were drawn toward the Kaaba, the House of Allah, in droves. The beauty of the sight of hajjis walking around

6.3. The courtyard of the Great Mosque during congregational prayer, 1885, by Snouck Hurgronje.

the Kaaba and kissing the black stone could hardly be surpassed. Daryabadi suggested that one should offer *namaz* near the stone on which Abraham stood while building the Kaaba.[46]

Mecca was the perfect setting to reveal the connections of Indian Muslims to the worldwide community of Islam. It had at least two important *madrasas* founded by Indians that Daryabadi visited. The Madrasa Saulatiya, named after a benevolent woman of Calcutta, Saulat Begum, was established by Maulana Rahmatullah of Kirana, Muzaffarnagar. The princely states of Bhopal and Hyderabad gave grants to it, but it did not find favor with the Saudi government. The Madrasa Fakhr-e-Usmania, named after Mir Usman Ali Khan

Bahadur, had Indian, Hejazi, and Javanese students in it. A high point of Daryabadi's hajj was his encounter with the famous Sheikh Sannusi, who had declared jihad against the Italians in Tripoli, and was now in Mecca. Daryabadi discussed with the leader of the Sannusi rebellion the degradation of the Muslim world, the political situation in India, the state of the Khilafat Committee, and the leadership of the Ali brothers, Mohamed and Shaukat. Daryabadi compared Sheikh Sannusi with Sayyid Ahmed of Rae Bareilly, who had launched his own jihad in northwestern India in the early years of colonial rule.[47]

"The twin dynamics of universalism and exclusivism, both in their outward and inward manifestations," Ayesha Jalal writes, "have coexisted in the thought of leading Muslim intellectuals since the inception of Islam in the Arabian peninsula." Muslims were unanimous in acknowledging "the *hakimiyat* or sovereignty of Allah over the entire world," which along with the concept of *tauhid* or unity of God underpinned "the Islamic view of universal brotherhood." While theoretically "no community or individual" possessed "a greater right to Allah's benediction," the political process of forging the *ummah* or a worldwide community of believers injected an element of exclusivism that counterbalanced the universal and egalitarian appeal of Islam. The age-old tension between an uncontested divine sovereignty *(hakimiyat)* and fiercely contested temporal sovereignty *(khilafat)* took on an added dimension after the formal loss of sovereignty in India, where Muslims were in any event outnumbered by nonbelievers.[48]

The pilgrims' quest under colonial rules bore the imprint of this coexistence between universalism and exclusivism. The hajj was the quintessential acceptance of *hakimiyat* open only to those who belonged to the *ummah*. The colonial regulation of the hajj from South and Southeast Asia, where most Muslims of the world lived, was galling enough. In the early twentieth century Western powers went a step further in reordering the terms of temporal sovereignty within the Hejaz itself. The removal of the authority of the Ottoman sultan-khalifa over the Holy Cities, the Hashemite interregnum, and the establishment of Saudi dominance widened fissures not just between Muslims and non-Muslims but also within the universal community of Islam. Yet a deep commitment to the highest level of divine sovereignty enabled the Muslims of the Indian Ocean world to cope with, if not transcend, the trials and tribulations in the realm of temporal sovereignty. So it was entirely appropriate for Daryabadi, for all his disenchantment with Western influence and Saudi bigotry in the Hejaz, to close his book with an invocation of two attributes of Allah. He observed that the ship in which he and his companions had traveled to the Arabian peninsula was named *Akbar* and the ship that brought them back to India was the *Rahmani*. This meant that when they were heading toward Mecca and Medina they were awed by Allah's greatness and on their return they brought back with them Allah's mercy.

7

A Different Universalism?

Oceanic Voyages of a Poet as Pilgrim

The metaphor of pilgrimage was widely deployed by poets and philosophers who set out on voyages across the Indian Ocean to retrace the footprints of India's overseas history. The pilgrimage as a religious duty might thus be transformed into a broader intellectual and cultural quest undertaken in its name. Rabindranath Tagore (1861–1941), the Bengali poet who won the Nobel Prize in Literature in 1913, made several oceanic journeys to distant lands. His contemporaries referred to him in Bengali as *biswakabi* (global poet). Yet this poet of the world also imagined the Indian Ocean interregional arena to be a common milieu invested with a distinctive unity of poetry and culture. In 1916—while Europe was experiencing the carnage of World War I—Tagore embarked on a global oceanic voyage. Traveling east from India, he made his first stop in Burma and then continued via Southeast Asia to Japan. He next made the long Pacific crossing to North America. In Japan and as he journeyed from the West Coast of the United States to the East, he delivered powerful strictures against worshipping the new god called Nation. "The Nation [with a capital 'N']," Tagore declared at Carnegie Hall in New York on November 21, 1916, "with all its paraphernalia of power and prosperity, its flags and pious hymns, its blasphemous prayers in the Churches, and the literary mock thunders of its patriotic bragging, cannot hide the fact that the Nation is the greatest evil for the Nation, that all its precautions are against it, and any new birth of its fellow in the world is always followed in its mind by the dread of a new peril."[1] He did not want Indian patriots to imitate the monstrous features of European nationalism and the territorially bounded model of the nation-state.

In 1924–1925, Tagore traveled in response to an invitation from Latin America across the Indian Ocean, the Mediterranean, and the Atlantic. This was another of the poet's global journeys, during which he glided with relative ease from one ocean into another. On this trip Tagore was a creative poet rather than a self-conscious pilgrim, but his poetry and prose diary of the journey, written on board ships, has enough insights into the notion of "foreignness" and the blurred line between cultural universality and specificity to make inclusion in this study valuable. It throws into sharp relief the journeys he undertook in 1927 and 1932, which may be described as his Indian Ocean cultural explorations—forays that gave expression to a form of universalism subtly different from an abstract globalism. The voyage to Southeast Asia in 1927 in response to an invitation from archaeologists in Java was explicitly described by Tagore as a "*tirthajatra* (pilgrimage) to see the signs of the history of India's entry into the universal."[2] It provided an occasion for testing the validity of a "greater India" thesis being put forth around that time in varied forms by leading scholars and thinkers. "My pilgrimage would have been incomplete without this visit," Tagore wrote of his sojourn in Iran and Iraq in 1932, emphasizing how an exploration of the historic unity of Indo-Persian culture had given new meaning to "the evening of his life."[3] He also reflected on the present and envisioned a future that would be illuminated by the convergence of different new lamps lit by an Asia reborn. Both searches—for the cultural contours of a "greater India" across the Bay of Bengal and the lineaments of a universal brotherhood of Sufi poets bridging the Arabian Sea—complicate recent discourses on the tensions among global and fragmentalist approaches to understanding the peoples and cultures of the Indian Ocean rim.

Wistful for the Far Beyond

While in Japan in May 1924, Tagore received an invitation to visit South America on the occasion of the centenary of Peru's independence. The traveler in him could not resist the temptation to visit a new people in a new land.[4] He was well-known among the Spanish-reading public through the translations of Juan Ramón Jiménez and Zenobia Camprubi, but so far had no direct experience of the Latin world. On September 19, 1924, the sixty-three-year-old poet set off from Calcutta in bad health on his trip around half the globe. "But the boons he received from the goddess of poetry in his tired frame," writes Prabhatkumar Mukhopadhyay with no exaggeration, "will remain immortal in the history of literature; these were *Purabi* in poetry and *Pashchim Jatrir Diary [Diary of a Westbound Traveler]* in prose."[5]

> It is 8 o'clock in the morning. There are dark clouds in the sky, the horizon is dim with pouring rain, and the moist wind like a peevish child refuses to be pacified. The unruly sea is sweeping across the concrete wharf of the harbour with its roar, as if wanting to catch somebody by the hair and then falling back in despair. Such a stormy weather at the time of departure makes one depressed . . . And yet I know, once we sail away from land, the tie that holds me back will dissolve of itself. The young traveller will come out on the royal path. This young man had once sung, "Restless am I, I am wistful for the far beyond."[6]

A profound sense of yearning and loss, even a wrenching pain in solitude, seems to have been the main impulse behind Rabindranath's creativity as a poet. It was this emotion somewhere in the depths of his being that must have enabled him to compose two of his greatest poems on board the ship *Harana Maru* in the Indian Ocean on October 1, 1924. In "Fulfillment" ("Purnata") he conveys his essence of the universal conversation between woman and man, which destiny had conspired to eavesdrop on and interrupt:

That whispered communion of ours
  The stars of the Pleiades heard;
    In the bushes of the evening rose
Off and on, in wafts it flowed,
  Then in stealth, came between us,
    In mask of death, a boundless breach.
Our meetings ended—no more speech
  Availed in that touchless infinity.
    Yet the void is not an empty void;
An anguished fiery vapour fills the sky
  And all alone, in songs glowing in the fire,
    I create a world of dreams.[7]

Rabindranath's ceaseless search for the woman of the mind had long been a recurring feature of his poetry. That search reached the zenith of poetic utterance in "The Call" ("Ahwan"), which began:

All through this life, and times without number,
Have I wandered crying for the woman who would
Call me to her.[8]

"The Call" is a long poem in which each stanza vies with another to excel in rhythm and imagery. If there is one that has an edge among the connoisseurs of Bengali literature, it is this one:

From the thunderbolt of Indra, bring forth
In your dark eyes the flash of lightning

Thou Summer Storm, light up the fire in the cloud
Within me eager to shed its rain. The still,
The dumb, the imprisoned bounty within its
Tear-laden bosom darkens. Set it free in a wild
Torrent, empty it, rob it of all and save it.[9]

In his abstract ruminations on man and woman, Rabindranath was not above broaching his own essentialized views on the difference of gender. He engaged in polemical disagreements with "the worshippers of solid realism" for their discomfort with "the disturbing ghost of this unreal woman" and their false faith that "once the woman is freed from illusion, solid truth will be found." Rabindranath for one was not sure that there was "anything that can be called solid truth in creation" or, if there was, that a "pure unwavering mind" could be found to "reflect its pure print." The way in which he then connected the power of illusion with poetic creativity is best given in his own words:

Man's imagination . . . finds its freedom . . . in a woman. The orb that surrounds a woman is made up with all the suggestivities of the indescribable; a man can enter there without difficulty with his imagination coloured by the hue of his own emotion and taking the form of his own thought. In other words, he finds there a scope for his own creation, which gives him a special pleasure. A man who is totally devoid of illusion may laugh at this, but then a man without illusion never knows the calamity of the creative urge; he lives in the midst of calamity.[10]

Less than a week after he wrote these lines, Rabindranath implored the ocean-sky to lift its "still and blue curtain" so that he could rediscover "the image" of his "momentary friend." "Mingled in shadow and light," she was "beyond infinity in some illusory land" and "the illusion of the unknown" yearned for "the fleeting vision":

> Lift, O, Lift, O Sky, thy still and blue curtain,
>   I will look among the stars for the jewel from
> The garland of the fleeting moment. I will seek
>   From where, in autumn, comes for an instant
> The twilight gleam, from where, along with rain,
>   descends upon the earth the evening jasmine, and
> From where the storm receives its diadem of lightning
>   With a sudden flare.[11]

Proving that it was possible to be mobbed by admirers in the middle of the ocean, Tagore was cheered by passengers on the *Suya Maru* traveling in the opposite direction. On October 11, 1924, the *Harana Maru* arrived in Marseilles. After spending a week in France, the poet set off for Latin America from Cherbourg on October 18, 1924. The *Andes* did not offer the same warm hospitality as did the Japanese vessel *Harana Maru*, but Rabindranath discovered that it was possible to let the poetic imagination fly even inside a cramped cabin. The three-week voyage across the Atlantic afforded time for twenty-three poems. The "Stranger" ("Aparichita") struck a rather plaintive note on the sorrow of the poet's solitude. "Hope" was not exactly robust in its optimism, but revealed his "heart's keen hunger," and "Grateful" returned to the theme of remembering loves past. As the *Andes* neared the shore, Rabindranath allowed himself one flight of ego in his poem "Future," sobered by a quick reflection, "The Past." By the time he arrived in Buenos Aires, the "ache of a time gone by" had deepened "the ache of the moment."

A variety of circumstances, not least the poet's frail health, led to the cancellation of plans to visit Peru. For nearly two months—from November 7, 1924, to January 3, 1925— Rabindranath stayed in Argentina and wrote another twenty-six poems. From November 12 he was the guest of Victoria Ocampo at her riverside garden house, Miralrío, in San Isidro. Upon his arrival, his poetry switched to the present tense.[12] His poem "Alien Flower" ("Bideshi Phul") reveals a new sense of joy in Rabindranath's life:

> O, alien flower, when I ask you, tell me,
>> Will you forget me ever?
>> You smile and nod, but this I know,
>> In your thoughts, every now and again
>>> Me you would recall.
>>> And when in a short while
>> I would be gone to a distant land,
>> The love of the far, in your dream
>> To you will make me known—and you will not forget.[13]

While Vijaya (Victoria) retrospectively came to be seen as the "alien flower" in the "last spring" of Rabindranath's life, the first poem directly addressed to her was "The Guest" ("Atithi") written on November 15:

7.1. Rabindranath Tagore with Victoria Ocampo in Argentina, 1924. Rabindra Bhavan, Viswa Bharati, Santiniketan.

> With what infinite sweetness you fill
> The days of my sojourn, Woman . . .
>
> . . . Blessed one, you gaze upon my face even as
>   Those stars and say in the same strain,
>   "You are no stranger, I know you fully well,"
>   And though I do not know the language you
>   Speak, I hear you sing, "The poet is a guest
>   Of love and a guest of mine for ever."[14]

Unquestionably, Tagore's most beautiful poem from his San Isidro phase is "Last Spring" ("Shesh Basanta"), which, according to Keataki Kushari Dyson, "would be very difficult to turn into modern English without making it sound trite and cliché-ridden." The difficulty, as she explains, is twofold. First, the poem embodies a sentiment that would most likely be unacceptable "to English-speaking Western readers" unaccustomed to making allowance for cultural differences. Second, "Shesh Basanta" is "an exquisitely musical, rimed poem in strict form, incarnating the kind of verbal loveliness which the idiom of twentieth-century English-language poetry tends to eschew and therefore cannot capture without caricaturing and trivializing what it is purporting to capture, without destroying its magic."[15] "The Key" is another quintessential poem from Tagore's "last spring." When Providence created his heart as "a mansion of many rooms," he had thrown away the key to "the silent solitary inmost chamber."

> I ponder, if ever I would meet the traveller
>   Who has picked up the key
>   On some unknown seashore . . .

. . . And she would open the door which nobody could
discover.[16]

Whether Vijaya opened the door to "the silent solitary inmost chamber" we cannot be absolutely sure, but she had almost certainly turned the key in the lock and threatened to
barge in. In any event, on the day of Rabindranath's departure
from Buenos Aires on board the *Giulio Cesare*—January 3,
1925—his cabin door had to be taken apart from its hinges so
that Vijaya could give him his favorite armchair as a token of
her love. He wrote to her on January 5: "I pass most part of
my day and a great part of my night deeply buried in your
armchair which, at last, has explained to me the lyrical meaning of the poem of Baudelaire that I read with you." She replied from San Isidro on January 15: "So, at last, you understood Baudelaire through my armchair! . . . I hope that you
may understand, through that same piece of furniture, what
the lyrical meaning of my devotion is! I hope, at least, *part* of
its meaning shall be revealed to you. The part a comfortable
seat can reveal . . . (Hélas! it is only a small part)."[17]

Rabindranath was probably feeling a little too comfortable
in Vijaya's armchair. He wrote only four poems during the
eighteen-day voyage from Buenos Aires to Genoa. But the last
of this quartet—"Exchange" ("Bodol")—is especially poi-
gnant. The wistfulness has returned. He had exchanged his
"basket of the wettest rains" with her "garland of the newest
spring." Yet melancholy had claimed victory and now at the
end of the warmest day "the flowers had withered." The rich-
est gift carried within it the inevitability of loss.

On January 21, 1925, Rabindranath set foot in Italy. He had

looked forward to this visit. "I know that in Italy I shall have a welcome," he had written to C. F. Andrews, "for from various sources I have heard that the people there are eagerly expecting me, and that my books are very widely read."[18] But Italy did not give him the inspiration Latin America had, as his poem "Italia" makes plain. Like many a poet, he had come to offer the queen tributes at her feet. But she had said from behind a veil,

> It is winter now,
> The sky is hidden in mist and my garden is
>   Without flowers.
>   . . . I've not yet donned my colourful robes,
>   Go back now, ardent poet,
>   I'll call you back by my side
> When in the sweet spring I'll take my seat
>   On a carpet of flowers.[19]

The flower garden at San Isidro was indeed where Rabindranath had spent his "last spring." The memory of its sights and scents would animate the final years of his life. In the autumn of 1925 the poetry book *Purabi* was published. On October 29, 1925, Rabindranath wrote to Vijaya, "I am sending you a Bengali book of poems which I wish I could place in your hand personally. I have dedicated it to you though you will never be able to know what it contains. A large number of poems in this book were written while I was in San Isidro. My readers who will understand these poems will never know who my Vijaya is with whom they are associated. I hope this book will have the chance of a longer time with you than its author had. *Bhalobasa* (Love)."[20] "During his stay at San Isidro," wrote Victoria Ocampo on the occasion of the poet's birth centenary in 1961, "Tagore taught me a few words of Bengali. I have retained only one, which I shall always repeat to India: *Bhalobasa.*"[21]

In Search of "Greater India"

Tagore's westward voyage in 1924–1925 had kindled an emotion that was to circumnavigate the globe, transcending all boundaries despite the challenges of literary and cultural translation. It was as an intellectual pilgrim that in July 1927 the poet traveled east from Madras on the French ship *Amboise.* "India's learning had once spread outside India," Tagore wrote to Nirmalkumari Mahalanobis on July 15, 1927, "but the people outside accepted it . . . We have embarked on this pilgrimage to see the signs of the history of India's entry into the universal."[22] His only motive in making this journey was "to collect source materials there for the history of India and to establish a permanent arrangement for research in this field."[23] His Bengali followers quickly established a Greater India Society in Calcutta on the eve of his voyage to Java. Tagore took with him on this journey a small but formidable team of intellectuals and artists, including Suniti Kumar Chattopadhyay, Surendra Nath Kar, and Dhirendra Krishna Brahma.

"It is necessary above all," K. N. Chaudhuri has admonished us, "to banish the term 'Indian colonization' from the vocabulary of social analysis." For the peoples of Southeast

Asia the "interweaving" of Indian and Islamic cultural patterns with preexisting local ones was "a more complex process than the simple transfer of social and cultural forms by people who [were] already part of these structures."[24] Chaudhuri's admonition and similar warnings by many scholars of Southeast Asia must be read in the context of a significant corpus of early twentieth-century European colonial anthropology—as well as the scholarship of a strain of colonized, nationalist intellectuals in India who narrated with an arrogant whiff of (sub)imperialism the story of the subcontinent's civilizational gifts to Southeast Asia. Yet the frontiers of colonies and nation-states, as well as the boundaries of area studies in the Western academy during the Cold War era, also obstructed the study of the process of "interweaving" that might legitimately lead to an insightful comparative and connective history. The complexity of the process did not go wholly unnoticed by the more perceptive minds involved in the quest for some kind of a "greater India." In other words, there was a recognized need to distinguish a loftier aspiration of universalism (not a universalist boast) from the haughtier expression of cultural imperialism, even though the line between the two occasionally became blurred. The universalist current was more creative and generous in its delineation of cultural commonalities and difference. Riding this current, Buddhist missionaries, Sufi mystics, anticolonial visionaries, and humanist scholars had traversed the Indian Ocean to Southeast Asia over the centuries.

One of Tagore's companions, the famous linguist Suniti Kumar Chattopadhyay, has left a vivid, detailed, and learned travelogue-cum-historical thesis on "greater India." "The foreign land to which we are travelling," Chattopadhyay wrote on July 16, 1927, "does not seem especially foreign to us. We are going with a conception that this *bidesh* (alien land) we are moving towards is part of our *desh* (homeland)—a conception born out of historical sense." The destination of *Amboise* was Haiphong in French Indochina. The five hundred or so passengers came from a variety of national and religious backgrounds. There were a good number of French citizens. Among Indians there were Tamils from Pondicherry as well as other Tamil Hindus, Tamil Muslims, and Tamil Christians; Mappilla Muslims from Malabar; a few Telegus; and, of course, Bengali Hindus who were part of Tagore's party. Among the "Annamese" there were two types: the "northerners" from Tonkin who "had painted all their teeth black," and the "southerners" from Cochin-China "whose teeth were natural white." Some sixty or seventy Arabs from Algeria and Aden worked in the machine room of the ship. In addition, there were Creoles from Madagascar and Mauritius, a few Africans ("Kafri" was the term Chattopadhyay used without seeming to be concerned about its possible pejorative connotations) who served in the canteen, and a handful of Chinese.[25]

At one end of the deck a Mappilla Muslim prepared a sheep roast as a group of French and "Annamese" soldiers looked on. Nearby, a Lakshminarayan was using a huge pestle from Madras to grind chilies, turmeric, ginger, cumin, and pepper into paste as Suniti-babu (as Suniti Chattopadhyay was known) chatted with him in Hindustani and with the French soldiers in French. Not too far away a Tamil Muslim chef diced a large quantity of potatoes, while another made huge piles of onion and garlic. Suniti-babu was not especially fond of the "Chettis," however good they might be at keeping accounts. He could not understand why, despite their obvious wealth evident from the ornaments of their womenfolk, they still chose to travel third class and bribed the deckhands to take fresh-water baths in the first-class section. The Tamil Hindus, he discovered, were mostly engaged in *tejarati* (moneylending), while the Tamil Muslims tended to be small retailers in Hanoi, Hue, Saigon, and Phnom Penh. Suniti-babu made friends with one Abdul Saheb who informed him in "Annami" that he had been running a cloth trade in Saigon for thirty years. The Hindu "Chettis" and the Tamil Muslim traders mixed quite easily, displaying no evidence of the well-known Hindu upper-caste notions of "untouchability." The ship, Suniti-babu concluded, was "the great leveller."[26]

While Suniti Chattopadhyay observed people with a keen eye, Tagore himself observed the sea. On a day bathed with sunshine he remembered Shelley's poem:

> The sun is warm, the sky is clear,
> The waves are dancing fast and bright.[27]

But he interpreted these lines as a form of lament reflecting the weariness of life. In the morning Tagore had seen the sky's eternal message on the edge of the ocean's horizon, a message of peace like a white lotus on a wave of tears. But at the end of the day there were dark clouds and the distant thunder of turmoil.[28] In a less pessimistic mood he could not but marvel at the audacious enterprise of human beings in conquering the sea:

> Standing by the shore, human beings saw the ocean in front of them. One cannot imagine a bigger obstacle . . . The day dwarf-like human beings boldly proclaimed: "We will climb on the back of the ocean," the gods did not laugh. Instead, they whispered the *mantra* of victory in the ears of these rebels and waited. The back of the ocean is under control, the ocean's bottom is now being prospected.[29]

The *Amboise* arrived at Singapore on July 20, 1927. All the arrangements for Tagore's tour of the Malay peninsula had been made by Ariam Williams (Aryanayakam), a Tamil Christian scholar of divinity who originally hailed from the Jaffna peninsula of Ceylon. The poet's stopover in the Malay peninsula afforded an opportunity for a rapturous welcome by Indian and Ceylon Tamils as well as Gujarati Khojas and Banias. The reception given to the poet by the Indian Association in Singapore attracted a large number of ordinary Indians—small traders; automobile drivers; security guards from a variety of communities including Sikh, Pathan, and Punjabi Muslims; Tamil Hindus and Muslims; and Gujarati Bhatias, Khojas, and Bohras. Tagore's gracious host in Singapore was Mohammed Ali Namazi, an Iranian businessman who had come to Southeast Asia via Madras. Suniti Chattopadhyay was struck by the admiration this Shia Muslim family had for "Hindu civilization" and found himself arbitrating in intrafamily debates on the precise nature and direction of the "Aryan" link between Iranians and "the Brahman and Kshatriya castes" of India.[30]

Tagore's moment in the Malay peninsula also gave him a chance to have a conversation with the Chinese literati. The Chinese had named the Indian poet Chu Chen-Tan ("Thunder and Sunlight of India," with the "Chu" derived from Thien-chu, meaning Heavenly Kingdom, an ancient Chinese name for India). Among the Malay Chinese whom Tagore met was the barrister Song Ong Siang, who in 1923 had authored the book *One Hundred Years' History of the Chinese in Singapore, 1819–1919*. Another was Lim Boon Keng, who along with Song had run the *Straits Chinese Magazine* from 1897 to 1907. In 1911 Lim had gone to Europe to take part in the Universal Races Congress in London. He was by this point the head of Amoy University, but as a product of the famous Raffles School retained close ties with the city founded by Raffles. Lim Boon Keng had recently completed an English translation of *The Li-Siao: An Elegy on Encountering Sorrows* by the fourth-century-B.C. Chinese poet Qu Yuan. Tagore was enchanted by the life, work, and death of Qu, who had in the end drowned himself in the Milo River in Hunan. When Lim sent Tagore a copy of his manuscript, Tagore wrote a foreword for the book in Penang.[31]

A trip to the Malay peninsula was unthinkable without including a visit to Malacca, and Tagore made his journey there from Singapore by sea. Suniti Chattopadhyay, always opinionated, decided to shun the "Tamil Chettis" wearing diamond earrings and Gujarati Khojas with their turbans wrapped in gold thread. Instead he went to that part of the deck where a few Hindustani Muslims donning Turkish caps were speaking in Bhojpuri mixed with Urdu. He learned from them that they traveled around on ships in the Malay world selling Islamic books, *taabiz*, as well as pictures of Mecca and Medina. They praised the religiosity of the Malays and reported that by Allah's grace they had made handsome profits in their trade. They then inquired whether the man who looked like a *pir* (spiritual guide) and had such a luminous appearance was indeed Rabindranath Tagore. The next question was about this *pir*'s faith. After prefatory remarks about how true religion was beyond all institutional religion, Suniti-babu divulged that Tagore was not a Muslim. His audience listened politely and then, disappointed, turned back to their *roti* and *kebabs*.[32]

From Malacca the sea presented a serene spectacle. The ocean beach was spread out in front of the poet in the shape of a half moon. The hue of the shallow waters made the sea look as if it was clad in the earth's saffron end of a sari. On the left were coconut trees leaning on one another as if for support.[33] While in the city, a group of Punjabi Hindu, Muslim, and Sikh men arrived to pay their homage to the poet. (According to the Muslims, Tagore was not only a poet of the highest caliber but by the grace of Khudatallah had also attained *tassawuf* or the enlightenment of a Sufi mystic.) The idyll and pleasantries, however, were soon rudely disturbed. Subbaya Naidu came to Malacca to tell Tagore about the dismal condition of Indian laborers on the rubber plantations— of whom 80 percent were Tamils, 9 percent Telegus, 4 percent Malayalam-speaking Mappilla Muslims, and the remainder Hindustanis and Punjabis. Moreover, some of the British rubber barons seemed unhappy with the Indian poet's "triumphal progress" through the Malay peninsula. On August 2, 1927, the *Malay Tribune* published an editorial on "Dr Tagore's Politics" that viciously attacked the poet for something he had purportedly written in the *Shanghai Times*. Tagore was quoted as having said: "Asia prepares her weapons in her armories for a target which is bound to be the heart of Europe."[34]

The poet had actually written or said nothing to the Chinese paper. When he had visited China in 1924, he had been greatly disturbed to see the brutal use of Sikh armed police against the Chinese in Shanghai and had written a Bengali article protesting against the British practice of using Indian troops overseas. An English translation of the article was published in the *Modern Review* in early 1927, which then was recycled in garbled form in the *Shanghai Times* and the *Malay Tribune*. An energetic young Tamil scholar in Malaya noticed the distortions, and the Indian paper *Malayan Daily Express* published a strong rejoinder under the title "Anti-Tagore Bubble Pricked: An Object Lesson in Dishonest Journalism." Tagore himself was as worried by the new aggressive forms of nationalism as he was about British imperialism. Before leaving Malaya, in a lecture at Penang on August 15, 1927, the poet issued a stern warning to anticolonial activists not to imitate the monstrous features of European nationalism.[35]

On August 16, Tagore set off from Penang on board the *Kuala,* bound for the Dutch East Indies by way of Singapore. He had always been less enthused by Indian military con-

quests in Southeast Asia than by the processes of cultural interaction facilitated by "Hindu Brahmanas" and "Buddhist
Shramanas." As his connecting ship, the *Plancius*, journeyed
from Singapore across the Strait of Malacca toward Batavia,
Tagore wrote his poem "Srivijayalakshmi," celebrating the
renewal of a bond after a thousand-year separation.[36] The
Srivijaya empire had granted patronage to the Buddhist university at Nalanda and enjoyed friendly ties with the Pala
kingdom of Bengal; both had suffered military defeat in the
1020s at the hands of the Cholas of south India. A leading Javanese poet, Doetadilaga (Timboel), composed a long and
classical response to Tagore's poem, whose fourth and fifth
stanzas reminisced:

> Remember how we never could believe in days past
> that our love would know separation;
> perfect was our harmony, one our thought, one our soul
>   and one our body,
> the unity of God and creature nigh.
> Verily I saw in you my elder brother
> guiding me in the ways of the world,
> teaching me scripture, tongue and behaviour,
> and all that we need to exist.[37]

The *Plancius* carried a varied contingent of Malays and
Chinese as well as Indian Tamils, Gujaratis, and Pathans. A
venerable Baghdadi Jewish merchant, who had migrated to
Surabaya via Bombay and Singapore, had read Tagore's books
and was delighted to have a private meeting with the poet.

And some forty or fifty Indians, many of them Sindhi merchants, came to greet Tagore at his hotel in Batavia. But Tagore's full exploration of Java had to wait until he had made a pilgrimage to Bali, the island where Dutch scholars claimed to have discovered a living museum of early Indian religion and customs.[38] Tagore was soon to discover how "Hindu" religious sentiment and ritual pervaded life in Bali, but in a very distinctive form.

During a silent drive with the "king" of Karangasem, a gap in the surrounding forest revealed the blue ocean. The king at once uttered the Sanskritic word *"samudra"* (ocean). Seeing that Tagore was astonished and thrilled, he gave further synonyms for ocean—*"sagara, abdhi, jaladhya."* He then recited: *"saptasamudra* (the seven seas), *saptaparbata* (the seven mountains), *saptavana* (the seven forests), *sapta-akash* (the seven skies)." Having given a rather obscure Sanskrit word *adri* for mountain, he then rattled off: "Sumeru, Himalaya, Vindhya, Malaya, Hrishyamuka"—all names of Indian mountains. At one place a small river was flowing below the mountain. The king muttered on: "Ganga, Jamuna, Narmada, Godavari, Kaveri, Saraswati"—names of key rivers in north and south India. Tagore reflected: "In our history Bharatvarsha (India) had realized its geographical unity in a special way." That mode of imagining the unity of natural and sacred space had crossed the great eastern ocean to reach distant islands. Tagore also noted that neither the names of the Indus and the five rivers of the Punjab nor that of the Brahmaputra flowing through Assam figured in Balinese vocabulary. He concluded that these regions were not culturally part of the ancient India that had spread its influence across the Bay of Bengal at a particular moment in history.[39]

Upon arriving at the palace, Tagore and his companions found four Brahman priests worshipping Buddha, Shiva, Brahma, and Vishnu.[40] The next day some Brahman *pandits* (learned men) arrived with a set of coconut-leaf manuscripts—one of them the "Bhishmaparva" (chapter on Bhishma) of the *Mahabharata*. Arjuna, the hero, was their ideal man. But there were subtle variations on the epic tale. In the Balinese version, Shikhandi, the half-man, half-woman who rode on Arjuna's chariot to undermine Bhishma's ability to fight, had turned into Srikanti, Arjuna's wife.

The differences in the Southeast Asian versions of the great epics *Ramayana* and *Mahabharata* enabled Tagore through comparative study to advance some very insightful interpretations of plains-forest tension as well as issues of race and gender that animate these stories. In the Malay world, Ram and Sita were portrayed as a brother and sister who were married. Tagore tended to accept this version as the original, something that had been suppressed in later renderings within India. Such an interpretation sustained Tagore's point about marriage as metaphor in the epics—in this case, Sita and Ram representing the line etched by the plough and the green of the newly sprouting crop, respectively, both children of mother earth and yet bound in wedlock.[41] If Malay literature had recreated the Indian epics as their own, Balinese dance depicted tales related in the Indian Puranas. But the "Hindu" ethos of the island was no bar to Arab Muslims, Gujarati Khoja Muslims, and Chinese merchants conducting trade.[42]

After his departure from the island, Tagore wrote one of his most beautiful poems, "Bali"—later renamed more generically "Sagarika" (Sea Maiden)—which opened with the following verse:

> Having bathed in the sea with your wet tresses
> you sat on the rocky beach.
> Your loose yellow robe
> drew a forbidding line around you on the earth.
> On your uncovered breasts and unadorned body
> the morning sun painted a gentle golden hue.
> With a *makara*-crested crown on my forehead
> bow and arrow in hand
> I appeared royally adorned
> And said, "I have come from another land."[43]

Tagore's pleasure in discovering India in Bali was disturbed only by news of the appearance of the American author Katherine Mayo's best-selling potboiler *Mother India*, which Gandhi characterized as a drain-inspector's report on his country. Sitting on a hilltop at Munduk, Tagore wrote an angry denunciation of the book that was published in the *Manchester Guardian* and later reprinted in J. T. Sunderland's book *India in Bondage*.

From Bali, Tagore traveled to Surabaya on the predominantly Muslim island of Java. It was sugar from here, he wrote in one of his letters, that went into the *sandesh* (Bengali sweet) made by the famous confectioner Bhim Chandra Nag of Calcutta. Hosted by the family of the seventh *monkonegoro*

7.2. Tagore with the Seventh Monkonegoro of Java, 1927. Rabindra Bhavan, Viswa Bharati, Santiniketan.

of Surakarta, he was amazed by the extent to which stories of the *Ramayana* and *Mahabharata* suffused the dance and drama of the Muslim Javanese. The islands known as the Dutch Indies could be more appropriately named, according to Tagore, "Vyas Indies," after the divine sage. One evening the theme of the dance would be the fight between Indrajit, the educated demon-prince of Lanka, and Hanuman, the monkey; on another, the sultan's brother would himself play the role of Ghatotkacha, a *Mahabharata* character who had been creatively transformed in the Javanese variant of the epic. The veranda of the raja's home was decorated with beautiful silk scrolls on which events of the *Ramayana* were painted.

Echoes of the Indian masterpiece *Ramayana* were also heard in Yogyakarta, where Tagore was a guest of the *paku-alam*. The sultan's daughters danced and the entire family gathered to perform the story of the killing of the great bird Jatayu in the epic. Tagore lamented the lack of more comparative studies of *Ramayana*. "One day some German scholar will do this work," he wrote. "After that by protesting against or substantiating that thesis we will earn Ph.D.'s in the university."[44]

A visit to the great Saiva-Buddhist temple complex of Borobudur proved to be something of an anticlimax; Tagore found it to be big in scale but not in majesty.[45] He was rather more generous in his assessment of the site in his poem "Borobudur." On the ship *Maier* traveling from Java to Singapore, Tagore wrote what was to become one of his most popular songs:

> Who goes playing that plaintive flute on a foreign boat?
> I can feel the touch of that melody.[46]

But it had been a hectic trip. Recalling Coleridge's lines about water everywhere in the ocean but not a drop to drink, Tagore felt he was drifting in the ocean of time and yet could not snatch even a moment of it.[47]

Tagore pursued the Buddhist connection further in Siam on the way home. In Bangkok, he met the prince of Chantabun, who had published multiple volumes of the Pali *tripitaka* in Thai script. His poem "Siam," composed on October 11, 1927, gave a final expression to Tagore's search for a greater India:

Today I will bear witness
   to India's glory
that transcended its own boundaries
   I will pay it homage
outside India at your door.[48]

Despite Tagore's obvious pride in "India's entry into the universal," three features of his perspective on Southeast Asia from the Indian Ocean deserve attention. First, Tagore makes a rather self-conscious attempt to downplay the episodes of Indian military aggression against Southeast Asia in an attempt to highlight the theme of cultural exchange. This strategic move ends up giving a partial view of the historical relations between the two regions, but seems clearly designed as a prescription for models that ought to be eschewed or followed in the present and the future. Second, Tagore does not treat India as a monolith in discussing the ways in which cultural influences radiated from the subcontinent to the shores of Southeast Asia. By contrast, there is a story of regional differentiation within India that is told along with an attempt at periodizing the spread of such influence. The thousand-year-old tie with Srivijaya was clearly one fostered by the Palas of Bengal and not by India as a whole. The attempt to date the forging of particular links across the eastern Indian Ocean is based on a study of the regionally differentiated literatures, cultural practices, and histories of India. Third, the Southeast Asian negotiations with Indian cultural forms and products are regarded throughout by Tagore as a creative process conducted by active historical agents. There is no sense of hierarchy, for example, in analyzing the many versions of the *Ramayana* and *Mahabharata*. "India's true history reflected in the many stories of the *Ramayana* and *Mahabharata* will be seen more clearly," he writes, "when we are able to compare with the texts that are to be found here [in Southeast Asia]."[49] Once "colonization" in its pernicious forms has been banished, it is hoped that the connections across the eastern Indian Ocean will form a valid subject for comparative, historical inquiry.

Shades of Aryanism, Depths of Sufism

Malaya and Java were great Muslim societies under European colonial subjugation, and it was Tagore's desire to see Muslim countries with Muslim sovereigns that led him to board a Dutch airplane to Iran and Iraq in April 1932.[50] Not only was Tagore too old and infirm by this time to withstand a long journey by sea, but also air transportation was beginning to revolutionize travel in the Indian Ocean arena. The Persian Gulf was now, as the British political resident in Büshehr put it, "the Suez Canal of the Air."[51] This was Tagore's second journey by air, the earlier one having been from London to Paris. On that occasion he had only felt a loose tie to the land, but his heart felt a wrench as the plane lifted off from the soil of Bengal. The airplane roared its way toward the west, touching down at Allahabad, Jodhpur, and Karachi. "The *jahaj* (ship) flew along the ocean's shore. Blue water on the left, hilly desert to the right." After one more stop at Jask on the Makran coast, the poet and his companions, including Amiya Chakravarty, Kedarnath Chattopadhyay, and Tagore's daughter-in-law Pratima Devi, landed in Büshehr. Tagore was as welcome in Büshehr as Curzon had not been in 1903. He was, in fact, treated as royalty.[52]

Tagore's *Parashye (In Persia)* is much more than a diary or a travelogue by an acute observer of cultures. It is the closest thing to a real history among Tagore's writings, based as it is not just on philosophical musings but also fairly solid empirical research. Tagore had set out many years before to watch the first stirrings of an awakening in easternmost Asia. Unfortunately, Japan had been infected with the European virus of imperialism. He had in the past, too, heard distant echoes of West Asia's tumultuous history, and when it seemed to him that Turkey was finally sinking, there suddenly appeared Kemal Pasha. He now wanted to see for himself how West Asia was responding to the call of the new age.[53]

In Iran, Tagore was not just any poet, but a poet of the east. "For the Persians," Tagore wrote, "my identity has another special feature. I am Indo-Aryan . . . I have a blood relationship with them." Governor Ferughi of Büshehr certainly claimed in his welcoming address that the "Aryan race" and "Aryan civilization" formed the basis of the bond between India and Iran. Word had also spread that Tagore had certain affinities with romantic and devotional Persian poets, and it was the brotherhood of Sufi poets that eventually turned out to be the more emotionally charged aspect of the relationship. European race theory took second place to Indo-Persian poetry as the ground for commonality. Shades of Aryanism were drowned in the depths of Sufism. There was absolutely no occasion, Tagore asserted, when the Persians made him feel that they belonged to another society or religious community.[54]

With Tagore's main identity established as a poet and an honorary Sufi, the highlight of his visit turned out to be the encounter with Saadi and Hafiz in their home town of Shīrāz. On the way from Būshehr to Shīrāz by car, the chief of the Bashkri tribe, Shakrullah Khan, came galloping on his horse to pay his respects. Meals on the journey consisting of *pulao* and *kebab* did not seem too different from the *mughlai* food of India. Shīrāz, the home of Saadi and Hafiz, appeared quite suddenly at the end of a plain. Tagore had made Hafiz's acquaintance as a boy through his father's translations from the Persian. Hafiz had also been a favorite of the nineteenth-century Bengali social reformer Raja Rammohun Roy, who quoted the Sufi poet to good effect in his *Tuhfat-ul-Muahuddin*. Overwhelmed by an effusive welcoming address with references to Saadi's soul wafting in the air and Hafiz's satisfied smile being reflected in the joy of his countrymen, Tagore responded by pointing out that the only weight on his side of the scale was that he was present in Iran in person. Hafiz had received an invitation in the fourteenth century from Ghiasuddin Azam Shah, the third Ilyasshahi sultan of Bengal, but if Persian traditions are to be believed, his ship had been forced to turn back. Bengalis generally believed that Hafiz responded to the Ilyasshahi invitation with a poem about Bengalis having taken to appreciating sugar now that they had tasted it in the form of Hafiz's Persian poetry.

At a reception in a carpeted garden surrounding Saadi's

7.3. Tagore at Hafiz's grave, 1932. Rabindra Bhavan, Viswa Bharati, Santiniketan.

grave, Tagore claimed to be akin to the Sufi poets and composers of yesteryears; the only difference was that he used the language of the modern age. At Hafiz's graveside, the custodian of the cemetery brought out a large square volume of Hafiz's *diwan* (oeuvre) and asked Tagore to open it with a wish and his eyes shut. Tagore had been agonizing about the blindness and prejudice that went by the name of religion and wanted India to be free of this terrible affliction. "Will the tavern's door be flung open," Tagore read when he opened his eyes, "and with it the tangled knots of life unfasten? Even if vain religious bigots keep it shut, have faith, that by God's will, the door will open."[55] On that glorious morning the *musafir* (traveler) had a vision of Hafiz's smiling eyes beckoning him from another distant spring. Tagore had no doubt that he and Hafiz were long lost friends who had in the same tavern together filled many cups of wine.[56]

Tagore stayed in Shīrāz at the garden house of a merchant named Shīrāzi who did business in Calcutta. In the evening Persian music was played with an instrument resembling the sitar and percussion on what looked like a tabla for the left hand. Both the instruments and tunes had resonances with India. The similarity with Bengali was that Persian music and poetry seemed inextricably linked.

From Shīrāz, Tagore was driven to Isfahan via Persepolis. On the outskirts of Isfahan, Tagore was greeted by civic elders as well as a poet from the village of Shahrezā who proclaimed:

The caravans of India always carry sugar but this time it has the perfume of the muse. O caravan, please stop your march, because burning hearts are following thee like the butterflies which burn around the flame of candles.[57]

Tagore was entranced by the gardens and mosques of Isfahan. He visited the Masjid-e-Shah started by Shah Abbas and the neighboring Masjid-e-Chahar-e-bagh. He also crossed the bridge to see the Armenian church and related how Shah Abbas had brought the Armenians from Russia and what made them migrate to India during the reign of Nadir Shah. Not surprisingly, Tagore compared Shah Abbas with India's Akbar.[58]

Having developed an ear for Persian music played on the

tar and *dambok* in Isfahan, Tagore set off for the capital Tehran. During his two weeks in Tehran, he participated in as many as eighteen public functions. Persian music continued to intrigue him with its elements of sameness and difference in relation to north Indian classical music. Tagore was often played melodies on the violin that sounded like the morning ragas of Bhairon, Ramkeli, and even the pure Bhairavi.

The poet's seventy-first birthday, on May 6, 1932, was celebrated with great fanfare in Tehran. In return for all the bouquets, Tagore gave a gift in the form of a poem, titled "Iran":

> Iran, all the roses in thy garden
>   and all their lover birds
> have acclaimed the birthday
>   of the poet of a far away shore
> and mingled their voices in a paean of rejoicing . . .
> And in return I bind this wreath of my verse
>   on thy forehead, and cry: Victory to Iran![59]

The next day Tagore met Iran's parliamentary leaders and the poet who had translated some of his poems. He received from them an exquisitely produced volume of the poetry of Anwari. Tagore summed up his Persian sojourn in these words: "Each country of Asia will solve its own historical problems according to its strength, nature and need, but the lamp that they will each carry on their path to progress will converge to illuminate the common ray of knowledge . . . it is only when the light of the spirit glows that the bond of humanity becomes true."[60]

The journey toward the Iraqi border took Tagore through Kazbin, Hamadan, Kirmanshah, Behistun, and Takibustan. The poet saw the various sights that had so enthralled visitors for centuries, including Darius's carvings on the mountainside in Behistun and the glorious sculpture of the Sassanid age in Takibustan.[61] The short distance from Kasrishireen in Iran to Kanikin in Iraq represented a transition from roads to railways. Iraqi officials and poets and Indian expatriates were on hand to receive Tagore on the Iraqi side of the border. Indian Hindus assured him that their relations with Muslims in Iraq were perfectly cordial.[62]

From his hotel room in Baghdad, Tagore could see the wooden bridge over the Tigris built by General Stanley Maude, and which the 28th Punjabis, 53rd Sikhs, 67th Punjabis, and the 2nd and 4th Gurkhas had crossed in March 1917.[63] A conversation with the Christian chaplain attached to the British air force in Iraq, which was engaged in a ferocious bombing campaign against Iraqi villagers, led Tagore to reflect on the shift from sea power to air power in human history. He could see that it was extremely easy to kill the desert dwellers from the air. The humanity of those who could be killed with impunity from afar was not especially apparent to the killers, who were also not at serious risk of facing retaliation. When the priest affiliated with the Iraqi air force asked him for a message, Tagore wrote:

From the beginning of our days man has imagined the seat of divinity in the upper air from which comes light and blows the breath of life for all creatures on this earth. The peace of its dawn, the splendour of its sunset, the voice of eternity in its starry silence have inspired countless generations of men with an ineffable presence of the infinite urging their minds away from the sordid interests of daily life . . . If in an evil moment man's cruel history should spread its black wings to invade that land of divine dreams with its cannibalistic greed and fratricidal ferocity then God's curse will certainly descend upon us for that hideous desecration and the last curtain will be rung down upon the world of Man for whom God feels ashamed.[64]

In a very early poem Tagore had wished he were an Arab bedouin. One day in Iraq he indulged his childhood fancy by visiting a bedouin tent. He was first served coffee—thick, bitter, black Arabic coffee. Then followed a feast to the accompaniment of delicate music. Tagore and his male companions were deprived of the pleasure of watching a dance by the bedouin women, which only Tagore's daughter-in-law could enjoy and report on. But he was treated to a war dance by the men with whirling sticks, knives, guns, and swords. Tagore was just reflecting on how different was his life, nurtured by the rivers of Bengal, from the struggle for existence in the desert, when the bedouin chief startled him with the language of universal humanity. "Our Prophet has taught us," the chief said, "that he is a true Muslim from whom no fellow human-being fears any harm."[65]

How should we interpret Tagore's intellectual journeys across the seas? Some tend to hear voices from the colonial world in

7.4. Tagore with a bedouin chief in Iraq, 1932. Rabindra Bhavan, Viswa Bharati, Santiniketan.

their writings' unbending insistence on claims to difference. Yet Tagore was an eloquent proponent of a universalist aspiration, albeit with a twist. Universalist claims from Europe in the modern age have rarely managed to avoid the taint of imperialism, which has led local cultures under siege in the colonial world to assert their difference. A discerning historical investigation makes clear, however, that universalism was hardly a quest over which European modernity had any kind of monopoly. Local, regional, and national cultures in different parts of the globe were not just jealous guardians of their own distinctiveness, but also wished to participate in and contribute to larger arenas of cultural exchange. In this process the lines

7.5. Poem-painting, Baghdad, May 24, 1932. Rabindra Bhavan, Viswa Bharati, Santiniketan.

that separated the large constructs of East and West, Asia and Europe, as well as the smaller communitarian categories came to be transcended in myriad ways. A certain sense of nostalgia for the bonds of the past need not be seen as a simple longing for a precolonial refuge in the hostile environment of the colonial world. It was very much part of a struggle in the present to try to influence the shape of a global future. The ideas that wafted across the Indian Ocean and beyond suggest that the age of empire may best be studied in the framework of multiple and competing universalisms rather than mutually exclusive and inherently conflictual cultural relativisms.

In late May 1932 the intellectuals of Baghdad organized a civic reception in Tagore's honor. An old poet recited his poetry in a sonorous voice, which sounded to Tagore like tumultuous waves on the ocean. Once the flow of Arabic poetry had ebbed, Tagore spoke about Hindu-Muslim conflict in India. He invited his hosts to resend their message, with its universalist ideal in the sacred name of their Prophet, once more across the Arabian Sea so that India could be saved from communitarian narrow-mindedness, inhuman intolerance, and the degradation of liberal religion and instead take the high road to unity and freedom. He expressed this sentiment even better in a poem-painting signed "Baghdad May 24 1932." It can be read today as an exhortation to people across the globe to awaken from their postmodern slumber and weave together communities and fragments into a larger and more generous pattern of human history:

The night has ended.
Put out the light of the lamp
   of thine own narrow corner
      smudged with smoke.
The great morning which is for all
   appears in the East.
Let its light reveal us
    to each other
  who walk on
    the same
  path of pilgrimage.[66]

The Indian Ocean Arena in the History of Globalization

This book may be read as a contribution to global history and, at the same time, as a cautionary tale against its recent excesses. It shares with the proponents of global history the desire to expand spatial scale beyond the contours of locality and nation. But it parts company with that historical version of global integration that hastily robs such interregional arenas as the Indian Ocean rim of any real meaning. The cross-cutting Indian Ocean stories narrated in this book have something to say about historical conceptions of both space and time. In particular, they underscore the relevance and resilience of the Indian Ocean space in modern times.

Michael Pearson, in his magisterial overview of the Indian Ocean from prehistory to the present, believes that he has discovered only one major temporal break. This break, which in his view occurs around 1800, constitutes the moment when all the deep structural elements underlying Indian Ocean history for millennia—monsoons, currents, and land barriers—are "all overcome by steam ships and steam trains in the service of British power and capital; the Indian Ocean world becomes embedded in a truly global economy and for the first time production, as opposed to trade, is affected." Borrowing a distinction between history *in* the Mediterranean (contingently so, but really part of larger histories of Islam or Christendom) and history *of* the Mediterranean—based on a firm sense of place requiring Mediterranean-wide comparisons—Pearson argues that from the turn of the nineteenth century the Indian Ocean became submerged in a larger global story.[1]

There can be little question that the global forces of imperial domination played out their historical drama on the Indian Ocean stage in the nineteenth and the twentieth centuries. This book about the Indian Ocean has been attentive to the global context and a larger set of global connections throughout. Yet it has also shown that Indian Ocean history in the age of global empire had elements of both history *in* and *of* the ocean. The British Empire—for all the power of steam it could bring to bear—may have in the end, to borrow Ranajit Guha's famous phrase, merely achieved "dominance without hegemony."[2] The peoples of the Indian Ocean made their own history, albeit not without having to contend with economic exploitation and political oppression, and the oceanic space supplied a key venue for articulating different universalisms from the one to which Europe claimed monopoly. Pearson does a wonderful job of leavening his prose with firsthand travelers' accounts. But he confesses to having "privileged European travelers, partly as their accounts give vivid impressions of life at sea when the ocean was a British lake, and partly as they have left so many quotable accounts behind them."[3] The Indian Ocean in the nineteenth and first half of the twentieth centuries both was a British lake and it was not, and there is certainly no dearth of quotable non-European travel accounts in this period. If "India was the fulcrum of the ocean around which all other areas swung" and thirty million Indians traveled overseas between the 1830s and the 1930s, Indian experiences and firsthand accounts assume some importance.[4] This book has tried to do some justice to them.

Even the almighty British Empire often paid more attention to colonial rather than metropolitan considerations when projecting its power across the Indian Ocean. Curzon's strategic vision for the ocean was largely that of Britain's Indian empire, and the sea change in sovereignty that was brought about in the late nineteenth and early twentieth centuries bore all the hallmarks of Indian and Indian Ocean specificities. It was the colonial British Indian empire that fought the first Gulf War of the twentieth century against the precolonial Ottoman Empire. The Indian soldiers who were sent out to fight played both a global and an Indian Ocean role and they understood the difference. Britain's global economic domination at the high noon of empire was undeniable. Yet it was this huge asymmetry in economic power relations on a world scale that led Indian and Chinese intermediary capitalists to build their own lake in the stretch of ocean from Zanzibar to Singapore. Highly specialized capital and labor flows connected different parts of the Indian Ocean rim. Migrant labor movements, indentured and otherwise, certainly had a global reach, but the

Indian Ocean dimension exhibited both similarities and differences with what went on in the plantation complex that also had the Atlantic and the Pacific in its web. It was the worldwide depression of the 1930s that upset the finely tuned interregional balance, but the social and political ramifications of this global economic crisis are best grasped through comparisons that span the entire Indian Ocean region.

Global and local communitarian histories have combined in recent years to rescue history from the nation, a wholly laudable historiographical enterprise. Yet the more overzealous attempts to put the nation in its place by directly juxtaposing the global to the local have not achieved much more than inventing the clumsy word "glocal." They have missed the continuing significance of the interregional arena for the crafting of an extraterritorial and universalist anticolonialism that coexisted and contended with territorial nationalism. The interplay between nationalism and universalism illuminated the thought and politics of expatriate patriots who counted no less a figure than Mohandas Karamchand Gandhi among their number. This retrieval of the nuances of patriotism in diasporic public spheres has been attempted without resurrecting a monolithic conception of the Indian nation. The focus has been on how the many fragments have connected to one another across the borders of colonies and would-be nation-states.

Votaries of the direct linkage of the local with the global have also grossly underplayed the importance of both religious communitarianism and religious universalism dear to Indians and others who traveled overseas. The duty of pilgrimage enjoined on the *ummah,* the worldwide community of Islam, remained a quintessentially Indian Ocean experience for Muslims from India, Malaya, and Java who braved colonial regulations to make it to Mecca and Medina throughout the period of British imperial domination of the seas. The reality of the Indian Ocean comes through most strongly in the imagination of creative thinkers and artists who believed that world to be blessed with an aura of cultural affinity. This was true of a "global poet," Tagore, who had no qualms about conversing with the West, but found that the trails of India's entry into the universal crisscrossed the Bay of Bengal and the Arabian Sea. That oceanic zone provided the fount for the inspiration of different universalisms that could challenge the European variants tainted by the power of colonial empires.

There was, then, something other than the "nation," narrowly defined, that intermediated the levels of the global and the local. One of the aims of this book has been to refine and embellish the more sophisticated contributions that have been made to conceptualize the process of globalization in history. Historians have by now reclaimed the phenomenon of globalization from the clutches of social scientists and journalistic commentators who saw it simply as a contemporary development about a quarter of a century old. Indeed, one collective project has identified four historical phases of globalization— the archaic, the proto-modern, the modern, and the postcolonial.[5] Despite the somewhat mechanical quality of the periodization, it retains some heuristic value. It has the added merit of being able to recognize the multiple sources of the process of globalization and the varied contributors to it, at least in the two early phases. In powering what C. A. Bayly calls archaic globalization, characterized by "notions of cosmic kingship, universal religion, and humoural understandings of the body and the mind," the peoples of the Indian Ocean arena can be seen to have played a creative role.[6] Even in the age of proto-modern globalization straddling the eighteenth and early nineteenth centuries, proponents of a "Muslim universalism" can be regarded as equal partners with Europeans in the authorship of the globalization process.[7]

An inherent danger resides in this schematic view of globalization, which gives the modern phase, as it were, to Europe and the West. But it has been avoided by the more perceptive modern historians of other regions of the world, even while acknowledging the political and economic supremacy that the West came to achieve in the age of global empire. T. N. Harper has shown through his examination of the twin themes of diaspora and language in Southeast Asia how even at the turn of the twentieth century the globalism of the colonized was different from the globalization of the territorial nation-state by colonial empires.[8] This calls for a modification of the claim that the century spanning the 1860s to the 1960s constituted the era of territoriality.[9] It may well have been in the form and structure of states, but alternative universalistic allegiances were never wholly disavowed and perhaps, for the colonized, became even deeper attachments than before. A diasporic perspective further reveals little that was fragmentary about colonized peoples' identities, shaped as these were by "links and flows in a global context" and "interconnected with other communities," which contributed to the creation of a "shared public sphere of the port cities that ringed the Indian Ocean in this period." A focus on hybrid language and the polyphony of translation in this period teases out "the inner history of globalization, of how people lived in a global society in which others had economic dominance and cultural primacy." The origins of anticolonial struggle "lay not in confronting European power, but in the power of translating itself."[10] What came out of this project of translation was a universalist anticolonialism that did not recognize the false binary of the secular and the religious.

Were the oceanic connections closed down in the interwar period? Perhaps too early a concession is made to the tyrants when a "global public sphere" of the decades from 1890 to 1920 is seen to be devoured in the aftermath of World War I by "la tyrannie du national." Colonial empires correctly recognized that the challenge to their dominance in the early twentieth century transcended the boundaries of particular colonies. World War I–era "orientalist images of underground India, of the secret society complex of the Chinese, echo in a sinister way present-day preoccupations with Islamicist conspiracies and bamboo networks."[11] Colonial powers cracked down on them and cracked down hard. But were they so successful in their suppression that they erased universalist dreams from anticolonial minds and planted in their place firm loyalties to territorial nationalism? If that is true, Tagore's evocations of a cosmopolitan Indian Ocean arena in 1927 and 1932 were merely the last gasps of a lost era. The Curzonian vision of an imperialist globalization with its Indian Ocean particularities must then be seen to have decisively won, with the Tagorean universalist aspiration reduced to no more than an idle fancy. Yet this book has demonstrated quite the opposite.

The decades spanning the two world wars were doubtless disruptive for Indian Ocean connections. We have read ample evidence of the wrecking of the specialized interregional flows of capital and labor during the depression of the 1930s. From the 1940s to the 1960s, as the Indian Ocean arena made the transition to postcolonialism, the model of territorial nation-statehood certainly won out over competing forms of univer-salism, especially of the Islamic kind. Yet what is striking is the contested nature of the hegemony of the nation-state even in its heyday and the remarkable brevity of its unquestioned dominance in the Indian Ocean arena. Studies of nationalism have tended in one way or another to have privileged the mo-ment of arrival, a practice that has retrospectively colored what came before. This book, written around a set of sea voy-ages, has been more concerned with the liminal stage of the journey that stretched from the point of departure to the point of arrival. There were many possibilities on the way, includ-ing, of course, shipwreck. From this perspective, the ship of anticolonial nationalism in the Indian Ocean arena on its tur-bulent historical voyage may be seen to have docked at the port of the state for the briefest of moments. More than a de-cade ago Homi Bhabha had called for a "travelling theory" of nation and narration that was "alive to the *metaphoricity* of the peoples of imagined communities" marked neither by hori-zontal space or simultaneous time. The "metaphoric move-ment" of these peoples required "a kind of 'doubleness' in writing; a temporality of representation that moves between cultural formations and social processes without a 'centred' causal logic."[12] This traveling history of mobile peoples and ideas in the Indian Ocean arena has delineated the broad contours of cultural liminality both within and beyond the nation—an organization of peoples that was only one of many expressions of imagined communities in the age of global empire.

Such a history of movement, migration, and memory for the "modern" phase of globalization may hold some lessons for understanding globalization and its supposed enemies in its postcolonial incarnation. The opponents of what are regarded as Western forces of globalization may not all be staking their position on unbending economic autarky or absolute cultural difference. The bolder and more imaginative challenges may flow from alternative universalist aspirations engendering competing visions of global futures. The architects of global empire in the era of colonial modernity elicited challenges that had both territorial and extraterritorial dimensions. Yet those who did not uncritically accept the nation-state model in the Indian Ocean arena were not necessarily antimodern, but more likely were votaries of multiple modernities in diasporic public spheres. If this was true of "modern" globalization, which hawked the nation-state in the world as one of its prized export commodities, how much truer it must be for globalization in its postcolonial phase, when colonial modernity has lost much of its sheen and value.

It would be a mistake, however, to underestimate the structural constraints of the nation-state form and an interstate system even at a time when it has lost much of its legitimacy. When the leaders of the newly independent countries of Asia and Africa gathered in Bandung, Indonesia, in April 1955, their ideology had taken a sharp statist turn. Jawaharlal Nehru, India's first prime minister, insisted that only nation-states, not anticolonial movements, should have seats at the table in Bandung. And this stance was taken even though Malaya just across the Strait of Malacca was still under British imperial rule and Vietnam, a year after the decisive victory of the independence movement at Dien Bien Phu, was beginning to see U.S. domination replace French colonialism. At the other end of the Indian Ocean, most of Africa was not yet free. The cult of the nation-state had its moment in Indian Ocean history in the third quarter of the twentieth century before turning out to be yet another god that failed.

On a visit to India in 1995, Nelson Mandela expressed the hope that "the natural urge of the facts of history and geography . . . should broaden itself to include the concept of an Indian Ocean Rim for socio-economic cooperation and other peaceful endeavours." "Recent changes in the international system," he argued, "demand that the countries of the Indian Ocean shall become a single platform."[13] In promoting the formation of an Indian Ocean Rim Association for Regional Cooperation (IOR-ARC) to bring together the littoral countries from South Africa through India to Southeast Asia, he had the right idiom and the wrong instruments. He had touched a historical chord that harked back to a kind of cosmopolitan harmony, but a regional organization made up of nation-states did not possess the skills to play that music. Yet the tune is embedded in the not-too-deep recesses of memory and history of the peoples of the Indian Ocean arena, and it is one, if it can be expressed and embellished, they will know how to enjoy. As for the relations of that oceanic realm with the world beyond its outer boundaries, modern history suggests that there may be scope for postcolonial conversations. If the globe at the dawn of the twenty-first century is indeed witnessing a new, ferocious round in the clash of civilizations, the prognosis will be one of deepening conflict and unending war. But if the history of the modern world can be interpreted to a significant degree as an interplay of multiple and competing universalisms, room can be created for understanding through intelligible translations. It was this task of creating hybrid and polyphonic languages of translation that the peoples of the Indian Ocean interregional arena had so successfully accomplished through the archaic and modern phases of globalization. It remains the only hope for a new cosmopolitanism in a postcolonial setting.

NOTES

INDEX

Notes

1. Space and Time on the Indian Ocean Rim

1. See Bruce Jaffe, Eric Geist, and Helen Gibbons, "Indian Ocean Earthquake Triggers Deadly Tsunami," *Sound Waves: Coastal Science and Research News from across the U.S. Geological Survey* 68 (December 2004–January 2005): 1–6.

2. Ibid., p. 2.

3. Michael Pearson, *The Indian Ocean* (London: Routledge, 2003), p. 27.

4. Fernand Braudel, *The Mediterranean and the Mediterranean World in the Age of Philip II*, vol. 1 (Berkeley: University of California Press, 1995), pp. 168–170.

5. Bernard Bailyn, "The Idea of Atlantic History," working paper no. 96001, "International Seminar on the History of the Atlantic World, 1500–1800," Charles Warren Center for Studies in American History, Harvard University, p. 22, 2.

6. For a dazzling example of Atlantic poetry in epic form, see Derek Walcott, *Omeros* (New York: Farrar, Straus and Giroux, 1990).

7. K. N. Chaudhuri, *Asia before Europe: Economy and Civilisation of the Indian Ocean from the Rise of Islam to 1750* (Cambridge, Eng.: Cambridge University Press, 1990), pp. 112–113. For an insightful discussion of the interaction of space and time in the mental domain and the distinctive characteristics of "perceived" space and time, see his chapter 5 on "The Structure of Space and Society."

8. I am aware that the term "arena" in its Greek etymology tends to connote a ring of conflict. I use it in its more diffuse, modern, applied meaning as a sphere of action and interaction.

9. For examples of the interesting revisionist work, see M. N. Pearson, *The Portuguese in India* (Cambridge, Eng.: Cambridge University Press, 1987); Om Prakash, *The Dutch East India Company and the Economy of Bengal, 1630–1720* (Delhi: Oxford University Press, 1988); and Sanjay Subrahmanyam, *Improvising Empire: Portuguese Trade and Settlement in the Bay of Bengal, 1500–1700* (Delhi: Oxford University Press, 1990).

10. The best-known exponent of the world-systems approach is Immanuel Wallerstein, *The Modern World System* (New York: Academic Press, 1974). See also his "The Incorporation of the Indian Subcontinent into the Capitalist World-Economy," in Satish Chandra, ed., *The Indian Ocean: Explorations in History, Commerce and Politics* (New Delhi: Sage, 1987), pp. 222–253.

11. For a notable exception written with great literary flair, see Amitav Ghosh, "The Slave of MS. H. 6," in Partha Chatterjee and Gyanendra Pandey, eds., *Subaltern Studies*, vol. 7 (Delhi: Oxford University Press, 1993), pp. 159–220, the scholarly nucleus of Ghosh's brilliant book *In an Antique Land* (New Delhi: Ravi Dayal, 1992). A second article on diaspora in the series is Sudesh Misra, "Diaspora and the Difficult Art of Dying," in Gautam Bhadra, Gyan Prakash, and Susie Tharu, eds., *Subaltern Studies*, vol. 10 (Delhi: Oxford University Press, 1999).

12. Like "the currents and the winds," the ocean "really knew no frontiers" and one has to proceed with certain rule-of-thumb sketches of the limits. See M. N. Pearson, "Introduction I: The State of the Subject," in Ashin Dasgupta and M. N. Pearson, eds., *India and the Indian Ocean, 1500–1800* (Calcutta: Oxford University Press, 1987), p. 11.

13. Kenneth McPherson, *The Indian Ocean: A History of People and the Sea* (Delhi: Oxford University Press, 1993), pp. 3–4.

14. Chaudhuri, *Asia before Europe*, p. 9.

15. Ibid., p. 23. Complicating a Braudelian intuitive approach to long-term structures that remained invariant over time with a Foucaultian reexamination of human cognitive logic and Cantorian set theory, Chaudhuri has presented a sharper analysis of boundaries, ruptures, and thresholds in Indian Ocean history than Braudel was able to offer in his work on the Mediterranean. He deploys as three key analytical instruments the concepts of topology, order, and metamorphosis in his engaging exploration of the historical interaction between units of space and society. See chapter 5 in ibid.

16. To be fair, in an earlier work Chaudhuri did pose the question: "Is the 'Indian Ocean' as a geographical space the same as Asia?" His answer, following Braudel, was to draw a distinction between a physical unit and a human unit. "Asia as a continent," he wrote, "was an abstract concept, and during the period with which we are concerned people were unsure where Europe ended and Asia began." He seems to suggest that the Indian Ocean was a more meaningful human unit for historical analysis. See K. N. Chaudhuri, *Trade and Civilisation in the Indian Ocean: An Economic History from the Rise of Islam to 1750* (Cambridge, Eng.: Cambridge University Press, 1985), p. 4. In the modern period, many staunch believers in the

human unity underpinning the Indian Ocean arena slipped almost unconsciously into a continental vocabulary.

17. Chaudhuri, *Asia before Europe*, p. 36.

18. J. de V. Allen, "A Proposal for Indian Ocean Studies," *Historical Relations across the Indian Ocean* (Paris: UNESCO, 1980), pp. 137–151.

19. Dasgupta and Pearson, *India and the Indian Ocean*, p. 17.

20. C. J. Baker, "Economic Reorganization and the Slump in South and Southeast Asia," *Comparative Studies in Society and History* 23, no. 3 (July 1981); C. J. Baker, *An Indian Rural Economy: The Tamilnad Countryside, 1880–1955* (Delhi: Oxford University Press, 1984); Sugata Bose, *Agrarian Bengal: Economy, Social Structure and Politics, 1919–1947* (Cambridge, Eng.: Cambridge University Press, 1986); Sugata Bose, *The New Cambridge History of India: Peasant Labour and Colonial Capital* (Cambridge, Eng.: Cambridge University Press, 1993).

21. Rajat Kanta Ray, "Asian Capital in the Age of European Expansion: The Rise of the Bazaar, 1800–1914," *Modern Asian Studies* 29, no. 3 (1995): 553–554.

22. Ibid., pp. 452, 554.

23. C. A. Bayly, "Beating the Boundaries: South Asian History, c. 1700–1850," in Sugata Bose, ed., *South Asia and World Capitalism* (Delhi: Oxford University Press, 1990), pp. 27–39; and Bayly, *Imperial Meridian, 1780–1830* (London: Longman, 1989), chapter 2.

24. McPherson, *The Indian Ocean*, p. 44.

25. *Jibanananda Daser Sreshtha Kabita* [The Best Poems of Jibanananda Das] (Calcutta: 1974), pp. 51–52, 65, my translation.

26. Ibid., my translation.

27. Ashin Dasgupta, *Malabar in Asian Trade, 1740–1800* (Cambridge, Eng.: Cambridge University Press, 1967), p. 7. Intimations of "modernity" in the Indian Ocean interregional arena are discernible as early as the sixteenth century.

28. See Blair B. Kling and M. N. Pearson, eds., *The Age of Partnership: Europeans in Asia before Dominion* (Honolulu: University Press of Hawaii, 1979); Sanjay Subrahmanyam, *The Political Economy of Commerce: Southern India, 1500–1650* (Cambridge, Eng.: Cambridge University Press, 1990); and Anthony Reid, *Southeast Asia in the Age of Commerce, 1450–1680* (New Haven, Conn.: Yale University Press, 1988).

29. Ashin Dasgupta, "Introduction II: The Story," in Dasgupta and Pearson, *India and the Indian Ocean*, pp. 28, 39.

30. See C. A. Bayly, "A presenca portuguesa no Oceano Indico e a emegencia do Estado Moderno, 1498–1978," *Oceanos* 34 (June 1998).

31. Andre Wink, *Al-Hind: The Making of the Indo-Islamic World*, vol. 1: *Early Medieval India and the Expansion of Islam Seventh to Eleventh Centuries* (Delhi: Oxford University Press, 1990), p. 3. See also Andre Wink, "Al-Hind: India and Indonesia in the Islamic World-Economy, c. 700–1800," in *The Ancien Regime in India and Indonesia*, reprinted in *Itinerario* 1 (1988), special issue, pp. 33–72.

32. Chaudhuri, *Trade and Civilisation in the Indian Ocean*, p. 211.

33. Dasgupta and Pearson, *India and the Indian Ocean*, p. 39.

34. McPherson, *The Indian Ocean*, p. 4; see also pp. 8, 198–200.

35. Sanjay Subrahmanyam and C. A. Bayly, "Portfolio Capitalists and the Political Economy of Early Modern India," in Sanjay Subrahmanyam, ed., *Merchants, Markets and the State in Early Modern India* (Delhi: Oxford University Press, 1990), pp. 259, 264.

36. Curzon's claim is cited in J. G. Lorimer, *Gazetteer of the Persian Gulf, Oman and Central Arabia*, vol. 1: *Historical* (Calcutta: Government of India, 1908–1915), p. 2638. For a British imperial statement on the piracy debate based on Francis Erskine Loch's 1818–1820 diary of his adventures in the western Indian Ocean, see Sir Charles Belgrave, *The Pirate Coast* (London: G. Bell, 1966). Belgrave served and lived in the Persian Gulf from 1926 to 1957. For an argument about the colonial construction of piracy, see M. Al-Qasimi, *The Myth of Arab Piracy in the Gulf* (London: Routledge, 1988).

37. Geoffrey Parker, *The Military Revolution: Military Innovation and the Rise of the West, 1500–1880* (Cambridge, Eng.: Cambridge University Press, 1988), p. 115.

38. McPherson, *The Indian Ocean*, p. 243.

39. Dasgupta and Pearson, *India and the Indian Ocean*, p. 13.

40. On Kashmir, see Mridu Rai, *Hindu Rulers, Muslim Subjects: Islam, Rights and the History of Kashmir* (Princeton, N.J.: Princeton University Press, 2004).

41. See C. A. Bayly, *Indian Society and the Making of the British Empire* (Cambridge, Eng.: Cambridge University Press, 1990).

42. Subrahmanyam and Bayly, "Portfolio Capitalists," p. 264.

43. See Ray, "Asian Capital."

44. Ibid., p. 522.

45. Some major Indian intermediary capitalists, for instance, wrote and published their autobiographies. See, for example, Nanji Kalidas Mehta, *Dream Half-Expressed* (Bombay: Vakils, Feffer and Simons, 1966). Mehta traveled from Gujarat to Mombasa in 1901 and eventually made it big in East African commerce. See also S. N. Hotchand, *Memoirs of Seth Naomul Hotchand, 1804–1878* (Karachi: Oxford University Press, 1982) for the life story of a Sindhi entrepreneur.

46. J. H. Parry, *The Discovery of the Sea* (Berkeley: University of California Press, 1981), p. xi.

47. See, for example, Marina Carter, *Voices from Indenture: Experiences of Indian Migrants in the British Empire* (London: Leicester University Press, 1996).

48. This perspective runs counter to the argument in Benedict Anderson, *Imagined Communities: The Origin and Spread of Nationalism* (London: Verso, 1989).

49. See Ayesha Jalal, *Self and Sovereignty: Individual and Community in South Asian Islam since 1850* (London: Routledge, 2000).

50. Chaudhuri, *Trade and Civilisation in the Indian Ocean*, p. 4.

2. The Gulf between Precolonial and Colonial Empires

Epigraph. Niall Ferguson, "Hegemony or Empire?" *Foreign Affairs* (September/October 2003).

1. J. G. Lorimer, *Gazetteer of the Persian Gulf, Oman and Central Arabia*, vol. 1: *Historical* (Calcutta: Government of India, 1908–1915), p. 2627.

2. Ibid., pp. 2638–2639.

3. Ibid., pp. 2636, 2644.

4. Curzon to Secretary of State, December 1, 1903, cited in Earl of Ronaldshay, *The Life of Lord Curzon*, vol. 2 (London: Ernest Benn, 1928), p. 317.

5. The Curzon quotation and Lorimer's report are both from Lorimer, *Gazetteer of the Persian Gulf*, p. 2648–2649.

6. The most eloquent historian in this legion is undoubtedly Niall Ferguson. See his *Empire: How Britain Made the Modern World* (London: Allen Lane, 2003) and *Empire: The Rise and Demise of the British World Order and the Lessons for Global Power* (New York: Basic Books, 2003). Note the pedagogical tone in the title of the American edition.

7. The debate over the appropriateness of "U.S." as an adjective of empire need not detain us here. I share Andrew Bacevich's view that the idea of "America as empire" may "make it possible to see America's global role in a new and clearer light." Andrew Bacevich, *The Imperial Tense: Prospects and Problems of American Empire* (Chicago: Ivan R. Dee, 2003), p. xiii.

8. G. W. Leitner, *Kaiser-i-Hind: The Only Appropriate Translation of the Title of the Empress of India* (Lahore, 1876). Leitner's scholarly rivals were unimpressed by this claim.

9. Bernard S. Cohn, "Representing Authority in Victorian India," in Eric Hobsbawm and Terence Ranger, eds., *The Invention of Tradition* (Cambridge, Eng.: Cambridge University Press, 1992), p. 172.

10. Ibid., p. 178. Cohn writes that the suppression caused "the desacralization of the person of the Mughal emperor."

11. See C. A. Bayly, *Indian Society and the Making of the British Empire* (Cambridge, Eng.: Cambridge University Press, 1990), chapter 1.

12. The phrase is Stanley Tambiah's. See his *World Conqueror and World Renouncer* (Cambridge, Eng.: Cambridge University Press, 1976) and *The Buddhist Conception of Universal King and Its Manifestations in South and Southeast Asia* (Kuala Lumpur: University of Malaya, 1987).

13. Sanjay Subrahmanyam, "Imperial and Colonial Encounters: Some Reflections on an Undigested Past," paper presented at the Social Science Research Council conference "Lessons of Empire," New York, September 26–27, 2003.

14. See Mridu Rai, *Hindu Rulers, Muslim Subjects: Islam, Rights and the History of Kashmir* (Princeton, N.J.: Princeton University Press, 2004), chapter 2.

15. This was Disraelispeak quoted in Cohn, "Representing Authority," p. 184.

16. Rai, *Hindu Rulers, Muslim Subjects*, pp. 90–93.

17. Lorimer, *Gazetteer of the Persian Gulf*, p. 2638.

18. Charles Belgrave, *The Pirate Coast* (London: G. Bell and Sons, 1966), p. 1.

19. Muhammad Al-Qasimi, *The Myth of Arab Piracy in the Gulf* (London: Routledge, 1988), p. xiii.

20. Lakshmi Subramanian, "Of Pirates and Potentates: Maritime Jurisdiction and the Construction of Piracy in the Indian Ocean," in Devleena Ghosh and Stephen Muecke, eds., *UTS Review: The Indian Ocean* 6, no. 2 (2000): 15, 14, 17.

21. On the notion of "hidden transcripts" and the backstage discourses of resistance, see James C. Scott, *Domination and the Arts of Resistance: Hidden Transcripts* (New Haven, Conn.: Yale University Press, 1991).

22. James Francis Warren, *The Sulu Zone, 1768–1898* (Singapore: Singapore University Press, 1981), pp. xii–xiii.

23. Lorimer, *Gazetteer of the Persian Gulf*, p. 197.

24. Belgrave, *Pirate Coast*, p. 129.

25. Ibid., p. 140.

26. Lorimer, *Gazetteer of the Persian Gulf*, p. 201.

27. Ibid., p. 2638.

28. Ibid., pp. 250, 265.

29. John S. Galbraith, "The 'Turbulent Frontier' as a Factor in British Expansion," *Comparative Studies in Society and History* 2, no. 2 (January 1960): 157–158.

30. Ibid., pp. 159–162.

31. See Frank Swettenham, *British Malaya* (London: Allen and Unwin, 1955).

32. C. A. Bayly, *Empire and Information: Intelligence Gathering and Social Communication in India* (Cambridge, Eng.: Cambridge University Press, 1996), p. 141. See also pp. 113–128.

33. Htin Maung Aung, *The Stricken Peacock: Anglo-Burmese Relations, 1752–1948* (The Hague: Martinus Nijhoff, 1965), pp. 87–89.

34. Amitav Ghosh, *The Glass Palace* (Delhi: Permanent Black, 2000), p. 47.

35. Aung, *Stricken Peacock*, p. 92.

36. Anil Chandra Banerjee, *Annexation of Burma* (Calcutta: A. Mukherjee & Bros., 1994), pp. 316–317.

37. This was also true of premodern European states.

38. See C. A. Bayly, *Origins of Nationality in South Asia* (Delhi: Oxford University Press, 1998), chapter 1.

39. W. W. Hunter, *The Indian Mussalmans* (1871; Lahore: Sang-e-Meel, 1999), p. 1.

40. See Thongchai Winichakul, *Siam Mapped: A History of the Geobody of a Nation* (Honolulu: University of Hawaii Press, 1994).

41. George N. Curzon, *Persia and the Persian Question* (1896; New York: Barnes and Noble, 1966), pp. 3–11, emphasis in the original.

42. Douglas Goold, "Lord Hardinge and the Mesopotamian Expedition and Enquiry, 1914–1917," *Historical Journal* 19, no. 4 (1976): 924.

43. This brief account of the Mesopotamian campaign is primarily based on the *Mesopotamia Commission Report* (Command Papers 1917–1918, XVI.773), which can be viewed in the Government Documents section of Widener Library, Harvard University.

44. Goold, "Lord Hardinge," p. 933.

45. A. J. Barker, *Townshend of Kut: A Biography of Major-General Sir Charles Townshend* (London: Cassell, 1967), p. 173.

46. For a graphic account of these horrors, unheard of since the Crimean War, see the section on "Medical Breakdown" in the *Mesopotamia Commission Report*, pp. 63–95. See also Edmund Candler, *The Long Road to Baghdad*, cited in ibid., pp. 173–174.

47. A. J. Barker, *The Neglected War: Mesopotamia, 1914–1918* (London, 1967), p. 266.

48. Barker, *Townshend of Kut*, p. 193.

49. Ibid., pp. 196–197. Emphasis in original.

50. War Diaries of the Mesopotamian Campaign, 1916–1917, General Staff Army Headquarters, India, vol. 2, parts 113, 114, and 117, L/MIL/17/5/3789 (India Office Records, British Library, London).

51. Daniel Barnard, "The Great Iraqi Revolt: The 1919–1920 Insurrections against the British in Mesopotamia," paper presented at the International History Conference, March 2004, Harvard University.

52. See Arnold T. Wilson, *Mesopotamia, 1917–1920: A Clash of Loyalties* (London: Oxford University Press, 1931).

53. Benedict Anderson, *Imagined Communities: Reflections on the Origin and Spread of Nationalism* (London: Verso, 1991); Partha Chatterjee, *Nationalist Thought and the Colonial World: A Derivative Discourse* (Minneapolis: University of Minnesota Press, 1993).

54. On the coming together of the Islamic crescent and the Indian charkha, see Ayesha Jalal, *Self and Sovereignty: Individual and Community in South Asian Islam since 1850* (London: Routledge, 2000), chapter 5; on Gandhi's reason for supporting the Khilafat issue, see Sugata Bose, "Nation, Reason and Religion: India's Independence in International Perspective," *Economic and Political Weekly*, August 1–8, 1998.

55. "The Turkish Question," *Young India*, June 29, 1921.

56. "Three National Cries," *Young India*, September 8, 1920.

57. F. W. Buckler, "The Historical Antecedents of the *Khilafat* Movement," *Contemporary Review* 121 (May 1922): 603–611.

58. S. M. Burke and Salim al-Din Quraishi, *Bahadur Shah: The Last Mogul Emperor of India* (Lahore: Sang-e-Meel Publications, 1996), p. 203.

59. Buckler, "Historical Antecedents of the *Khilafat* Movement."

60. Sisir K. Bose and Sugata Bose, eds., *Azad Hind: The Collected Works of Netaji Subhas Chandra Bose*, vol. 11 (Calcutta: Netaji Research Bureau, 2002), p. 6.

61. Subhas Chandra Bose, "The Great Patriot and Leader," in his *Blood Bath* (Lahore: Hero Publications, 1947), p. 65.

62. David Marquand, "Playground Bully," in Andrew Bacevich, ed., *The Imperial Tense: Prospects and Problems of American Empire* (Chicago: Ivan R. Dee, 2003), p. 113.

63. Ferguson, "Hegemony or Empire?"

64. Sheldon Pollock, "Empire and Imitation," paper presented at the Social Science Research Council conference "Lessons of Empire," New York, September 26–27, 2003.

3. Flows of Capitalists, Laborers, and Commodities

1. This attitude toward India is confirmed by minutes of the meeting of the Persian Gulf Subcommittee of the Committee of Imperial Defence, July 2, 1928,

and "Oil Interests in the Persian Gulf," June 28, 1928, communicated by the Board of Trade (file no. 262-N, "Reports of the Committee of Imperial Defence on Matters Affecting the Persian Gulf," Foreign and Political Department, Government of India, National Archives of India, New Delhi; hereafter FPD, NAI).

2. Michael Pearson, *The Indian Ocean* (London: Routledge, 2003), p. 223.

3. Claude Markovits, *The Global World of Indian Merchants, 1750–1947: Traders of Sind from Bukhara to Panama* (Cambridge, Eng.: Cambridge University Press, 2000), pp. 17–18.

4. Ibid., p. 24.

5. See Rajat Kanta Ray, "Asian Capital in the Age of European Domination: The Rise of the Bazaar, 1800–1914," *Modern Asian Studies* 29, no. 3 (1995): 449–554, which is discussed more fully in Chapter 1. Markovits has an academic quibble with Ray's position, suggesting that he falls prey to the same "dual economy" model he sets out to critique. It seems to me that Ray's formulation about European and Asian capital as a dialectic between two *Gesellschaften*—as distinct from a dual economy model of a *Gesellschaft* and a *Gemeinschaft*—is clear and compelling.

6. "Local history" is "combined with world history" in Markovits's study while the level of "national history," which the author contends is "largely meaningless in this case," is deliberately "ignored." Markovits, *Global World of Indian Merchants*, p. 8.

7. Ray, "Asian Capital," p. 552.

8. Hugh Tinker, *A New System of Slavery: The Export of Indian Labour Overseas, 1830–1920* (London: Oxford University Press, 1974).

9. Marina Carter, *Servants, Sirdars and Settlers: Indians in Mauritius, 1834–1874* (Delhi: Oxford University Press, 1995), p. 2.

10. For claims that seem more optimistic than is warranted by the evidence, see David Northrup, *Indentured Labor in the Age of Imperialism, 1834–1922* (Cambridge, Eng.: Cambridge University Press, 1995), and P. C. Emmer, "The Meek Hindu: The Recruitment of Indian Indentured Labourers for Service Overseas, 1870–1916," in P. C. Emmer, ed., *Colonialism and Migration: Indentured Labour before and after Slavery* (Boston: Martinus Nijhoff, 1986), pp. 187–207.

11. Ralph Shlomowitz, "Mortality of Indian Labour on Ocean Voyages, 1843–1917," *Studies in History* 6, no. 1 (January 1990): 35–65.

12. Carter, *Servants, Sirdars and Settlers*, p. 298.

13. Philip D. Curtin, *The Rise and Fall of the Plantation Complex: Essays in Atlantic History* (Cambridge, Eng.: Cambridge University Press, 1998).

14. Carter, *Servants, Sirdars and Settlers*, p. 295.

15. C. J. Baker, "Economic Reorganization and the Slump in South and Southeast Asia," *Comparative Studies in Society and History* 23, no. 3 (July 1981): 325–349.

16. J. G. Lorimer, *Gazetteer of the Persian Gulf, Oman and Central Arabia*, vol. 1: *Historical* (Calcutta: Government of India, 1908–1915), pp. 2644–2645.

17. Political Agent, Bahrain, to Political Resident, Persian Gulf, Büshehr, November 4, 1905; Political Resident, Persian Gulf, Büshehr, to Political Agent, Bahrain, November 15, 1905; Political Agent, Bahrain, to Political Resident, Persian Gulf, Büshehr, August 30, 1907; Political Agent, Bahrain, to Political Resident, Persian Gulf, Büshehr, March 7, 1908; Political Agent, Bahrain, to Political Resident, Persian Gulf, Büshehr, June 8, 1910; Political Agent, Bahrain, to Political Resident, Büshehr, August 22, 1910, in "Hindu Merchants at Qatif," R/15/2/24 (India Office Records, British Library, London; hereafter IOR, BL).

18. Lorimer, *Gazetteer of the Persian Gulf*, vol. 1, pp. 2630, 2633, 2640–2641.

19. "Trade of UK and India with Persian Gulf Ports," L/P&S/18/B205 (IOR, BL).

20. "Note on the Trade in the Persian Gulf," L/P&S/18/B411 (IOR, BL).

21. Ibid.

22. "Persian Gulf Administration Report, 1929," R/15/1/714/5 (IOR, BL), pp. 5–6, 23, 26, 46, 50, 65–66.

23. "PGAR, 1930," R/15/6/529 (IOR, BL), pp. 6–7, 21, 42, 51.

24. "Pearl Industry," Charles Belgrave, Political Adviser, to Political Agent, Bahrain, R/15/2/1344 (IOR, BL). See also "Report on the Economic Situation in the Persian Gulf," file no. 294-N, 1929, National Archives of India, pp. 10–14.

25. "PGAR, 1930," R/15/6/529 (IOR, BL), pp. 57–58. See also Political Resident, Persian Gulf, Büshehr, to Foreign Secretary, Government of India, November 16, 1930 (FPD, NAI).

26. "PGAR, 1931," R/15/715/1 (IOR, BL), pp. 11–12, 31, 42, 48–49, 66.

27. "PGAR, 1931," R/15/715/2 (IOR, BL), pp. i, 10, 23.

28. Ibid., pp. 36, 54.

29. Political Agent, Bahrain, to Political Resident, Persian Gulf, Büshehr, November 26, 1932, "Indian Trade Interests in Bahrain," file no. 241-N, 1933 (FPD, NAI).

30. "Pearl Industry," Charles Belgrave, Political Adviser, to Political Agent, Bahrain, December 19, 1928, R/15/2/1344 (IOR, BL).

31. Political Agent, Bahrain, to Political Resident, Persian Gulf, Büshehr, May 30, 1932, "Disturbances by Pearl Divers at Bahrain," file no. 276-N, 1932 (FPD, NAI).

32. H. J. von Bassewitz, "Swan Song of the Pearl Divers," in ibid., p. 5.

33. Political Agent, Bahrain to Political Resident, Persian Gulf, Büshehr, May 30, 1932, "Disturbances by Pearl Divers at Bahrain."

34. "PGAR, 1933," "PGAR, 1934," and "PGAR, 1935," R/15/1/715 (IOR, BL).

35. "Gamble's Report," R/15/2/1345 (IOR, BL); *The Near East and India*, March 28, 1935.

36. Bahrain Trade Reports (annual), R/15/2/1344–1347 (IOR, BL).

37. "Aden: Brief for Secretary of State," L/P&S/18/B462 (IOR, BL).

38. "Mesopotamia: Question of Indian Immigration," August 1919, L/P&S/18/B331 (IOR, BL).

39. "Exclusion of Prosperous Indians from Kuwait (1936)," R/15/5/201 (IOR, BL).

40. Rabindranath Tagore's statement is in "Fears of Indians in Iraq—Legal Status: Alleged Attempt to Oust Traders," *Statesman*, November 7, 1935.

41. "Gamble's Report," *Petroleum Times*, March 30, 1935, R/15/2/1344 (IOR, BL).

42. Alan Villiers, *The Indian Ocean* (London: Museum Press, 1952), pp. 87, 92.

43. Political Agent, Kuwait, to Political Resident, Persian Gulf, November 16, 1939, R/15/5/201 (IOR, BL).

44. Political Resident, Persian Gulf, to Deputy Secretary, External Affairs, Government of India, April 6, 1938, in "Indian Interests in Bahrain," R/15/2/344 (IOR, BL).

45. Political Resident, Persian Gulf, to Political Agent, Bahrain, September 17, 1939, in ibid.

46. Political Agent, Bahrain, to Political Resident, Persian Gulf, Kuwait, October 18, 1939, in ibid.

47. Ministry of External Affairs, Government of India, to Persian Gulf Residency, April 12, 1948, in ibid.

48. Nanji Kalidas Mehta, *Dream Half-Expressed* (Bombay: Vakils, Feffer and Simons, 1966), pp. 17, 34, 36–39.

49. Ibid., pp. 40–41.

50. Ibid., pp. 67–71. The later career of Nanji Kalidas Mehta is discussed well in Savita Nair, "Moving Life Histories: Gujarat, East Africa and the Indian Diaspora, 1880–2000," Ph.D. diss., University of Pennsylvania, 2001, pp. 125–140.

51. Nair, "Moving Life Histories," pp. 21–22, 222.

52. Cynthia Salvadori, ed., *We Came in Dhows* (Nairobi: Paperchase Kenya, 2000), vol. 1, p. 15 and vol. 3, pp. 56–57, 156–157.

53. "Report on the Zanzibar Dominions" by Lt. Col. C. P. Rigby, Bombay Army, Her Majesty's Consul and British Agent at Zanzibar, July 1, 1860, reprinted in Mrs. Charles E. B. Russell, ed., *General Rigby, Zanzibar and the Slave Trade* (London: George Allen & Unwin, 1935), pp. 326–353, quotations from p. 329.

54. J. Forbes Munro, "Shipping Subsidies and Railway Guarantees: William Mackinnon, Eastern Africa and the Indian Ocean, 1860–93," *Journal of African History* 28, no. 2 (1987): 209–230.

55. Bartle Frere, Zanzibar, to Earl Granville, Poona, May 7, 1873, Foreign Office 84, vol. 1391, no. 58, cited in Haraprasad Chattopadhyaya, *Indians in Africa: A Socio-Economic Study* (Calcutta: Bookland, 1970), p. 386.

56. Frere to Granville, March 31, 1873, cited in ibid., p. 389.

57. H. R. Crofton, *A Pageant of Spice Islands* (London: John Bale, 1936), p. 91, cited in Chattopadhyaya, *Indians in Africa*, p. 395.

58. Winston Churchill, *My African Journey* (1908; London, 1962), pp. 33–34.

59. "Report of Mr. K. P. S. Menon, I. C. S., on the Effect on Indian Interests of Certain Decrees Passed by the Government of Zanzibar, 10 Sep, 1934," file no. 102(2), 1935 (FPD, NAI), p. 2.

60. These were (1) Alienation of Land Decree, 1934, (2) the Moneylenders' Decree, 1934, (3) the Clove Growers' Association Decree, 1934, (4) the Clove Exporters' Decree, 1934, (5) the Adulteration of Produce Decree, 1934, and (6) the Agricultural Produce Decree, 1934.

61. "Report of Mr. K. P. S. Menon," pp. 3–4.

62. "Comments of the Government of Zanzibar on Mr. K. P. S. Menon's Report, 12 December 1934," file no. 102(2), 1935 (FPD, NAI), pp. 18–19.

63. "Report of Mr. K. P. S. Menon," pp. 5–6.

64. "Comments of the Government of Zanzibar," pp. 20, 27.

65. "Report of Mr. K. P. S. Menon," pp. 9–10.

66. Cited in Chattopadhyaya, *Indians in Africa*, pp. 400–401.

67. Salvadori, *We Came in Dhows*, pp. 56–57.

68. Rabindranath Tagore, *Japane-Parashye (In Japan and Persia)* (Calcutta: Viswa Bharati, 1941), pp. 18–19.

69. Ibid., pp. 14, 17–25.

70. David Rudner, *Caste and Capitalism in Colonial India: The Nattukottai Chettiars* (Berkeley: University of California Press, 1994), p. 69.

71. Michael Adas, *The Burma Delta: Economic Development and Social Change on an Asian Rice Frontier, 1852–1941* (Madison: University of Wisconsin Press, 1974), p. 22.

72. *Report of the Burma Provincial Banking Enquiry Committee, 1929–30,* vol. 1 (Rangoon: Government of Burma, 1930), p. 190.

73. Ibid., p. 93.

74. Ibid., p. 203.

75. A. Saviranatha Pillai, "Monograph on Nattukottai Chettis' Banking Business," *Madras Provincial Banking Enquiry Committee,* vol. 3 (Madras: Government of Madras, 1930), p. 1170. These figures are approximate at best. For a careful discussion of the difficulties in assessing the Chettiars' net worth, see Rudner, *Caste and Capitalism,* pp. 69–70.

76. *Report of the Burma Provincial Banking Enquiry Committee, 1929–30,* vol. 1, p. 211.

77. Raman Mahadevan, "Pattern of Enterprise of Immigrant Entrepreneurs: A Study of the Chettiars in Malaya, 1880–1930," *Economic and Political Weekly,* January 28–February 4, 1978, pp. 146–152.

78. Kingsley Davis, *The Population of India and Pakistan* (New York: Russell and Russell, 1968), p. 101.

79. Adas, *Burma Delta,* pp. 86, 89, 98–99, 101, 162.

80. Kernial Singh Sandhu, *Indians in Malaya: Some Aspects of Their Immigration and Settlement, 1786–1957* (Cambridge, Eng.: Cambridge University Press, 1969), pp. 304, 313.

81. Baker, "Economic Reorganization and the Slump in South and Southeast Asia," p. 339.

82. Adas, *Burma Delta,* p. 205.

83. Sandhu, *Indians in Malaya,* pp. 314–317.

84. *Report of the Burma Provincial Banking Enquiry Committee, 1929–30,* vol. 1, p. 189.

85. Ibid., pp. 198–199.

86. Adas, *Burma Delta,* pp. 172, 188.

87. Rudner, *Caste and Capitalism,* p. 87.

88. Jomo Kwame Sundaram, "Plantation Capital and Indian Labor in Colonial Malaya," in K. S. Sandhu and A. Mani, eds., *Indian Communities in Southeast Asia* (Singapore: Times Academic Press, 1993), p. 301.

89. Lim Teck Ghee, *Peasants and Their Agricultural Economy in Colonial Malaya, 1874–1941* (New York: Oxford University Press, 1977), pp. 215–216.

90. Adas, *Burma Delta,* pp. 197–199, 207–208.

91. James C. Scott, *The Moral Economy of the Peasant: Rebellion and Subsistence in Southeast Asia* (New Haven, Conn.: Yale University Press, 1976), p. 149.

92. Adas, *Burma Delta,* pp. 194, 203.

93. Scott, *Moral Economy of the Peasant,* p. 155.

94. Amitav Ghosh, *The Glass Palace* (Delhi: Permanent Black, 2000), p. 468.

4. Waging War for King and Country

Epigraph. L/MIL/5/825, part 4, folio 570 (IOR, BL).

1. See Sugata Bose and Ayesha Jalal, *Modern South Asia: History, Culture, Political Economy* (London: Routledge, 2004), chapter 7.

2. Ibid., chapter 10.

3. This letter was translated from its original in Hindi. See L/MIL/5/825, folio 568 (IOR, BL).

4. Nur Muhammad, 129th Baluchis, now in hospital (K. I. H. Brighton) in England, to Jamadar Muhammad Baksh at the regimental depot at Karachi (Urdu dated July 26, 1915), L/MIL/5/825, folio 618 (IOR, BL).

5. Risaldar Hidayat Ali Khan, Persian Gulf, to Jamadar Ali Khan, Persian Gulf 4th Cavalry, I.E.F. (Urdu dated June 11, 1915), L/MIL/5/825, part 4, folio 566 (IOR, BL).

6. Lance Naik Sherafuddin, 40th Pathans, Kitchener's Indian Hospital, Brighton, to Mirza Hasan Ali Khan, Jhelum, Punjab (orig. Pathan, Urdu dated July 17, 1915), L/MIL/5/825, part 4, folio 586 (IOR, BL).

7. Jamadar Ghulla Singh, Mesopotamia, to Jamadar Bachittar Singh, 6th Cavalry, France (orig. Sikh, Urdu dated December 19, 1916), L/MIL/5/827 (IOR, BL).

8. Badshah Khan in Meerut Stationary Hospital to Tarai Khan serving with the 57th Rifles in France (Urdu dated July 26, 1915), L/MIL/5/825, part 4, folio 615 (IOR, BL).

9. Santa Singh, Ressaidar, 23rd Cavalry, Mesopotamia, to Ujagar Singh, 23rd Cavalry attached to 36th Jacob's Horse, France (Gurmukhi dated January 26, 1917), L/MIL/5/827 (IOR, BL).

10. Badan Singh, 10th Lancers, Mesopotamia, to Pertab Singh, 36th Jacob's Horse, France (Gurmukhi dated January 28, 1917), L/MIL/5/827 (IOR, BL).

11. Mahmud Khan, Sowar, Isfahan, attached 11th Lancers, to Mahomed Khan, Dafadar, 18th Lancers, France (orig. Punjabi Mahomedan, Urdu dated October 18, 1916), L/MIL/5/827 (IOR, BL).

12. Lance Dafadar, Karman Rifles, Persia, to Dost Mahomed, Risaldar, 18th K. C. Lancers, France (orig. Punjabi Mahomedan, Urdu dated December 7, 1916), L/MIL/5/827 (IOR, BL).

13. Lance Dafadar Mahomed Khan, 15th Lancers, Shīrāz, Persia, to Dafadar Mahomed Khan, 18th Lancers, France (orig. Punjabi Mahomedan, Urdu dated December 16, 1917), L/MIL/5/827 (IOR, BL).

14. Naik Firoz Khan, Indian Contingent, Somaliland, to Sowar Bhawan Khan, 18th Lancers, France (orig. Punjabi Mahomedan, Urdu dated January 2, 1917), L/MIL/5/827 (IOR, BL).

15. Syed Asghar Ali, Sub-Assistant Surgeon, British East Africa, to Abdul Jabbar Khan, Dafadar, 6th Cavalry, France (orig. Hindustani Mahomedan, Urdu dated January 30, 1917), L/MIL/5/827 (IOR, BL).

16. "War Diaries of the Mesopotamian Campaign," part 57, L/MIL/17/5/3788 (IOR, BL).

17. Ibid., part 220, L/MIL/17/5/3789 (IOR, BL).

18. Abdul Rauf Khan, 2nd Combined Field Ambulance, Mesopotamia, to Abdul Jabbar Khan, Dafadar, 6th Cavalry, France (orig. Hindustani Mahomedan, Urdu dated February 19, 1917), L/MIL/5/827 (IOR, BL).

19. Kazi Nazrul Islam, *Byathar Dan (The Gift of Pain)* in *Nazrul Rachanabali (Collected Works of Nazrul)*, vol. 1 (Dhaka: Bangla Academy, 1993), p. 610. Muzaffar Ahmed, editor of *Bangiya Muslim Sahitya Patrika,* later reminisced that Nazrul had had Dara and Saif join the "lal fauj" (Red Army) in his manuscript, but that Ahmed thought it prudent in the context of 1919 in colonial India to change that to "a liberation army." In the version that was serialized in the journal, the hero was named Nurannabi (a name in its shortened form, Nuru, often used by Nazrul himself), but in the book published in March 1920 the name was changed to Dara. See ibid., pp. 931–932.

20. Ibid., p. 612.

21. Paul Ricoeur, *Time and Narrative,* cited in Hayden White, *The Content of the Form: Narrative Discourse and Historical Representation* (Baltimore: Johns Hopkins University Press, 1987), p. 171.

22. Islam, *Nazrul Rachanabali,* vol. 1, p. 34.

23. Syed Sajjad Husain, "Nazrul Islam: An Assessment," in Rafiqul Islam, ed., *Kazi Nazrul Islam: A New Anthology* (Dhaka: Bangla Academy, 1990), pp. 207–208.

24. See Ayesha Jalal, "Exploding Communalism: The Politics of Muslim Identity in South Asia," in Sugata Bose and Ayesha Jalal, *Nationalism, Democracy and Development: State and Politics in India* (Delhi: Oxford University Press, 1997). For a detailed discussion of conceptions of rights and sovereignty during the Khilafat movement, see Jalal's *Self and Sovereignty: Individual and Community in South Asian Islam since 1850* (New York: Routledge, 2000), chapter 5.

25. See Mohamed Ali's statement in R. M. Thadani, *The Historic State Trial of*

the Ali Brothers (Karachi: n.p., 1921), pp. 63–87. I am grateful to Ayesha Jalal for bringing Mohamed Ali's line of contestation to my attention.

26. Memorandum dated October 20, 1945, p. 369, doc. 154, in Nicholas Mansergh, ed., *India: The Transfer of Power, 1942–47*, vol. 6 (London: H.M.S.O., 1970–1983). For a fine study of the Indian National Army that weaves in participant narratives of Prem Kumar Sahgal, one of the Red Fort trio, and Lakshmi Swaminathan Sahgal, commander of the Rani of Jhansi Regiment of the INA, see Peter Ward Fay, *The Forgotten Army: India's Armed Struggle for Independence, 1942–1945* (Ann Arbor: University of Michigan Press, 1993).

27. Quotations from Shah Nawaz Khan's statement are taken from Moti Ram, *Two Historic Trials in Red Fort: An Authentic Account of the Trial by a General Court Martial of Captain Shah Nawaz Khan, Captain P. K. Sahgal and Lt. G. S. Dhillon and the Trial by a European Military Commission of Emperor Bahadur Shah* (New Delhi: Roxy Printing Press, 1946), pp. 103–111.

28. Ibid., pp. 104–105.

29. According to estimates later made by British intelligence, of 45,000 Indian soldiers gathered at Farrer Park on February 17, 1942, only 5,000 remained nonvolunteers. See Monograph no. 3, "The Incidence of Volunteers and Non-Volunteers," compiled by Lt. Col. G. D. Anderson and his staff in May 1946, L/WS/2/45 (IOR, BL).

30. Ram, *Two Historic Trials,* pp. 105–106.

31. Ibid., pp. 109–110.

32. Ibid., pp. 110–111.

33. S. A. Ayer, *Unto Him a Witness: The Story of Netaji Subhas Chandra Bose in East Asia* (Bombay: Thacker, 1951), p. xiv. Ayer's migratory route took him from a small village in Tamil Nadu to Madras and Bombay and from there to Southeast Asia.

34. Ibid., pp. xxvi, xxii.

35. Ibid., pp. 17–18. For a moving account of another retreat by a participant, see Abid Hasan Safrani, *The Men from Imphal* (Calcutta: Netaji Research Bureau, 1971, 1995).

36. Ibid., p. 23.

37. Ibid., p. 25.

38. Mohammad Zaman Kiani, *India's Freedom Struggle and the Great INA* (New Delhi: Reliance Publishing House, 1994).

39. Ibid., pp. xiv, xvii.

40. Ibid., pp. xiii–xiv.

41. Ibid., p. 216.

42. See Safrani, *Men from Imphal*, p. 11.

43. Ibid., pp. 7–9.

44. Kiani, *India's Freedom Struggle*, pp. 168–169.

45. Ibid., p. xiv.

46. Ayer, *Unto Him a Witness*, p. xiv.

47. Kiani, *India's Freedom Struggle*, pp. xv, xvi.

48. Ibid., pp. 244–245.

49. Ibid., p. 222.

50. Some have been published in the Calcutta-based journal *The Oracle*, while others can be read in the archives of the Netaji Research Bureau.

51. See Ranajit Guha, "The Prose of Counter-Insurgency," in Ranajit Guha and Gayatri Chakravorty Spivak, eds., *Selected Subaltern Studies* (New York: Oxford University Press, 1988), pp. 45–86.

52. See Gayatri Chakravorty Spivak, "Subaltern Studies: Deconstructing Historiography," in Guha and Spivak, *Selected Subaltern Studies*, pp. 3–32.

53. For one of these rich intellectual dividends, see Partha Chatterjee, *Nationalist Thought and the Colonial World: A Derivative Discourse* (Minneapolis: University of Minnesota Press, 1993).

54. See Sisir K. Bose and Sugata Bose, eds., *Chalo Delhi: The Collected Works of Netaji Subhas Chandra Bose*, vol. 12 (Calcutta: Netaji Research Bureau, 2006).

5. Expatriate Patriots

Epigraph. Mohandas K. Gandhi, *An Autobiography: The Story of My Experiments with Truth* (Boston: Beacon Press, 1957), p. 186.

1. For such a blinkered approach to diasporic patriotism in an otherwise fine economic history of Sindhi merchants, see Claude Markovits, *The Global World of Indian Merchants, 1750–1947: Traders of Sind from Bukhara to Panama* (Cambridge, Eng.: Cambridge University Press, 2000).

2. Peter van der Veer, ed., *Nation and Migration: The Politics of Space in the Indian Diaspora* (Philadelphia: University of Pennsylvania Press, 1995).

3. C. A. Bayly, *Origins of Nationality in South Asia: Patriotism and Ethical Government in the Making of Modern India* (Delhi: Oxford University Press, 1998), chapters 1 and 2.

4. Benedict Anderson, *Imagined Communities: Reflections on the Origin and Spread of Nationalism* (London: Verso, 1991). See also Partha Chatterjee, *Nationalist Thought in the Colonial World: A Derivative Discourse* (Minneapolis: University of Minnesota Press, 1993).

5. Gandhi, *An Autobiography,* pp. 182–195.

6. Maureen Swan, *Gandhi: The South African Experience* (Johannesburg: Ravan Press, 1985), pp. 1, 19.

7. Uma Dhupelia-Mesthrie, *From Cane-Fields to Freedom: A Chronicle of Indian South African Life* (Cape Town: Kwela Books, 2000), photo and caption no. 16.

8. Haraprasad Chattopadhyaya, *Indians in Africa: A Socio-Economic Study* (Calcutta: Bookland, 1970), p. 139.

9. Gandhi, *An Autobiography,* pp. 138, 142, 149.

10. Chattopadhyaya, *Indians in Africa,* p. 143.

11. Gandhi, *An Autobiography,* p. 153.

12. On Gandhi's war medal and for the quotations, see ibid., pp. 214–216, 315–316.

13. Swan, *Gandhi,* p. 113.

14. *Indian Opinion,* September 22, 1906, cited in ibid., p. 120.

15. Gandhi, *An Autobiography,* pp. 318–319.

16. Swan, *Gandhi,* p. 137.

17. *Indian Opinion,* January 25, August 1, and August 8, 1908, cited in ibid., p. 147.

18. *Indian Opinion,* January 4, 1908, cited in Dhupelia-Mesthrie, *From Cane-Fields to Freedom,* photo and caption no. 183.

19. Chattopadhyaya, *Indians in Africa,* pp. 151, 174.

20. *Indian Opinion,* February 15, 1908, cited in Swan, *Gandhi,* p. 163.

21. M. K. Gandhi, *Satyagraha in South Africa* (Ahmedabad: Navajivan, 1928, 1950), p. 187.

22. On communitarian discourses on identity in the Punjab, see Ayesha Jalal, *Self and Sovereignty: Individual and Community in South Asian Islam since 1850* (New York: Routledge, 2000), chapters 2 and 3.

23. Swan, *Gandhi,* pp. 198–203.

24. *Indian Opinion: Honourable Mr G. K. Gokhale's Visit to South Africa* (special edition, 1912).

25. Swan, *Gandhi,* pp. 235–236.

26. Ibid., pp. 247–248.

27. Ibid., p. 250. For details of the individuals who played a key role in this struggle, see *Golden Number of "Indian Opinion," 1914: Souvenir of the Passive Resistance Movement in South Africa, 1906–1914* (Pietermaritzburg, South Africa: Africana Book Collectors, facsimile edition, 1990).

28. Swan, *Gandhi,* pp. 251–254.

29. Chattopadhyaya, *Indians in Africa,* pp. 165, 168.

30. Ibid., p. 172.

31. Savita Nair, "Moving Histories: Gujarat, East Africa and the Indian Diaspora, 1880–2000," Ph.D. diss., University of Pennsylvania, 2001, pp. 96–122.

32. Gandhi, *An Autobiography*, p. 187.

33. Abid Hasan Safrani, "A Soldier Remembers," transcript of a taped interview, 1976, part 5, in *Oracle* 7, no. 1 (January 1985): 21.

34. Ibid., p. 22. For further details of the submarine voyage, see Sisir Kumar Bose, Alexander Werth, and S. A. Ayer, *A Beacon across Asia: A Biography of Subhas Chandra Bose* (Bombay: Orient Longman, 1973), pp. 158–164; and Leonard A. Gordon, *Brothers against the Raj: A Biography of Indian Nationalists Sarat and Subhas Chandra Bose* (New York: Columbia University Press, 1990), pp. 488–492.

35. Bose, Werth, and Ayer, *Beacon across Asia*, pp. 163–164.

36. "Link up Indian Nationalists All over the World," message to the Bangkok conference, June 15, 1942, in Sisir K. Bose and Sugata Bose, eds., *Azad Hind: Writings and Speeches, 1941–1943. Collected Works of Netaji Subhas Chandra Bose*, vol. 11 (Calcutta: Netaji Research Bureau, and Delhi: Permanent Black, 2002), pp. 115–116.

37. "Why I Left Home and Homeland," speech at a mass meeting in Singapore, July 9, 1943, in Sisir K. Bose and Sugata Bose, eds., *Chalo Delhi: Writings and Speeches, 1943–1945. Collected Works of Netaji Subhas Chandra Bose*, vol. 12 (Calcutta: Netaji Research Bureau, and Delhi: Permanent Black, 2006).

38. Gordon, *Brothers against the Raj*, p. 498; Peter Ward Fay, *The Forgotten Army: India's Armed Struggle for Independence, 1942–1945* (Ann Arbor: University of Michigan Press, 1993), pp. 214, 525–526.

39. Lakshmi Sahgal, "The Rani of Jhansi Regiment," in *Oracle* 1, no. 2 (April 1979): 15–19, and author's conversations with Lakshmi Sahgal *(née* Swaminathan).

40. Puan Sri Datin Janaki Athinahappan, "The Rani of Jhansi Regiment," *Oracle* 2, no. 2 (January 1980): 29–32, and author's conversations with Janaki Athinahappan *(née* Davar). See also Fay, *Forgotten Army*, pp. 219–221; "Broadcast by Protima Pal," *Young India: Journal for Indian Youths in East Asia*, January 23, 1944, archives of the Netaji Research Bureau, Calcutta; Shanti Majumdar, "Netaji's Rani of Jhansi Regiment," *Oracle* 2, no. 3 (July 1980): 21–26; Maya Banerjee, "My Life with the Rani of Jhansi Regiment" and "Convention of the Rani of Jhansi Regiment Proceedings" both in *Oracle* 2, no. 2 (April 1980): 21–24, 63–65.

41. Abid Hasan Safrani, *The Men from Imphal* (Calcutta: Netaji Research Bureau, 1971, 1995), p. 13.

42. "Proclamation of the Provisional Government of Azad Hind," in Bose, *Chalo Delhi.*

43. Bhulabhai Desai, "Address of Counsel for Defence, Red Fort Trial, Delhi, 1 December, 1945," *Oracle* 15, no. 4 (October 1993): 34.

44. "Where Is Your Bank Book?" speech at the All Malai Chettiars and Other Indian Merchants Conference, October 25, 1943, reprinted in Bose, *Chalo Delhi*.

45. Fay, *Forgotten Army*, p. 215. For detailed reports of contributions collected at local branches in Malaya, see, for instance, *Young India* (September 19, 1943), archives of the Netaji Research Bureau, Calcutta, pp. 12–13.

46. Hasan, *Men from Imphal*, pp. 11–12.

47. "Unification of the Indian Nation," resolutions of the meeting of the Council of Ministers of the Provisional Government of Azad Hind, December 9, 1943, in Bose, *Chalo Delhi*.

48. "Netaji in Andaman, December 29–31, 1943: A Report," *Oracle* 16, no. 1 (January 1994): 11–13.

49. "Independent Burma," press statement on the achievement of Burma's independence, August 1, 1943, in Bose, *Chalo Delhi*.

50. Sarat Chandra Chattopadhyay, *Pather Dabi*, 3rd ed. (Calcutta: Mukhopadhyay, 1947), p. 68.

51. Subhas Chandra Bose, "At Bahadur Shah's Tomb," speech on September 26, 1943, in Bose, *Chalo Delhi*.

52. Ibid.

53. Gordon, *Brothers against the Raj*, p. 510; Bose, *Chalo Delhi*.

54. Bhulabhai Desai, "Address of Counsel for Defence," p. 42.

55. "Father of Our Nation," speech broadcast to Mahatma Gandhi, July 6, 1944, in Bose, *Chalo Delhi*.

56. Gordon, *Brothers against the Raj*, p. 511.

57. Krishna Bose, *Prasanga Subhaschandra* (Calcutta: Ananda, 1993), pp. 72–81, and author's conversations with Naga Sundaram.

58. Subhas Chandra Bose, "The Great Patriot and Leader," speech at Bahadur Shah's tomb, July 11, 1944, in Bose, *Chalo Delhi*.

59. Fay, *Forgotten Army*, p. 556.

60. Hasan, *Men from Imphal*, pp. 7–9. See also Raja Muhammad Arshad, "The Retreat" (written at the Red Fort, October 1945), *Oracle* 16, no. 4 (October 1994): 1–56.

61. William Slim, *Defeat into Victory* (London: Cassell, 1956).

62. Fay, *Forgotten Army*, p. 399.

63. Hasan, *Men from Imphal*. See also Gurbaksh Singh Dhillon, "The Nehru Holds the Irrawaddy," *Oracle* 5, no. 4 (October 1993): 1–30.

64. Gurbaksh Singh Dhillon, "The Indo-Burman Relations during World War II," *Oracle* 7, no. 3 (July 1985): 15–22; "Aung San's Reply to the Address of Sarat Chandra Bose, 1946," in Sisir K. Bose, ed., *Netaji and India's Freedom* (Calcutta: Netaji Research Bureau, 1974).

65. "Posterity Will Bless Your Name," last message to Indians in Southeast Asia, August 15, 1945, in Bose, *Chalo Delhi.*

66. Cyril John Stracey, "How I Came to Join the INA," *Oracle* 4, no. 1 (January 1982): 53–56.

67. Fay, *Forgotten Army*, pp. 493–524.

68. Cited in S. A. Ayer, *Unto Him a Witness* (Bombay: Thacker, 1951), p. xvi.

69. "Unity of India, Past and Present," INA platoon lecture, archives of the Netaji Research Bureau, Calcutta.

6. Pilgrims' Progress under Colonial Rules

Epigraph. Abdullah Yusuf Ali, *The Holy Quran: Text, Translation and Commentary* (1934; Brentwood, Md.: Amana Corporation, 1989), p. 1042.

1. Khwaja Hasan Nizami, *Safar-e-Misr wa Sham wa Hejaz* (Delhi: K. Indian Press, 1911), pp. 1–2.

2. For a discussion of autobiographical accounts of the hajj, see Barbara Daly Metcalf, "The Pilgrimage Remembered: South Asian Accounts of the *Hajj,*" in Dale F. Eickelman and James Piscatori, eds., *Muslim Travellers: Pilgrimage, Migration, and the Religious Imagination* (Berkeley: University of California Press, 1990), pp. 85–107.

3. The shift from sea to air transport in the conduct of the hajj took place only in the 1970s. Indian law did not address this shift until the twenty-first century. See "Report on the Haj Committee Bill, 2000, of the Parliamentary Standing Committee on External Affairs," presented to the Lok Sabha by Chairperson Krishna Bose, August 23, 2001 (New Delhi: Lok Sabha Secretariat, 2001).

4. Ibid., pp. 4–6.

5. Ibid., p. 8. *Pas-e-anfas* is the practice of repeating "La-Ilaha (there is no God) Il-Allah (but God)" while breathing in and out.

6. Ibid., pp. 10, 12–13, 15, 17–18.

7. Ibid., pp. 23–26, 39–40. A recent history of Sindhi merchants by Claude Markovits, *The Global World of Indian Merchants, 1750–1947: Traders of Sind from Bukhara to Panama* (Cambridge, Eng.: Cambridge University Press, 2000), grossly underplays the importance of religion in their overseas identity.

8. Ibid., pp. 43–45, 54–55, 70–80.

9. No translation can capture the ring of the original Urdu; see ibid., pp. 90–94.

10. Ibid., p. 97.

11. Ibid., pp. 98–99.

12. See F. E. Peters, *The Hajj: The Muslim Pilgrimage to Mecca and the Holy Places* (Princeton, N.J.: Princeton University Press, 1994), pp. 301–302; David Arnold, "The Indian Ocean as a Disease Zone, 1500–1950," *South Asia* 14, no. 2 (1991): 1–21; and Takashi Oishi, "Friction and Rivalry over Pious Mobility: British Colonial Management of the Hajj and Reaction to It by Indian Muslims, 1870–1920," in Hidemitsu Kuroki, ed., *The Influence of Human Mobility in Muslim Societies* (London: Kegan Paul, 2003).

13. "Haj Enquiry Committee Report," file no. 97-N, 1930, FPD, NAI, pp. 124–125.

14. The disincentives associated with British "regulation" contrasting with the facilitation of travel by Mughal "patronage" probably explains why the absolute number of pilgrims was not much higher in the early twentieth century than in the late sixteenth. Michael Pearson makes a "conservative estimate" of 15,000 Indian Muslims annually making the hajj under Mughal auspices between the sixteenth and eighteenth centuries—see his *Pilgrimage to Mecca: The Indian Experience, 1500–1800* (Princeton, N.J.: Markus Wiener, 1996), p. 57. Poorer Muslim agriculturists clearly formed a larger proportion of the total pilgrims in the twentieth century than before.

15. The figures are drawn from the following source: "Haj Enquiry Committee Report," file no. 97-N, 1930, FPD, NAI, pp. 21–22.

16. Ibid., p. 22.

17. "Haj Pilgrimage Report, 1927," file no. 448-N, 1926, FPD, NAI, p. 9.

18. "Haj Enquiry Committee Report," p. 88.

19. Ibid., p. 69.

20. Ibid., pp. 24, 22–23.

21. Hossein Kazemzadeh, *Relation d'un pèlerinage à la Mecque en 1910–1911* (Paris: Leroux, 1912), pp. 192–193, cited in Peters, *The Hajj*, p. 275.

22. "Haj Enquiry Committee Report," pp. 25–28, 30–31, 38–39.

23. Ibid., pp. 21, 80–81, 112, 118.

24. Ibid., p. 70.

25. Acting British Agent and Consul to the Foreign Office, London, no. 100, August 26, 1926, enclosing "Pilgrimage Report, 1926," file no. 448-N of 1926, FPD, NAI, pp. 1–2, 5–6, 13, 18.

26. Ibid., pp. 13, 20.

27. Ibid., pp. 16–17, 21.

28. Ibid., pp. 16–18.

29. His Britannic Majesty's Agent and Consul, Jeddah, to the Foreign Office, London, no. 109 (2), September 24, 1927, enclosing "Report on the Pilgrimage, 1927," file no. 448-N, 1926, FPD, NAI, pp. 1–3, 6–7, 9, 14, 21.

30. A total of only 115 ships brought the 39,346 pilgrims in 1931 compared to 194 ships carrying 84,821 pilgrims in 1930 (with the number of British ships declining from 116 to 63). The figures from Egypt and the Dutch East Indies showed a 70 percent and 50 percent decline, respectively. The number of pilgrims from British India and the princely states was down to a mere 7,292 in 1931. Bengal, which had sent more than 15,000 pilgrims in 1927, supplied only 1,261 pilgrims in 1931; for Punjab, the figure was down from the 1927 high of 4,572 to 1,351 in 1931.

31. Sir A. Ryan to Sir John Simon, November 26, 1931, enclosing "Report on the Pilgrimage of 1931 (A. H. 1349)," file no. 566-N, 1931, FPD, NAI, pp. 2–4.

32. Memorandum from His Majesty's Chargé D'Affaires, British Legation, Jedda, no. 2203/1177/2, July 29, 1933, enclosing "Report on the Pilgrimage of 1933 (A. H. 1351)," file no. 279-N, 1933, FPD, NAI, pp. 2–5, 13.

33. Ibid., pp. 6, 18–19.

34. As many as 5,891 Indian pilgrims visited Iraq this year, 4,894 of them traveling by sea and landing at Basra. See "Iraq Pilgrimage Report: Report on the Work of Indian Section of the British Consulate at Baghdad for the Year 1935," National Archives of India, New Delhi.

35. Printed Despatch no. 2351/402/12, August 11, 1934, from His Majesty's Chargé D'Affaires, British Legation, Jedda, enclosing "Report on the Pilgrimage of 1934 (A. H. 1352)," file no. 323-N of 1934, FPD, NAI, pp. 2–6.

36. Ibid., pp. 5, 15–16.

37. Ibid., p. 23.

38. *Surah Al-Baqarah*, verses 196 and 197, in Ali, *Holy Quran*, pp. 79–81. For Daryabadi's book, see Abdul Majid Daryabadi, *Safar-e-Hejaz* (Azamgarh, Uttar Pradesh: Maarif Press, 1929).

39. *Surah Ali Imran*, verses 96 and 97, in Ali, *Holy Quran*, pp. 152.

40. Daryabadi, *Safar-e-Hejaz*, pp. 82–91.

41. *Surah Al Nisa*, verse 64, in Ali, *Holy Quran*, p. 204.

42. Daryabadi, *Safar-e-Hejaz*, pp. 92–100. The quotation is my translation.

43. Ibid., pp. 111–122.

44. Ibid., pp. 196–214.

45. *Surah Al-Qasas,* verse 57, in Ali, *Holy Quran,* p. 976.

46. Daryabadi, *Safar-e-Hejaz,* pp. 215–250.

47. Ibid., pp. 352–355. On Sayyid Ahmed of Rae Bareilly's *jihad* see Ayesha Jalal, *Partisans of Allah: Meanings of Jihad in South Asia* (forthcoming).

48. Ayesha Jalal, *Self and Sovereignty: Individual and Community in South Asian Islam since 1850* (London: Routledge, 2000), pp. 188–189.

7. A Different Universalism?

1. See Prabhat Kumar Mukhopadhyay, *Rabindrajibani (Life of Rabindranath)* (Calcutta: Viswabharati, 1987), pp. 577, 583.

2. Rabindranath Tagore to Nirmalkumari Mahalanobis, July 15, 1927, in Rabindranath Tagore, *Java Jatrir Patra (Letters of a Traveler to Java)* in *Rabindra Rachanabali (Collected Works of Rabindranath Tagore),* vol. 19 (Calcutta: Viswabharati, 1957), p. 456.

3. Rabindranath Tagore in *Parashye (In Persia)* in *Rabindra Rachanabali,* vol. 22, and cited in J. N. Sarkar, "Tagore and Iran: A Few Side-Lights on Tagore's Discovery of Persia," *Indo-Iranica* 39, nos. 1–4 (1986): 81–82.

4. This discussion of Tagore's journey across the Indian Ocean, the Mediterranean, and the Atlantic in 1924–1925, especially the analysis of the poems published in *Purabi* (*Of the East,* also the name of an evening *ragini,* or melody) draws on the much more extended treatment of the subject in Sugata Bose and Krishna Bose, "The East in Its Feminine Gender: An Historical and Literary Introduction," in Sugata Bose and Krishna Bose, eds., *The East in Its Feminine Gender: Poems and Songs of Rabindranath Tagore,* trans. Charu C. Chowdhuri (Calcutta: Seagull, 2006). Unless otherwise noted, all verses from Tagore are translated by Chowdhuri and taken from this forthcoming book.

5. Mukhopadhyay, *Rabindrajibani,* vol. 3, p. 147. The book *Purabi* actually had two parts: the poems composed in the spring of 1924 were contained in the first section called "Purabi," while the poems written during his travels in late 1924 and early 1925 made up the second section, called "Pathik" ("Traveler").

6. Diary entry for September 24, 1924, on board SS *Harana Maru,* Rabindranath Tagore, *Pashchim Jatrir Diary (Diary of a Westbound Traveler),* trans. Indu Dutt as Rabindranath Tagore, *The Diary of a Westward Voyage* (Westport, Conn.: Greenwood, 1975).

7. "Fulfillment," in Rabindranath Tagore, *Purabi (Of the East)* (Calcutta: Viswabharati, 1925), pp. 67–69.

8. "The Call," in ibid., pp. 70–76.

9. "Pathik," in ibid.

10. Rabindranath Tagore, *The Diary of a Westward Voyage (Pashchim Jatrir Diary)*, trans. Indu Dutt (Westport, Conn.: Greenwood, 1975), pp. 38, 40, 42.

11. Tagore, *Purabi*, pp. 84–86.

12. There is some doubt about whether Rabindranath came to stay at San Isidro on November 11 or whether it was actually November 12. See Ketaki Kushari Dyson, *In Your Blossoming Flower-Garden* (New Delhi: Sahitya Akademi, 1988), p. 87. Dyson's is the most extended essay on the Tagore-Ocampo relationship, and it benefits from a good deal of detective work and a thorough examination of the letters of Tagore, Ocampo, and Leonard Elmhirst, Tagore's secretary who was present throughout in San Isidro. See also Victoria Ocampo's own memoir in Spanish, *Tagore en las Barrancas de San Isidro* (Buenos Aires: Sur, 1961).

13. Tagore, *Purabi*, pp. 151–153.

14. Ibid., p. 154. Chowdhuri translated the Bengali word "nari" in the second line simply as "Woman," but chose to render "kalyani" as "Blessed one." "Lady" (for "kalyani"), used in William Radice's version, does not capture the nuances of the term. Compare Rabindranath Tagore, *Selected Poems*, trans. William Radice (Harmondsworth, Eng.: Penguin, 1986), p. 91. Rabindranath's own English rendering for Vijaya translated both "nari" and "kalyani" as "Woman." See Dyson, *In Your Blossoming Flower-Garden*, p. 121. The concept of "bideshini," literally foreign woman but meant more in the sense of a distant and elusive woman, had appeared in Tagore's poetry and songs for many decades. A very famous song composed in 1895, which Rabindranath translated for Vijaya, began: "I know you, I do know you, bideshini; you live beyond the ocean, bideshini."

15. Dyson, *In Your Blossoming Flower-Garden*, p. 137. But see Charu Charu C. Chowdhuri's translation, which attempts to convey some of that magic without abandoning a "musical rimed" form, in Bose and Bose, *The East in Its Feminine Gender*.

16. Tagore, *Purabi*, pp. 167–168.

17. Rabindranath Tagore to Victoria Ocampo, January 5, 1925, and Victoria Ocampo to Rabindranath Tagore, January 15, 1925, in Dyson, *In Your Blossoming Flower-Garden*, pp. 384–385, 394. The Baudelaire poem in question was "L'invitation au Voyage" in *Les Fleurs du Mal*. Tagore refused initially to grasp the relevance of furniture imagery to an erotic theme and referred to Baudelaire as "your furniture-poet." For an analysis of Baudelaire's Indian Ocean experience, see François Lionnet, "Reframing Baudelaire: Literary History, Biography, Postcolonial Theory, and Vernacular Languages," *Diacritics* 28, no. 3 (Fall 1998): 63–85.

18. Rabindranath Tagore to C. F. Andrews, December 22, 1924, cited in Prabhat Kumar Mukhopadhyay, *Rabindrajibani*, vol. 3, p. 159.

19. Tagore, *Purabi*, pp. 223–224.

20. Rabindranath Tagore to Victoria Ocampo, October 29, 1925, in Dyson, *In Your Blossoming Flower-Garden*, pp. 416–417. The word "bhalobasa," love, was written in Bengali script.

21. Victoria Ocampo, "Tagore on the Banks of the River Plate," *Tagore Centenary Volume* (New Delhi: Government of India, 1961), p. 47.

22. Tagore to Mahalanobis, July 15, 1927.

23. Rabindranath Tagore to Ramananda Chattopadhyay, May 28, 1927, cited in Prabhat Kumar Mukhopadhyay, *Rabindrajibani*, vol. 3 (Calcutta: Viswabharati, 1991), p. 312.

24. K. N. Chaudhuri, *Asia before Europe: Economy and Civilisation in the Indian Ocean from the Rise of Islam to 1750* (Cambridge, Eng.: Cambridge University Press, 1990), p. 58.

25. Suniti Kumar Chattopadhyay, *Rabindra-Sangame Dweepmaya Bharat O Shyama-desh (With Rabindranath in Island India and the Country of Siam)* (1940; Calcutta: Prakash Bhawan, 1964), pp. 4, 21.

26. Ibid., pp. 22, 41, 44–45.

27. P. B. Shelley, "Stanzas Written in Dejection Near Naples," in *The Golden Treasury* (1907; London: Oxford University Press, 1947), p. 227.

28. Rabindranath Tagore to Nirmalkumari Mahalanobis, July 16, 1927, in Tagore, *Java Jatrir Patra*, p. 461.

29. Rabindranath Tagore to Nirmalkumari Mahalanobis, July 17, 1927, in ibid., pp. 462–463.

30. Chattopadhyay, *Dweepmaya Bharat*, pp. 61–69. Susan Bayly has recently pointed out the connections between British ideas about caste and ethnological race science in the later nineteenth century. See her *Caste, Society and Politics in India from the Eighteenth Century to the Modern Age* (Cambridge, Eng.: Cambridge University Press, 2000). The extent to which Indian and Iranian intellectuals, Hindu and Muslim alike, imbibed and internalized nineteenth-century European theories about the Aryan race is not yet fully appreciated. Ayesha Jalal shows how the great Urdu poet Muhammad Iqbal described Indian Muslims as having combined "the sterling qualities of their Semitic father and the softness of their Aryan mother." See her *Self and Sovereignty: The Muslim Individual and the Community of Islam in South Asia since 1850* (London: Routledge, 2000). The Aryan issue is discussed further in the next section.

31. Chattopadhyay, *Dweepmaya Bharat*, pp. 83–86, 124–126, 235–238.

32. Ibid., pp. 155–159.

33. Tagore, *Java Jatrir Diary*, p. 467.

34. Chattopadhyay, *Dweepmaya Bharat*, pp. 198–199.

35. Ibid., pp. 203–207, 237.

36. See Mukhopadhyay, *Rabindrajibani*, vol. 3, pp. 314, 323.

37. The translation is by Chattopadhyay; see *Dweepmaya Bharat*, pp. 690–694.

38. Ibid., pp. 259–261, 272. On the Dutch invention of Balinese tradition, see Adrian Vickers, *Bali: A Paradise Created* (Ringwood, Australia: Penguin, 1989); and Henk Schulte Nordholt, "The Making of Traditional Bali: Colonial Ethnography and Bureaucratic Reproduction," *History and Anthropology* 8 (1994): 89–127.

39. Rabindranath Tagore to Mira Devi, August 31, 1927, in Tagore, *Java Jatrir Patra*, pp. 483–489.

40. The king himself, however, held that the rituals were inconsequential in comparison with the ultimate goal of striving for *nirvana* (salvation). See Suniti Kumar Chattopadhyay, "Gleanings," *Maha-Bodhi* 40, no. 8 (August 1932): 383–384.

41. Rabindranath Tagore to Nirmalkumari Mahalanobis, August 1, 1927, in Tagore, *Java Jatrir Patra*, pp. 472–474.

42. Rabindranath Tagore to Rathindranath Tagore, September 7, 1927, and Tagore to Amiya Chakravarti, September 9, 1927, in Tagore, *Java Jatrir Patra*, pp. 489–501.

43. The beauty of the Bengali original is inevitably lost in my translation. For the original version, see Rabindranath Tagore, *Mahua* (Calcutta: Viswabharati, 1929), pp. 70–73.

44. See Rabindranath Tagore's letters to Pratima Devi, September 14 and September 17, 1927; to Amiya Chakravarti, September 17, 1927; to Rathindranath Tagore, September 19, 1927; to Nirmalkumari Mahalanobis, September 20, 1927; and to Pratima Devi, September 26, 1927, in Tagore, *Java Jatrir Patra*, pp. 501–519.

45. Rabindranath Tagore to Mira Devi, September 26, 1927, in Tagore, *Java Jatrir Patra*, pp. 19–521.

46. See Mukhopadhyay, *Rabindrajibani*, vol. 3, pp. 330–331. My translation.

47. Rabindranath Tagore to Amiya Chakravarty, October 2, 1927, in Tagore, *Java Jatrir Patra*, p. 526.

48. Mukhopadhyay, *Rabindrajibani*, vol. 3, p. 332.

49. Rabindranath Tagore to Nirmalkumari Mahalanobis, August 1, 1927, in Tagore, *Java Jatrir Patra*, p. 474.

50. Tagore also wanted one of the Muslim sovereigns to endow the chair in

Persian Studies at his university in Santiniketan. Reza Shah Pahlavi obliged. "My pilgrimage would have been incomplete without this visit,—especially when this ancient [Persian] people has been reborn and is feeling an irresistible urge of creative activity and moving to complete fulfilment of the grandeur and freedom of a positive self-expression. It is a source of inspiration in my life. This evening of my life has been filled to the brim." (Rabindranath Tagore in *Parashye (In Persia)* in *Rabindra Rachanabali,* vol. 22 and cited in Sarkar, "Tagore and Iran," pp. 81–82.

51. *Persian Gulf Administration Report* (1932) p. i, R/15/715/2 (IOR, BL).

52. Rabindranath Tagore, *Parashye (In Persia)* in *Rabindra Rachanabali,* vol. 22, pp. 434–439. Another account of this trip is in Kedarnath Chattopadhyay, *Rabindranather Sange Parashya o Iraq Bhraman (Travels in Persia and Iraq with Rabindranath).*

53. Tagore, *Parashye,* pp. 445–447.

54. Ibid., quotation on p. 451.

55. I am grateful to Sunil Sharma for locating the original Persian lines for me. Tagore had rendered "tavern's door" as "heaven's door" *(swargadwar)* in Bengali.

56. Tagore, *Parashye,* pp. 457–461.

57. Ibid., pp. 462–469.

58. Ibid., pp. 469–480.

59. Tagore's own translation in *Parashye,* p. 480.

60. Ibid., pp. 480–488, 511–520.

61. Ibid., pp. 488–493.

62. Ibid., pp. 493–494.

63. On the Indian troops' entry into Baghdad, see "The War Diaries of the Mesopotamian Campaign," L/MIL/17/5/3789 (IOR, BL).

64. Tagore, *Parashye,* p. 440.

65. Ibid., pp. 499–502.

66. Ibid., pp. 495–496 (Tagore's own bilingual poem-painting); see also Rabindranath Tagore, *Sphulinga,* in *Rabindra Rachanabali,* vol. 27 (Calcutta: Viswabharati, 1965), p. 3.

Conclusion

1. Ibid., pp. 9, 12. The *in* and *of* distinction is drawn from Peregrine Horden and Nicholas Purcell, *The Corrupting Sea: A Study in Mediterranean History,* vol. 1 (Oxford, Eng.: Blackwell, 2000), p. 43.

2. Ranajit Guha, *Dominance without Hegemony: History and Power in Colonial India* (Cambridge, Mass.: Harvard University Press, 1997).

3. Pearson, *Indian Ocean*, pp. 9, 224, 243.

4. Ibid., pp. 10, 196.

5. A. G. Hopkins, ed., *Globalization in World History* (London: Pimlico, 2002).

6. C. A. Bayly, "Archaic and Modern Globalization in the Eurasian and African Arena, c. 1750–1850," in ibid., pp. 47–73, quotation from p. 50.

7. Amira K. Bennison, "Muslim Universalism and Western Globalization," in Hopkins, *Globalization in World History*, pp. 74–97.

8. T. N. Harper, "Empire, Diaspora and the Languages of Globalism, 1850–1914," in Hopkins, *Globalization in World History*, pp. 141–166.

9. Charles S. Maier, "Consigning the Twentieth Century to History: Alternative Narratives for the Modern Era," *American Historical Review* 105, no. 3 (June 2000): 807–831.

10. Harper, "Empire, Diaspora and the Languages of Globalism," pp. 150–151, 154, 156.

11. Ibid., pp. 156–159.

12. Homi Bhabha, "DissemiNation: Time, Narrative and the Margins of the Modern Nation," in Homi Bhabha, ed., *Nation and Narration* (London: Routledge, 1990), p. 293.

13. "Indian Ocean Rim Association for Regional Cooperation (IOR-ARC)," http://www.dfa.gov.za/foreign/Multilateral/inter/iorarc.htm, accessed April 19, 2005.

Index